Tal

Dedication i
Thank You iii
Author's Preface v
Editor's Note vii

PART 1: Breaking Down 1

Chapter 1 – Sweet Sixteen 3
Chapter 2 – Back to School 13
Chapter 3 – Vanishing Monsters 19
Chapter 4 – Get Up and Attack 29
Chapter 5 – Patriarchal Blessing 37
Chapter 6 – Linebackers 45
Chapter 7 – No More Fist Fights? 51
Chapter 8 – In the Den of Hope 57
Chapter 9 – The Fear of Hopelessness 61
Chapter 10 – Sergeant of Pain 71
Chapter 11 – Zombies 75
Chapter 12 – The Offering 79
Chapter 13 – A Lamb to the Slaughter 83
Chapter 14 – Get Up or Stay Down 97

PART 2: The Hospital 99

Chapter 15 – Attacking the Problem 101
Chapter 16 – Kindness 109
Chapter 17 – Yoga and Life 113
Chapter 18 – Hoping for Home 119
Chapter 19 – Movie Madness 125
Chapter 20 – In-and-Out 135
Chapter 21 – Time Removes a Problem 143
Chapter 22 – Psychotherapy 149
Chapter 23 – My Reaction Is to Keep Getting Up 153

PART 3: Going Home 157

Chapter 24 – My Attack Plan: Heal Myself, Then Others 159
Chapter 25 – Change for Junior Year 165

Chapter 26 – The Real World ... 171
Chapter 27 – Cheerleader ... 177
Chapter 28 – Christmas ... 181
Chapter 29 – The Problem Is Lithium Is Good, Bad & Ugly .. 189
Chapter 30 – A Friend Brings Hope ... 193
Chapter 31 – Where Puzzles Lie ... 197
Chapter 32 – Life's Story ... 201
Chapter 33 – Winning by Living ... 205

PART 4: Living in a Dream ... 207
Chapter 34 – Senior Year Distractions ... 209
Chapter 35 – Gym Time ... 215
Chapter 36 – Sunlight Fades ... 217
Chapter 37 – Headache ... 225
Chapter 38 – Will You Marry Me? ... 229
Chapter 39 – Teeth ... 233
Chapter 40 – Predator ... 239
Chapter 41 – Cult Character ... 243
Chapter 42 – Death Follows Me ... 251
Chapter 43 – The Problem Is Pregnancy ... 255
Chapter 44 – Told to Get Up ... 259

PART 5: Life After School ... 265
Chapter 45 – No More School ... 267
Chapter 46 – Christmas Is Coming ... 271
Chapter 47 – College Brings Hope ... 277
Chapter 48 – A Snowflake in the Flames ... 281
Chapter 49 – What If? ... 283
Chapter 50 – Thou Shalt Not Bear False Witness ... 287
Chapter 51 – Humble Pie ... 291

PART 6: Don't Lose Hope ... 295
Chapter 52 – The Meek and the Afflicted ... 297
Chapter 53 – Missionary Training Center ... 299
Chapter 54 – Elder Green ... 303
Chapter 55 – Meet the President ... 307
Chapter 56 – On Bended Knee ... 311

Beating the Adversary:

A True Story of Schizoaffective Disorder

By Richard David Price

Edited by Vrinda Pendred
Illustrations and Cover Image by Stephen Leaver

Published by Conditional Publications

ISBN: 978-0-9564529-1-7

This book is also available in digital format
For information, visit www.conditionalpublications.com

Chapter 57 – A Few Days Later ... 317
Chapter 58 – A Depressed People ... 319
Chapter 59 – Missionary Life ... 323
Chapter 60 – Bad News ... 329
Chapter 61 – Sorry, Elder ... 333
Chapter 62 – The Letter or the Spirit of the Law ... 337
Chapter 63 – I Can't Swallow ... 343
Chapter 64 – An Hour with Mr Keaton ... 349
Chapter 65 – Winding Down and Breaking Down ... 353
Chapter 66 – Homecoming ... 359

PART 7: Returned Missionary ... 363

Chapter 67 – After the Silence ... 365
Chapter 68 – Adam ... 369
Chapter 69 – Beautiful Depression ... 377
Chapter 70 – The Problem Is a Plug ... 381
Chapter 71 – Getting Up ... 389
Chapter 72 – Attack the Grief ... 393

Appendices ... 397

Useful Resources ... 399
About Conditional Publications ... 401
Links and Social Media ... 401
Also from Conditional Publications: *Check Mates* ... 402
Also from Conditional Publications: *The Ladder* ... 404

Dedication

This book is dedicated to my friend Adam Perry, who died in an accident on the job; and to Kade Rosemann, who was struck by a bus and killed while riding his bike. This was witnessed by many of his peers in junior high, and I gave a talk in church to help the survivors. This was what overwhelmingly inspired me to write my story. I would not feel right without dedicating the book in Adam and Kade's honor, and know they continue their good works on the other side.

Thank You

First and foremost, I would like to thank my mother, Marcia Hinckley Willes Price, who stood by me throughout what most would consider a very hard life. I would also like to thank my father, W David Price, who is a great artist and a better person.

The biggest help with this book has come from Vrinda Pendred and Professor Colleen Whitley, whom the Lord brought into my life. Both of these marvelous people were like finding a diamond in the rough or winning the lottery.

Last but not least, I met a lady by the name of Mary Halbostad, who is like a second mother to me. Mary worked with me to help me find my voice in written form, as I gathered lost memories and dug up emotions.

Author's Preface

Inspired by true events, *Beating the Adversary* is the story of a young man, Rick, who is fighting insanity. This book profiles Rick's mind and takes you on the terrifying journey of a life and death struggle that changes his life. Rick must discover a way to find happiness living in the present and not be trampled by the demons of his past. Remember: the darkest parts of life are the unknown ones, so if you only take one thing from this book, let it be to stay alive.

I hope you will enjoy the book, which highlights the need for medical benefits for the mentally ill, to treat others with kindness and know this message is truly greater than the man.

Editor's Note

Until I met Richard (Rick) Price, I confess I had never heard of Schizoaffective Disorder – and I consider myself more informed about these things than the average person on the street. That alone told me the subject demanded more 'publicity', if you will.

I have now learned it is a condition that affects an estimated 0.5-0.8% of the population, which adds up to quite a number of people – almost as many as those who struggle with more commonly talked about conditions such as Tourette Syndrome.

The term *Schizoaffective Disorder* was first coined in 1933 by a doctor named Jacob Kasanin as a way of addressing the frequent overlap between psychosis and mood disorder – *psychosis* referring to a difficulty in determining what is real and what is not.

Symptoms of psychosis include delusions and hallucinations – which, as you will see from Rick's story, can be startlingly vivid. At times, it's difficult even for the reader to be certain what is really happening in his personal account. Imagine what it must have been like for him to *live* through that.

The mood disorder element of the condition can take the form of either major depression or bipolar disorder (fairly regular cycles of depression and mania). Rick has struggled with bipolar disorder, which can be a very serious condition presenting itself by turns through poor concentration, sleep problems, apathy, feelings of worthlessness, impulsiveness, racing thoughts, hyper- or hypo-reactions to events and people, and – at worst – suicidal thinking or behaviour.

I think the racing thoughts and disorganised thoughts may have been the biggest challenge in putting this book together. We wanted to make sure the reader got a clear picture of Rick's struggle; but equally, we wanted to make a book that accurately portrayed the condition, in order to educate people (including me!) about something that deserves more understanding. As a compromise, the racing thoughts are still included, but have been abridged to ease reading.

Living with such a condition can, predictably, affect one's social life. Making friends and starting a family is a challenge; and anyone with a mood disorder (such as myself) will know it affects your ability to focus and succeed in school. And after all that, imagine how hard it is to hold down a job when you're subject to unpredictable tormenting hallucinations, or if you have a major depressive episode that leaves you struggling to get out of bed, much less be productive.

Many sufferers of the condition don't receive a diagnosis for years. This is because psychotic episodes can be caused by all sorts of things – drug abuse, delirium, blood and thyroid problems, epilepsy, extreme stress, sleeping pills, anti-depressants, ADHD medication and even some dietary supplements. To achieve the correct diagnosis can be a laborious and frustrating process. Once diagnosis is established, patients can expect to be treated through medication, exercise regimes (Rick self-medicated through exercise, something I think helped him get through adolescence intact) and, in extreme cases, hospitalisation – like Rick.

The first part of this book focuses on Rick's time in high school. The middle section concentrates on his time in hospital, his diagnosis, and his rehabilitation into school. The final section is the story of his 'healing'. In earlier drafts, Rick shied away from speaking too much about his faith. He was adamant that he didn't want to sound preachy. However, I didn't feel his story would be complete without giving this more attention.

Something I noted in *Check Mates: A Collection of Fiction and Poetry about OCD, by People with OCD* was that interestingly, it seems these conditions frequently play on our most deeply held beliefs and values. Indeed, in many ways OCD can be viewed as a break from reality. And for Rick, the hallucinations targeted his faith. So it only makes sense that in order to grow beyond his diagnosis, he had to reach inside and hold that faith as tightly as he could. That is what the final section of his story is about.

Many people with such diagnoses can't write a book; it's a project that demands structure and clarity. That Rick has done this is a tremendous achievement – something I cannot stress enough. He has gone through more than most people have, but he has refused to let it hold him back. Instead, he has channelled his trauma into a positive message, teaching us all that no matter what our 'Adversary' may be, we have the power to beat it.

Vrinda Pendred
Editor and Founder of Conditional Publications
22 January 2014

PART 1:
Breaking Down

Chapter 1 – Sweet Sixteen

Saturday: July 11th, 1987 – Age 16

Mom once told me a story about me when I was very young. I had a lot of trauma. I was born without an esophagus and then fed through a tube for 18 months, splitting my nose open. I had every major childhood illness and actually died on the operating table after I knocked my head on the floor by falling off a chair. Yet she still decided to let me find out some things the hard way.

She said it started with the rocks. There I was, this little kid with a rock in each hand, coming upon an outside step. She watched as I crouched down with my rocks and leaned forward, falling. Then I picked the rocks back up and went on my way. It's like what's happening now – only now it's like the rocks keep getting thrown at me. But I just keep going.

* * *

Symptoms of a setting sun flow through an opening made in the closet; natural light doesn't find my room easily. For a child, darkness means bedtime. But darkness means something different in my world. It brings unfathomable misery and shadows that stalk me as a lion would its prey, creatures of the night that come out with only one reason: to unify and make me suffer. Yet the sounds of the house fill the air with hope that tonight may be peaceful, and that when I lie down, I'll sleep.

I live with four sisters and my brother, which means there are always two TVs on and three or four people talking at any given moment. Not to mention Mom and Dad. Even parents make noise, and for some reason the noise blends into static, making the nightmare stick out and life more painful.

I hide in my room, giving me some relief from the disorder and the prying of eyes that bear witness to the world passing in and out our front door. I lean against my bed. It has a storage chest and four drawers, which give it the impression of a coffin – a big wooden box with a mattress flung on top. I sit with comic book at hand and my pitch-black dog, Badger, at foot. Badger doesn't resemble his namesake in the least, being a Labrador, but he does carry a white badge on his chest.

I'm feeding upon visions of ninjas battling our slinging champion of justice when a call comes:

"Rick, come up here!"

It's Mom, in her close-but-not-quite-yelling tone.

Out the bedroom door I go, passing my brother Thomas. Thomas, age 14, is tall with a slender build, or what I would consider normal, and he's loved by all the girls for (as our family says) his Kevin Bacon-like looks. Behind Thomas' blue eyes lies the heart of an angel embodied in a mortal temple that has him moving up the sports ladder. What is most striking about Thomas is that he seems to be the man in any crowd, always finding friendship, and I have always loved him dearly.

However, that doesn't stop me feeling jealous. Thomas is everything I'm not. For one, I got the comedian Tom Hanks as my family-suggested lookalike. The worst of it is that Thomas is my ***younger*** brother.

It's not right to be shown up by a little brother.

I pass by Thomas and find the family room with its staircase. Badger cruises by me on his way for some dog food, most likely, or maybe to try to escape.

I hurry up the stairs, replying to the call. "What do you need, Mom?"

I reach the top of the stairs. Mom looks at me in confusion, pauses a moment and then says, "I didn't call you."

I twist back, heading down the stairs, crammed with raw fear.

"What's happening to me? I heard her. I heard her," I mumble to myself.

I sink back into my room. *I heard her, just like I've heard her a thousand times before.* I'm reeling, trying to figure it out. Shock courses through my body and weakness slams my knees, forcing me to the floor in a daze. I've lost logic as visions of a world filled with good and bad turn all bad. My thoughts race, getting worse and worse. I'm losing control.

Nobody's going to find out that anything's wrong with me, I vow to myself. *I have too many problems already.* I decide I'll ignore any calls for me if I can't see the person speaking.

I'm on the floor. My head falls between my legs and I perceive that I'm rocking back and forth with anxiety, but can't seem to stop.

Why would I start hearing things? I'm not crazy. I can fix this.

It was sophomore year when the nightmares started – nightmares that were horror films brought to life – and then the paranoia kicked in. That year seemed to last for time and all eternity.

Now junior year at East Valley High School is looming just around the corner. I want to be able to live normally and at least somewhat successfully. But I'm in such pain I feel I should be seeing blood.

If only I had power over what's happening to me.

***

Today, as on many days, I sit isolated in my room amongst my comic books, debating my puzzle for hours. *How did I let this happen to me?* I think, as if it's somehow my fault. I find no answers.

I see codes that act as links to my life. I find myself comparing my circumstances to those of the characters in my comic books. Some voice in the back of my mind tells me comics are a key to finding something that will help; they are the nexus between who I am and who I could be.

I flip through the pages of the book I now hold, mentally bonding to the storyline, which makes the story come to life. *These ideas come from* somewhere*, and if that's possible, then maybe it's possible for me to transform and become like them. I can figure it out.*

When I read my comics, I'm immersed in artwork, going to places that are free from worry, pain, and free from anybody else.

I mask myself in my alternate reality, much like the infamous Dr Jekyll, who became the monster Mr Hyde. I too begin a journey that brings me to Hyde, to rage. My Mr Hyde is also cloaked in darkness, but he wears my face and his every instinct is to fight for survival. His persona has the temperament of a wild beast. Hyde finds a way of handling what is going on all around me when I can't. He confronts my problems with my anger, my rage, and my evil. When Hyde comes out, he doesn't comprehend the aftermath; he simply reacts.

Hyde is very different from Joseph Smith. I'm a Mormon, and Joseph is a hero of mine. The Church of Jesus Christ of Latter-Day Saints (LDS) history shows that he took many beatings. He was even tarred and feathered. Yet he remained a good person, all for God.

God, I now pray, *I've lost you in this world of ghosts. Joseph, how it must have been for you when you were enduring such pain, and all for the sake of something nobody else saw. You did so much, for something that could not be proven.*

A dark thought enters my mind:

God is not answering my prayers.

How can this God be listening to me, when he knows how much pain I'm in, physically and mentally? Why is he doing nothing?

I'm empty inside, like after a death.

Did he ever listen to me? Or have I fallen into the cracks and I no longer count?

These questions never terminate, never go silent, and always take my concentration away from any part of real life that might try to creep in. I'm a man in a maze of mystery, where there's no asking for help, and only in struggling to break out will I remain alive. As soon as I solve one problem, that leads to something else, and again to something else. I'm in a never-ending story, a nomad shielded from the world by a wall of interrogation.

This new reality is suffocating, and I can't even trust the safety of my own house.

I need to push out the pain. I have to keep my moods in check. I need to remain in control of myself.

* * *

I flop into bed and put my hands behind my head to rest on the pillow. I listen to the house and think of fun times when I would play neighborhood football with the guys. It seems so long ago, but it was only last season. We played like the pros; it was savage and fun. I was the smallest player on the field by far, but that didn't matter. I was so determined to be the toughest player on the field at all times. I would get creamed, then pop right back up or run, dodging or dragging a guy.

My best friend was Malcolm, whom I still know. He has curly black hair and he's the prototype for a sprinter: five-foot-seven and full of muscle. He should have been named "Bullet". Malcolm was retro before there was retro, and it showed in his way of life. Malcolm was raised to be old school, giving him a swagger that's as good as a signature. Malcolm's family is large like mine, and is also LDS.

Malcolm would play quarterback and I was his number one target. It was amazing how he could hit me even without his thick-lens glasses. I learned this after the game that heralded one of the greatest Hail Mary passes the game had ever seen. Malcolm and I sat down to talk, Malcolm with his swagger and me with the inner happy spirit my face has never managed to show.

Malcolm said with a smile, "After I threw you the ball, all I could see was this hand coming up, surrounded by the other team, and I pulled it down for the touchdown."

"Yeah, that was a nice pass, man," I proudly enthused.

"I saw your hand and I knew you'd end up with the ball somehow. You just had to. I mean, it was like we were linked somehow and I just knew where to put the ball."

"Yeah, I don't think I'll ever be able to forget it."

"That was so cool when you rolled off Jim's back. How'd you do that?"

"I just sort of did it. I don't know. I didn't really think about it. What about you with that battling ram running of yours?"

"Just what I do, man."

We sat and talked about one of the greatest moments in our lives. Now, I look in the mirror and I see something completely foreign. I'm not whole. I no longer have control over myself or the events in my life.

***

I have a huge wishbone sticking out of my chest, like an extra set of bones just starting to be covered up with muscle. This has always caused me to act differently and given me an unbelievable fear of being touched, especially by a girl. To make things worse, I was born without an esophagus, requiring extensive long-term surgery in infancy, sometimes done without painkillers, due to the fact that when the tube in my neck slipped out, I was in danger of drowning. It's something worthy of Dr Shadow or some other brilliant doctor, but permanently having my shirt partially un-tucked to hide the wishbone will have to do for now.

I had so many surgeries as a child that I finally stopped crying, but now I feel the tears surface.

It's crazy to think of all I've been through already. There are my learning disabilities and all the tests that have gone along with them, then on to attending the special classes. I can't even count all the trips to the hospital. My mother has always been at my side, but she doesn't seem to have a clue now.

My mother, Marcia Hinckley Willes by birth, has always been a pretty lady, a brunette version of Margaret O'Houlihan from one of my favorites shows, *M*A*S*H.* Her parents are Ruth, a humanitarian, and Joseph, a historian who wanted to keep an attachment to the Hinckley side of the family and therefore gave it as his daughter's middle name. My mother was born as the Great Depression was ending, and so she was raised to be levelheaded. She would grow to be an English teacher, and I, making a thousand mistakes per assignment, would get frustrated with myself and reflect much of that frustration onto her. She also had so many kids that "Doctor Mom" fits like a glove – plus, she's currently the Relief Society President for the ward she always used to take me to.

Mom would know what to do to help me, but that would mean explaining what I think is happening to me.

How do I ask for help?

I throw my hands to my forehead and course my fingers through my hair. My head pounds. Darkness closes in around me. I'm in a living hell. Thoughts race through my mind like a train and my heart pulses.

Where is the air? I need to run!

I head out the front door, running as hard as I can. I run on the instinct of fight or flight. I run and run, not caring who I see or where I go. I want freedom, but freedom can't be found. I'm trapped inside myself and there's no way out.

What if I just end it all?

I hit my stride like a two-legged horse, and my vision blurs from the sweat streaming off my forehead.

Who would get my room? What would happen to my comics?

I round a corner, jumping over something, a loose mutt. The sweat burns my eyes.

I can't do that. I can't think this. It's not me. The Devil did this to me and I'm going to get even.

Visions of pain and torment fade from my mind as my emotions turn to anger. I continue to run, finishing about half a block away from home, and then walk it off.

I'm going to beat this out of pure stubbornness and spite. The Devil can't mess with me. Not as long as I stay strong and have something to say about it. I'm still here and I'm strong. Come after me and you'll see. You will lose in the end.

***

I open the front door to the house, careful not to let Badger out, and see my dad, who is a master shake-maker, making one of his peanut-butter-banana shakes. Walter David Price is his name, raised by Annie, who supported her newlywed husband Walter on his mission, before he became a Patriarch in the church.

To describe Dad as just another man would be to describe a gentleman as any other man. Dad is a worthy Priesthood holder, something that can't be measured in his six-foot frame, and he wants me to be one too.

Dad has always been a people person, from his earliest years to his days at Price Brothers Auto Parts, and then to becoming an insurance salesman. Insurance was his way of showing he would do anything to feed the family, and with his boyish good looks, dark hair, and blue eyes sitting under black steel frames, he made it work. Dad is also the original family movie maniac; this is the reason our vacations happen as if Chevy Chase were driving.

The ever sweet Melissa, age 11, is watching TV while doing her homework at the kitchen table. Melissa is somewhere between blond and brunette, and she's often described as being "hot". She's way ahead of the pack when it comes to kindness, which can always be seen in her hazel green eyes. Melissa is also a workhorse when it comes to school and, of course, has it easy when in a group of friends.

Tiffany, the youngest, sits on the couch watching TV with Melissa. Tiffany, 6, is a beautiful little brown-haired busybody with blue eyes, who looks like she will become Samantha from *Who's the Boss?* Tiffany is the younger version of me when it comes to accidents in the family, starting with breaking her leg sliding out of bed as a toddler. She has a knack for getting hurt when landing from any jump, but she has a winning smile.

Dad, on the other hand, isn't big on smiles. What he does have, however, he shows me as I near him: one of those fatherly gazes that says, "You're doing okay." Then he asks me one of the most important questions a father can ask:

"Do you want a shake?"

"Sure," I respond quietly.

"Can I have a shake, too?" Melissa asks with her ears perked for the answer.

"Dad, can I have one? Dad. Dad, can I have one?" Tiffany says excitedly, running into the kitchen to be right next to him.

"Okay, shakes all around," Dad says, grinning because he has something in his arsenal that we kids like. The blender starts up as passing car lights shine through the family room window of our corner rambler nestled in Sandy, Utah. The hum of the blender brings cold delight to my always-ready mouth and sometimes-uncertain stomach. I sit in a place called "home" not knowing where my heart lies, now that the world has changed.

Things aren't going to be the same for me anymore. This is just the start of something bad. I need to prepare myself for anything and I have no idea how to do that.

I need to keep my head clear so I'm ready for anything strange, and be able to recognize as best I can when something is real...and when it's not.

Chapter 2 – Back to School

Wednesday: October 14th, 1987 – Age 16

A hemorrhage of agony hits my gut as East Valley High comes into sight, and a sole thought fills my mind: *I hate that place.*

A loud squeal fills the air as the bus lurches to a stop in front of the school. There's only one way off and I wait my turn. I take a deep breath that fills me with peace, although it's short-lived. I anchor the line out onto the sidewalk and begin the hike into the building, as wisps of exhaust fumes fill my not-stuffy-enough nose. Reluctantly, I move toward the front doors. I try to shake the shadows that loom overhead, mind torn from body as thoughts begin to race.

It's not a school. It's a prison where its inmates have some kind of survival of the fittest game going on. They're just trying to ensure their position in the afterlife, even if it means entrenching a place in the depths of Hell, a process they call "Ranking".

Why was Mr Smith talking with Jessica in the hall? They were standing really close to one another. Is he in on this thing too?

I feel sick to my stomach.

Why do I have to be here? Nobody likes me anyway, so shouldn't I be able to stay home or something? It's not right, this place isn't right. I can't make it right, I don't know what to do. There has to be a way to beat this, to beat them, to beat ***him****.*

To process everyone else's way of thinking brings a pain of its own. Small things on this side can equal big points on the other. Those who are joined to the Ranks try to keep the cryptic messages amongst themselves, but this isn't always the easiest thing to do when you have to complete tasks that involve innocent people from the outside. They call it "hazing" but I think there's more to it.

I've seen some of them scoff at others for the pleasure of it, while others raise mocking to such a punishing level that the only goal could be peer-driven suicide. Others engage in simpler tasks, tripping the weak to laugh at them and then pouring it in when the victim is down. Later, when the prey has been weakened from the onslaught, the Ranks go in for the kill.

I walk into the building and see John Wilde, who reminds me of Theodore Huxtable from *The Bill Cosby Show*, in looks and manner, styling in his leather jacket. John could be best described as "cool", but not because of his jacket; because he's my friend. John is also, as far as I know, the only African-American in the school. So I guess on some level I can relate to him and he relates to me, since we both stand out as some kind of minority.

I wave my hand. "Hi, John," I say.

"Hi, Rick," John says with a smile brimming with confidence.

"Are you going to play football?"

"Yeah, I am. If you bulk up, I'm sure Coach would look at you next season. Or maybe you could try the wrestling team or track." John gives me a look of encouragement.

"Yeah, I know, but I'm not big on sports," I say. It's not true, but I feel unsure of myself, so I need an excuse.

John nods. "Well, some sports are different from others. Look at those guys who do the Ironman. They're awesome. If you started off with running, you could be one of those guys some day." He checks his watch. "Well, I'll catch you later."

"Okay."

John rushes off to class, so I go toward my own class, thinking. John stands out as an individual at this school because of his race. I would imagine that being the only black kid here would give him cause to defend himself once in a while. Maybe that's why he's my friend. But you can never really be sure why somebody wants to be your friend. John may only be putting on a face like everybody else, just a different face. It's impossible to tell in this place.

***

Since the school year started, I've been overlooking the actual schoolwork. Mr Smith, my second period teacher and a 1960s throwback, has that very subject on his mind. This is evident when I walk near his desk and hear, "Rick, come over here."

I move closer to the desk, knowing he wants to remind me of the missing schoolwork, which is almost all the work since school started. I'm forced to listen to him ramble on about something. I imagine someone trying to do homework in the middle of a tie-dyed version of World War II and then look at him with my right eyebrow crooked down to question his reasoning, completely still, before finally looking Mr Smith in the eyes.

"I'll try to do better," I say, not really believing it myself.

"Rick, what would you like to do for a living after high school?" Mr Smith asks in an attempt to lead me down a path.

"I'd like to be a comic book artist," I say, a little sheepishly.

"That would be awesome," he says, and I perk up. "I've never heard anybody mention that one. But I'm thinking they'll probably still want you to have gotten through high school. You know what? You should read *Beowulf.* It's kind of like a classic comic book, and it's not too long, either." His tone turns. "Anyway, Rick, I'm concerned. I'd like to see you achieve your goals, but I haven't seen any work from you this year and we need to change that."

I look at the ground. "I'll try," I say.

"Okay, good, but I want to be sure about this, so I'm going to mention it to Vice Principal Rush. I wanted to give you a heads up, first."

"Why do I have to talk to him?" I ask.

Mr Smith looks at me with sincerity, like he can see the depression I'm sinking into. But he would never come right out and say that, so instead he tells me, "I think you need some help and he may be able to do that better than I, because he can deal with your classes as a whole and I only have you for one class."

"Whatever," I say, almost under my breath.

"Well, you'd better take your seat. We need to get started."

Head down, I walk to my seat and slump into it. Mr Smith begins the class, speaking of who knows what, while I wonder when this information will be useful to me. I know he just finished talking to me about applying myself more, and yet I don't care. To me, school just isn't a place of learning anymore.

From my seat, I have a view of the hallway. I see a girl there whom I have never seen before. As she walks by, she turns, looks right at me, and smiles. "Wow. Who is that?" I whisper to myself.

I had girls smile at me in middle school, but in high school not one has even given me a sign that I'm alive. I'm not dating anybody and I don't go to dances. It's like I was standing still and all of a sudden everything around me became about sex – but I got left behind. I've felt like a void in a school of faces, but now I've had some real acknowledgement.

She was really cute. I should have gone out and said hi. No, maybe next time I see her is better. Wait, was Mr Smith checking her out? Not sure. I need to watch him.

***

My classes and time melt away, and I'm swallowed up in the movement all around.

When things normalize, it's time for Geometry and Jessica. She's one of the most beautiful girls I've ever seen, with long black hair, dark auburn eyes, and Malaysian skin. On a scale of "pretty" to "wow" she's a "wow", meaning vocabulary is lost when you see her. Jessica's figure could be in Webster's Dictionary showing what girls should look like: the right curves for a young man's eye, and she dresses simply in a t-shirt or sweater of just one color and some sort of jeans. She looks best in her red t-shirt and black jeans. I start daydreaming about her in my typical way.

Her beauty transcends that of angels descending to touch my soul. Her song carries my hopes across the mountains, across the deserts, across the seas. In the eyes of her beauty, no man can stand his ground. The soft touch of her shadow dances slowly in time. Faster I climb to catch the beauty, upon the cliffs, the mountains high. I try to reach the sky, for there ascends that beauty.

I will not – must *not – give in to temptation. Finally, no higher can I climb. I jump, falling, falling swiftly to the jagged rocks below. With all my might I cry aloud!*

In a twinkle, two lights flashing in Heaven become one, as we slip into the night. Beauty is the star in Heaven that will forever shine, tonight.

Chapter 3 – Vanishing Monsters

Wednesday: October 14th, 1987 – Age 16

At home, I have just eaten dinner and now I'm poised over my comics, ready to hunt.

Maybe I'll make up new superheroes.

I wonder about one of the characters. *What if he came out in real life?* When I next glance at the comic, I blink in astonishment. That character has disappeared from the page.

I survey the room frantically, gasping. *What have I done? I've ruined my comic! Plus, what if someone finds out it was me who let him escape?*

I close the comic book and then reopen it.

Nope, still gone.

I'm startled by a noise. Blinking my eyes again, I review the page once more.

He's back! Oh, good, my comic is going to be okay. What a relief. A seven-foot, two-thousand-pound monster could really wreck the city.

Shaken, I set the comic on the ground and get to my feet. I walk through the house, heading upstairs to get a drink of water, and then watch some TV with the family before I go to sleep.

It seems like my head has only just hit the pillow when my beautiful sister Mary Ann's alarm clock radio wakes me up. Mary Ann is about my height, with blue eyes, and looks like that girl from *Dirty Dancing.* She's extremely determined and very organized. Mary Ann is also very clean and when she goes off, it's like a bomb made to clean everything in sight.

Mary Ann is my opposite. I'm not very clean at all. Plus, I don't like to shave and can't let my hair be cut, and I take way too long in the shower, just standing there, not really getting clean. But my sister would still do anything for me and I know it.

Naturally, Mary Ann always gets ready for school on time. I, on the other hand, have no yearning to go to school, so I drift back to sleep and, as far as I know, go unnoticed.

The entire day goes by without anyone asking me any questions. In my current state, I wouldn't answer anyway.

***

Friday: October 16th, 1987 9:16 A.M. – Age 16

I sit in Vice Principal Rush's office waiting to find out what's going to happen to me. It seems like he's in a good mood – from the brief moment I saw him, anyway.

I look over my shoulder to see if he's coming back. I catch a glimpse of potbelly returning to the room. He's just some old guy who's bald, with a gut I'm sure is made of beer, and an old button-down collar shirt with brown slacks – but he's in control of the next stage of my life. It's my life, *my life*. He probably really likes that he can exact some kind of power over others. I have no choice but to sit and listen. I don't want to, but what are my other choices? Dropout high or whatever they call that last-chance high school…and who knows what?

Rush sits down in his worn-out chair. He sways in his seat and begins to explain my life. Only what he says doesn't sound that bad.

He starts, "I'm thinking we should get you into a class that will give you time to study and give you some kind of credit at the same time. I have a study hall that does that, though it's not one we usually just give out. But I've spoken with a couple of your teachers and I feel we need to do something to help you."

"Okay, that sounds good," I reply, surprised.

He smiles at me. "Now, I want you to get back on track. This is an opportunity for you. You can start your first time in the class today. This will be your new fourth period class. It will be held in room 111 just before lunch. Your new schedule is waiting for you at the front desk." He bears a look of confidence that this change will help.

"Okay," I say, eager to get out of his office.

"Do you have any questions about the changes?" Rush asks with a look of sincerity.

"No." I wouldn't ask one even if I did.

"Well then, you better get to class, and remember to stop by the front desk on the way for your new schedule."

"Thanks."

I jump from my seat, entranced by the idea that finally something good is happening.

***

In class, for once time seems to fly. Already I find myself watching the clock tick down the final minutes before study hall. The bell rings and the crowd pours through the door. I make my way down the hall toward the new classroom. The hallway is teeming with people I want nothing to do with.

A student named Jarvis catches my eye. *I hate that guy. He thinks he's the best thing to come to girls since Elvis.* Jarvis, who is the perfect prototype for a rocker with his skin-tight Levis, long hair, some kind of band t-shirt, and of course the cursing.

What's worse is that Jarvis is walking my way and looking at me like he has something in mind. *He's going to do the stiff shoulder move.*

BAM!

"Stupid Jarvis," I mumble to myself as the distance between us grows and I renew the search for my next class.

Room number 111 is in the northeast wing of the school, close to the door leading outside to the basketball court and weight room. I open the door and walk into the room. The wretch of a teacher is slumped at his desk. He catches a glimpse of me over his paper and his jaw drops. He sits up in his chair and beckons me to come up to his desk. He's wearing a dress shirt with the top button undone and a tie that's been loosened as if the strain of it is too much to bear.

I scan the room and realize what this class is: it's designed for the football team. Members of the team are playing poker, probably because their sport either hasn't yet started or has just ended.

As I reach his desk at the front of the class, the teacher says his name, which I don't catch, and then asks, "Do you know where you are?" I hand him my paperwork. He reads it thoughtfully and says, "Take a seat."

Many of the desks have been arranged in a circle for the game. I see some of the heads of what must be the varsity football team members turning to get a better look at me. In my head, I spin a picture of how these guys came to be.

It's like a clone machine spat out the same basic person over and over: gator golf shirts, denim jeans, and each one trying to boast their muscles in exactly the same way.

I walk over and sit next to them, close enough to see they're playing for money. A quick count tells me there are nine players in total. This is the first time I see Steve, who looks to be in the money. Steve's size and demeanor reek of linebacker. His hairline is receding a bit, which seems odd for someone in high school. He hasn't taken notice of me yet, but I have the attention of most of the other guys. Outright scrutiny is more like it, the kind a dog would get after having an accident in the middle of the room. I guess that means I don't look like a football player.

I look back at the teacher. He gets up from his seat and moves toward the door in a hurry. When he leaves the classroom, he shuts the door rather hard behind him. One thought crosses my mind: *Somebody is going to be the tough guy here and he wants nothing to do with it.*

I know better than to roll my hands into fists, posturing for what could be a fight. Instead I decide to play it cool and see what happens. Sure as the sun will set, a friendly face looks my way.

"Do you have any money?"

"I have a nickel," I respond.

"Come and play," another says as they make some room.

I push in my desk, as they want my nickel in the pot and I want to make some friends. The name of the friendly face is Leo. Aside from being gracious, Leo is Hispanic and a bit on the heavy side. By the look in his eyes, he's someone who could be a true friend, not just while you're in the room. The cards are dealt with a penny ante. Someone across the table is good enough to sport me so I can go in with my full nickel. The guys start fussing over their hands.

"I've never really played," I say, trying not to make an odd face.

"I'll help you if you need it," says a tall, muscular guy on my left who looks more like a basketball player.

"Thanks, man."

The time comes to take cards before we bet. Rounding the table one-by-one, the dealer comes to me. "How many do you want?"

"I'll take two."

My time to bet draws close as the table is rounded once more. I throw down my nickel, waiting for the other nickels to roll out. I can't bet again, and I'll lose if anybody raises the pot, so I make my move and hope for the best.

"I'm not very good at cards. Is four of a kind good?" Everybody folds and I begin to pull in the money when Steve looks at my cards.

"He was bluffing!" Steve exclaims in astonishment that he was taken.

I continue to pull in the money and ask, "Is bluffing not allowed?"

A big laugh starts up, with Steve almost pounding his chest. "I should beat the crap out of you for that."

With a bluff and some extra money, I become a member of the group. By the end of the game I've won enough money to get something for lunch. Food is a favorite of mine and buying a meal for a nickel seems like a good deal. The only thing is the lunchroom and snack machines are at the other end of the building.

The expedition to get food won't be simple. The distance is no longer an easy journey to travel. Every time I walk the halls, I'm risking my life. I now not only see things in the building, but at times the true faces of the Ranks are revealed before my eyes, and it feels like I'm in a movie. One second, they look like normal students walking the halls; the next, their faces are those of ghouls, vampires, or the walking dead – the darkness they carry inside. I have no idea how these people live with that.

The journey to the cafeteria comes to an abrupt halt when I'm blocked by a considerably cute blond girl with her hair pulled back in a ponytail, except for a few curls outlining the sides of her face. She's dressed like something from a magazine, with the looks of a cherub, but the first words out of her mouth don't exactly match her demeanor.

"You're a racist!" she says, anger pouring over her face.

Stunned, I stammer, "I – I'm not a racist. Why are you saying that?" All around me, time seems to pause.

My accuser continues, "You, I'm talking to you. You're a racist!" I feel like I've been set up as one of Hitler's henchmen and now it's time for mob justice.

"I'm not a racist. I'm friends with John," I blurt out, hardly able to think.

A gathering crowd starts chanting away: "Racist! Racist!"

I don't know what to say or how to react. Shrouded in confusion and feeling run under, I head toward the lunchroom. Once again, I go the rounds with all eyes focused on me leaving the scene.

Now I'm being attacked by some girl I've never laid eyes on before.

It's bad enough that coming home from school each day feels like returning from war and walking the halls means having to deal with demons that creep out of the cracks in the walls – girls calling me "fag" and often being pushed around, unable to tell anybody who I feel I am – dealing with the fact that dark corners hold demons with knife-like claws ready to gut an unknowing victim – not to mention the "Ranking" going on all around me. Now I'm a "racist".

What lurks behind any of us in the darkness? Unseen dangers of the spirit world assaulting mind and body, with no room for words like "mercy" or "enough".

***

When day finally turns to night, I'm in my room, exactly where I should be. I have a knack for doing the right thing most of the time, like being in the house on time, which is something mothers love. My mom, however, seems to be looking at me more and more with different eyes. *How much does she know? I don't want her to know.*

It just doesn't make sense that she would know what's happening. I've been able to keep it inside so well. I mean, I'm not any different from how I used to be, yet more and more people are staring at me. I don't understand why people don't leave me alone. I just want everybody to leave me alone!

I want to be seen and not seen, at the same time. If I had friends who stuck, I could take an eraser to the rest of the world. Maybe then my pain would terminate. I know when I'm in school all eyes are on me and they're looking to hurt me.

Adults always tell you to run before you get into a fight. I try not to fight, but when it's you against the world and your world is becoming completely deranged, it can get hard to figure another way to solve the problem.

Our world is a world of survival of the fittest and I can't change that. What happened to humans acting like humans, instead of animals? I may never know the answer to that.

The walls feel like they're closing in, and I have an overpowering need to exercise. I get up and begin what is becoming routine shadow rope jumping. This continues for a half hour or so. I can't stop until I feel some relief. I have to keep going; I need the rush. It's a primal force screaming inside, wanting release. It helps me forget my problems.

I can't keep going on like this. Somebody or something needs to show up where I can see it. And when it does, I'm going to pound it.

Chapter 4 – Get Up and Attack

Saturday: October 17th, 1987 – Age 16

I lie in the dream world of a superhero saving the day, when my stomach leaps into my throat and the mattress evaporates from beneath me. I clutch the sides of the bed, spread-eagle. An immense pull spirals beneath me. The room is completely dark except for the eerie light coming up from the cavernous hole. I hear wailing as if from nowhere and everywhere at the same time, followed by an intense voice:

"So you think you can beat me!"

Deranged screams cry, ***"Drop and burn, drop and burn!"***

The punishment from the noise grows more intense, and I'm grabbed by reptilian hands. Rage boils to the surface of my stretched body and pours off into the abyss. My hold tightens and my heels bite into the wooden bed as the pull increases from the vortex. Hell's hounds wail for blood.

I turn my head to the left and the light is extinguished. I see only darkness where my mattress should be, as if I'm not worthy to witness Hell. I must escape. I grab hard onto the left side of the bed. I launch myself onto the floor and look up, but I see nothing but my bedroom, as always.

I'm now drenched in sweat, my muscles throbbing. I sit on the floor and search for some sign of explanation. I know this was no nightmare; whatever it is, it has changed my life. This thing I'm tied up in has been taken to a whole new level. This is a reality I'm not prepared for. How am I supposed to go through this every night? This is very different from seeing things move in the dark.

Remembering a film I once saw on TV, I think:

Nightmare on Elm Street *said you can't control your dreams; you can only stay awake. But I can't avoid sleeping forever.*

If I'm to be attacked in my sleep, I need to become a dream warrior so I'll know when a dream is about to be taken to something more.

And what if it isn't *a dream, but an attack by the Adversary coming out of nowhere?* Then *what should I do?*

Only wait and try to fight.

A great deal of time passes before I fall asleep on the floor. It's an uneasy sleep with room inspection taking place whenever I'm startled. When morning breaks, I awaken wounded, but deeper still is the emotional disfiguration.

I go to the bathroom without putting on a t-shirt and I see something out of the corner of my eye in the big outer bathroom mirror: scratches on my back where none were before. The only reason for scratches would be last night.

Could I have been so out of it last night that I didn't feel being scratched? Or is it worse? Did the Devil and his Angels only give me a taste of what's to come?

Mary Ann comes in. "What happened to your back?" she asks with concern.

So she can see them, too.

People often look into space for answers; I have no answer for Mary Ann and I'm looking any place I can think of. I can't say it was an attack from the Devil.

"Rick, did you hear me? What happened to your back?" Mary Ann repeats, determined to get an answer as always.

I'm taking way too long. I have to offer something.

"Badger must have done it," I mutter.

"Doesn't look like something he could've done."

"Well. I need to eat something. Later, Annie."

I walk off angry, not wanting to be bothered by her again while I'm trying to figure this out.

I have to be strong. I can't change what others think or how they feel, but by sheer force of will I can change my physical body. It doesn't matter how much pain it takes to make that change, if it's the key to my freedom. I'll never give in to the Adversary. I must be an Avenging Angel – and besides strength, I may have other powers, if I can figure them out.

If Angels have done certain things in the scriptures, then maybe some of those things can be found in my comics. I need to consider the fact that I'm involved in something bigger than normal life, and so all the rules are going to be different – not just for the world I'm now in, but for myself as well.

Hunger overwhelms me, so I throw on a shirt and head upstairs where my mom is in the kitchen.

"Richard," Mom calls me. This sounds serious. "I'd like to talk to you."

"Okay."

Mom points me into the living room and we sit down together. I wait while she tries to find the words to explain or ask what is wrong with her son. Being an English major and a teacher, Mom isn't usually at a loss for words. Badger joins us in the room looking rather puzzled, but that's not unusual for him.

Finally, Mom says, "It seems you've become more unfocused than usual. You're mouthing off more and just not acting like yourself. I want to talk to you to find out what's going on with you. I know you don't want to talk about it, because I've noticed you're also talking even less than normal, and for you that means you're pretty much not talking."

I look at her with nothing to say, but I think, *Where's this coming from? And where is she going with it?*

She continues. "Other times, I see you walking around the house tapping the walls, looking like a zombie, and it scares me. What's going on with you?"

I look at the ground, having no answer.

"And every time I ask you what's wrong, you say, 'Nothing.' I'm not sure what to do with that," she says.

The funny thing is that if she asked at this moment, "What are you thinking about?" I would give the same reply and it would be true. My mind is void of activity.

Or maybe it's just the opposite; maybe it's on overload.

I look into her eyes and say, "I don't know what's going on." Which is a lie, but only to a point. I do know my life is different.

I'm the same person, but I don't want her to know how much is going on in my life, so I continue with a half-truth. "I guess I'm just having problems at school. You know, with the other kids there."

"Why are you having problems? You've always been pretty good at making friends. Is high school so different for you?"

That's a loaded question.

"It's not just the students. I don't like the school itself."

She frowns. "You mean the building?"

"Yeah, I always get really uncomfortable there. It's so old."

A look of bewilderment crosses Mom's face as she replies, "Oh, I see. Okay."

I turn my focus to the floor.

Mom sighs and changes the subject, defeated. "Well, tomorrow night can you watch Tiffany? I have some things to do."

"Mom, I have too many things on my mind to worry about somebody else right now," I say, not at all concerned about what she might say in response.

"Well, okay." She tries not to look shocked and then says, "It's almost time for dinner. Why don't we pick this up another time? I need to get things done. Everybody will be hungry. Go and watch TV or something."

***

Without another word, I make my way downstairs, deciding to work the channels. I become a potato on the couch as my mind runs through the events that have just taken place. It seems like even when I have a really bad episode, I've managed to keep a fairly normal profile at home, so far – maybe because in having so many kids, Mom and Dad have too much to deal with. Or maybe it's because I keep my mouth shut enough of the time that they don't know the crazy things happening in the house. They're mostly at night, anyway.

If I could witness the other side of the veil, or if Mom or Dad could see it, then maybe I could learn what is beginning to oppress my life. There's a great deal of damage already done. Try and follow, if you will:

First, there's Rick who is known and loved by many people.

There's Rick who can't function, but is physically awake anyway. Trouble stirs within the bowels of Rick's soul.

There's his Mr Hyde. Mr Hyde, as we all know, has his own brand of powerful control.

And lastly, there's Coma Guy, who might as well be a snapshot of Rick sleeping, because that's all he ever does. He has already shown the ability to sleep for 24 hours straight.

Then there's that high school and the battle that hangs overhead. School will come again on Monday.

I leave the sofa and work out as hard as I can. Sunday is no day of rest. I'm at war with an unseen enemy. I can't let my body recover; I have to keep pushing. These workouts are beginning to show more and more in the form of compounded muscle swelling that looks like I'm taking steroids.

Nothing makes sense anymore. If nothing is really happening to me, why am I in such pain all the time? And if it's all in my head, why can't I just stop it?

What runs a tingle up my spine? Me.

I can't find any answers in the darkness, and yet I try and try. I'll push and fight, even if I can't see what's there. Wherever I go, no matter how far I run, it's never enough. In the end, I'm alone in the dark with no answers.

I reach down into the inner darkness of my soul to find the anger to fuel my stubborn mind. I pour over the recent events, giving me new hope, because I'm still here, alive, and ready to fight. Nobody can take that away from me. A wall may stand between me and everybody else who could help me, but I will not back down.

There's a difference between death and suicide, I think.

My father works in insurance and picks up a lot of death stories, which he often relays to his kids so we don't do stupid things.

These stories are all well intended, but they haven't always served their purpose, because we've still done tons of stupid stuff. Like rock climbing in our Rocky Mountains without any gear; or the thing most teenagers do, driving too fast and then jumping the car. To say I should have died many times is an oversimplification. By far, the best thing I've ever done when faced with a stupid choice was choose life. I've seen death come and take grandparents from me; I've heard many stories of people who were passed on by an act of God, if you will; and I've heard of some who just couldn't take the pain and ended it.

Choice! The choice of suicide says to the Adversary, "You win and I lose."

I refuse to let anybody or anything have power over me – nobody has the power to make me take my life! Especially someone who won't show their face in the light of day – not the King of Demons, not the Queen of Black Magic, and not the Devil.

So they want me dead. They'll have to kill me.

Chapter 5 – Patriarchal Blessing

Monday: October 19th, 1987 – Age 16

Monday hits me right in the face. Another day of school. Now study hall is the only place that seems normal – the way normal is supposed to feel. Plus, I usually win at poker and I can always use the money.

I make like a slug when getting myself ready for school, dressing and having something to eat, and doing my best to brace myself. Grotesque things have become commonplace, so ducking out for part of the day has become the norm. At this point, expecting something unusual to happen is just commonsense.

Time passes. I mumble to myself, "I guess I'd better get going or I'll miss the stupid bus."

I board the bus along with the other kids all gathered for the ride. The bus is slow and, to me, painful to be on, as it's a reminder that from here on, no one really knows me.

Once inside the school, I stand amongst the crowd, trying to fade into it, when I'm approached by an unfamiliar face: a pale underweight female holding a piece of paper. Blue eyes peer out from her silky blond hair. I scan my options for escape in case I need to leave in a hurry. I'm in a main artery of the school, with plenty of routes to get away, so I decide not to worry and then edge toward the girl. I glimpse a student with a broken leg crutching his way by.

The girl now stands directly in front of me. "I'm supposed to marry you," she says with complete confidence. "You're going to be my eternal companion. I can't believe I've finally met my soul mate."

I look into her blue eyes with astonishment. "What?" I blurt.

"I'm supposed to marry you. Look. This is you, right?" Her finger points to part of a typed-out paper. I look closely and see what seems to be a Patriarchal Blessing – a personal prayer typed out for later use. I read the name: Richard David Price. *It's my name.*

"That's you, right?" she says with a smile.

"No. I go by Rick. I have no idea what you're talking about."

"What? But that's just what you go by; this is you. Look, this is you!" she says as the frustration builds throughout her body.

A sense of darkness engulfs me and blocks me from laughing at my facetiousness. A dull feeling gains strides and shock drills into my gut.

Who are you?

I can't get the words out of my mouth. Then fate steps in: the crowd bumps somebody in between us. I take my chance to slip off around the corner and down the hall.

I quickly survey the area over my shoulder. I can tell I'm not being followed, which is good because I need a few minutes to think over what just happened.

That was so weird. I can't even get a girl to look at me, let alone a girlfriend. Then some girl comes out of nowhere and says she's supposed to marry me and she has it in her blessing? It just doesn't make sense. Girls don't do things like that. I should tell somebody. They'll get a laugh out of this or something....

Or maybe I should just hold onto it.

Then, as if nothing happened, the day goes on as normal…well, until study hall, that is.

***

Once the group is seated, the tournament is on, with all the colorful language that goes along with it. I've become the newest poster child for swearing, though all the glory is found in the title, because nobody took my picture.

Ten minutes into the game, a guy named Brent looks infuriated with me. He jumps from his seat and grabs me by the shirt with his left hand, clenching a fist with his right. “Cheater!” he yells. “Nobody is that good. I’m sick of you taking my money!”

I pause to consider how much money that would be. Then I shoot back with, “Wow, dude. Your forearm is really developed. Do you pitch or something?”

I know full well that he does; he was the pitcher when I tried out for Babe Ruth one summer, which perhaps rings a bell in his head since I did hit off him three times in a row. I couldn’t get the distance afterward that Coach wanted. Sometimes getting on base just isn’t enough.

Brent’s anger turns into questions and he releases my shirt.

“I do? Do you really think I’m developed or are you just trying not to get knocked out? Did somebody tell you I’m a pitcher?”

“No. Seriously, you have real definition. The curve in your forearm is massive. It goes right up into your wrist.”

Brent’s tone grows serious as he says, “If you’re messing with me, you’re toast.”

“Brent, I’m not messing with you.”

The other guys look at me like I’m either insane or an exposed treasure trove of knowledge, or maybe something else altogether. The truth is: if I set my mind to something, I don’t just do it; I *really* do it. I’ve read all the muscle magazines I can and learned all about muscles and how they work.

I need to seal the deal, so I add, “I’ll bet your girlfriend thinks your arms are pretty big.”

“She has told me she likes them,” Brent replies with a small grin.

Steve leans in and asks, “Do you think I should wear my shirt sleeves rolled up like this, or down? Which way’s better to show off my arms?” Steve rolls up one sleeve on his golf shirt with the other still down.

Maybe Steve is trying to help me.

I take the easy way out, even though it's far from macho, and answer the question. "I'd just leave it down, if I were you. Your arm is already so big that you don't need to roll it up. That'll make you stand out more, because it will look like you're not *trying* to stand out."

Steve's question and my reply seem to ease the room. At least, I hope so.

"Thanks, man."

"No problem."

More questions come my way. Each of the guys wants to know his strength. I'm fulfilling a need, and since my own need is to get out of a conflict, I play along.

Then, as if somebody said "hike", I'm free and clear…but my mind brings me back to the girl in the hallway from earlier in the day, and I want to make sure the previous subject has completely changed, so my own comment comes out, ready or not.

"Some girl showed me her Patriarchal Blessing today and it said she was supposed to marry me."

They look at me. One of them asks, "What's that?"

"It's a blessing from God," I explain.

Mouths open and Leo says, "Are you serious?"

"Yes. I read it right off the paper. It was my full name."

Brent says, "Are you sure? I've never heard of such a thing happening." Eyes gaze around at each other.

"Yes, I'm sure. It was right in front of me."

Brent continues, "Who was this girl?"

I answer, "I don't know." *Why are you always bothering me? You're such a pain. Okay, think.* "I never saw her before."

I finish my sentence just as the bell sounds. Nobody moves for a moment, which leaves me wondering what to do.

Then they start to leave before I have to say anything else.

***

Tick-tock go the hands of my master. The events of the day have taken their toll and it's becoming increasingly difficult to concentrate or even stay awake.

At the sound of Hell's final bell, I make my way to the bus and, step-by-step, I reach a seat. The bus starts clocking the miles that take me to a place called home.

"Home" has become a bittersweet word in its own right. A place of solitude is becoming a dynamic battlefield from which there's no place to hide.

The bus comes to a stop at our church, near my house. I snap back to life at the thought of a good meal. I get off the bus and see all the guys I know walking off, except for one.

No Malcolm.

My friend Malcolm has been going to his dad's office after school to do homework, and following the homework he starts his actual work with his dad. Malcolm is the kind of guy who doesn't take any bull. I've always respected him for that, but I don't like that he's not around very much.

I head across the parking lot on the way home, kicking rocks as I go. When the rocks hit the curb, it means I'm close – only a street and the lawn to go.

In a New York minute I'm opening the door to the kitchen and sitting on a stool at the counter. My attention drops and I hit space not long before Mom walks into the room.

"Rick...Rick, are you okay?" she asks, tying to gauge where I'm at mentally.

I'm not really sure how I am at this point, so I simply answer, "Yeah."

"Do you want to watch TV while I make dinner?"

I say, "Okay," but somehow don't leave the stool.

"Do you need help?"

"No, I can do it."

I follow my mom, who is already heading through the dining room and into the family room, where she pulls back my favorite chair and places it in front of the TV. "Sit down," she says.

Katie is already sitting in the room. She's a dark-haired stunner with blue eyes, and she's one of the brains in the family. Katie can get all her homework done in what seems like a minute, and then she's off to her friends. Katie's biggest fault is that she's fun to tease and has the unfortunate distinction of once being run over by Thomas on his bike, because he wanted to test his brakes. Katie, who will most likely breeze through college, will take the world by storm, because she has a keen eye for art and will be able to move mountains with it.

Right now, Katie is learning patience as I follow Mom's directions. I sit down and take hold of the remote she hands me. I aim the remote at the TV. I flip through the channels at three- to five-second intervals, but find nothing to watch. Without cable, the channels go by quickly.

After a few minutes, I vaguely hear my beautiful sister Katie saying in the background, "Mom, can you tell Rick to stop teasing?"

"I don't think he's teasing you. I'm sorry, Katie, but I need to watch what he does."

"What's going on?" little sister Tiffany comes in and asks, but no one answers.

The flipping continues as that part of the conversation is recorded in my subconscious, not grasping the weight of it in my current state. The channels bring me little hope; I find nothing to watch.

I get up from my seat and start making rounds. I hit the "touch spots" on the walls – places I just feel *must* be touched – and flip the lights that need to be worked, off and then on again.

If I don't do one of these things, bad things will happen and disorder will be brought to the forefront of the world – a world that contains no thoughts, no emotions, and no signs of outward affection. In this world, servant and master become the same and the pain from the hours blends into nothing but mist. In this world, people can come and go and never be thanked for their acts of kindness, or even noticed at all. To live here is to die alone, but free of the pain of so many of the other worlds that have befouled my life.

Spark!

Life returns to my mind's eye and travels down to my physical eyes, which now focuses on the chair.

Time to get back to the chair, where I can find the remote.

The remote is there, ready to be picked up, my remote. I exercise the channels again.

This goes on for some time, until a single thought comes: *Sleep.* Time for bed.

I head through the halls, toward my room. When I reach it, I open the door and see it's dark, lit only by the dim glow of the alarm clock.

I step inside, looking around for any other potential life signs that may be waiting for me. I'm especially wary of the ones that hide in the shadows and only want to come out when nobody else is around as witness.

I lie down, believing that I'll wake if I need to fight.

Weary from the day, sleep finally comes.

Chapter 6 – Linebackers

Tuesday: October 20th, 1987 – Age 16

Someplace out in the world a baby is being born, somebody is in need of help, somebody is falling in love, and somebody is dying. But my world revolves around me and trying to figure out the big question: why are bad things happening to a good person?

There's no hope in knowing God's punishment is as endless as He is Eternal, when tears streak across your face from the blinding pain of a damaged soul

The alarm sounds the call of the wild. I coax my legs to put my feet on the floor, and then look at the clock with a scowl.

I prepare for school, which should be a very mundane event. I brush my teeth and hair, and use the bathroom. However, as I get closer to going to school, it just doesn't seem the right thing to do. It seems like going to school could cause harm to come upon me.

My reflection in the mirror brings me to pause. My eyes are glazed over, and even I know that's a surefire red flag for depression.

I wish I could see the future, even if I could only see my own. Instead, what I see are misfortunes and lost hope – misfortunes that are mine as well as everybody else's, and they're trying to link together into some kind of nexus where I'm finally pulled in at different points. Nothing is simple anymore and my mind has to travel a million miles per second to keep up.

At least I woke up this morning. Because there was the question of whether I would or not.

***

After readying myself, and being dropped at school by Mom, I make my way inside. The almost-still air brings the scent of the aged building and the sounds are of people who are all happier than

I am. I walk over to a pillar and lean on it, in an effort to look cool. I must gather myself and generate a plan of action.

Mr Crutch from the day before happens by. He's yet another example of the nexus of all living things that are connected to or interfering with my life. It was Mr Crutch who was on hand during the blessing episode. Perhaps he had something to do with the delivery of the blessing, or with the girl finding me.

I'd better keep an eye on him.

What shakes me more is that some time before he broke his leg, he once invaded one of my dreams telling me I could have his girlfriend, who was hot. So there's ample cause to consider him an enemy, because nobody would give away a hot girlfriend.

For all I know, his leg isn't actually broken. It could be part of something bigger, or maybe he was trying for a Ranking.

I see all the familiar faces, hear the same old sounds and am surrounded by different perfumes. *Hell on Earth holds many mysteries.*

I pivot and head for my first class. The crowd in the hallway thins, which means I'm running late. I pick up the pace and find my way to my classroom, and then my desk, amongst other students who look at me as if I'm not supposed to be here.

Why is everybody looking at me like that? Did I do something wrong? Bunch of idiots! I can take on any one of them.

When study hall finally rolls around, I'm the first one in the class. In fact, it seems I'm going to be the only one in the class. Then the guys slowly start to come in. I guess they were lifting weights.

Steve comes running in. Excitedly, he lets out, "Rick, I'm glad you're here!" He hurries over, pushing back on my shoulder, and then he KISSES ME ON THE MOUTH!

In complete shock, I ask, "Why did you do that?"

"For helping me get my new girlfriend. What's the problem?" Steve asks as if he's done it a thousand times.

"You jerk, that was my first kiss. You kissed me!" I let out with total disgust.

Everybody starts laughing as my face draws shock in spades. Shy and introverted, I may be, but the romantic in me thinks that's not the way I wanted to remember being kissed by another person.

Then I hear Jeff. "That would mean the coach was my first kiss."

"Coach kissed you?" asks Travis.

"I threw a no-hitter."

"Yeah, okay, but Coach? Come on, man."

"Hold up, you guys. Didn't you hear what Rick said? He said he's a virgin," Steve reminds them, holding up his hand to quiet them. The laughter dissolves into awkward silence, which then turns into an even more uncomfortable conversation. It's directed right at me and I don't know how to evade it.

"Rick, we need to get you with a girl," Parker says with a smile, as similar comments come at me. Some even say I can borrow their girlfriends, like girls are only playthings. I don't know how to explain that I'm so not ready for something like that right now – that to me, a girl is something like gold, not a toy.

The next question comes from Brent, and it makes me even more uncomfortable:

"How come you're in and out of school so much?"

His observation strikes not just at my heart, but at the very fears I'm living with. I'll need to cover my tracks with lies – lies that become easier and easier to tell each time. I pull one out for cover.

"I just have bad allergies and asthma," I say. "Sometimes...I just can't leave the house."

"You don't ever seem that sick," Brent responds, more questioning than commenting. He's always wondering what he's not seeing.

"Thanks, man," I say. "I try not to let that stuff show. It's never cool to be known as the sick kid, you know."

But inside, I think, *Brent must be watching my behavior pretty closely to ask this type of question. He must keep tabs on me all the time. I don't want anybody watching me.*

Still, my cover story is perfect, since none of them know my background. The story is also true, in a way. Since we moved into our current Mayfield Place house, every year for about three days I pick my spot by the piano and just sleep, because of allergies.

"Anybody know whose hand is it?" queries Leo, and I'm finally off the hook. I guess I'm lucky these guys aren't that deep or personal by nature. Nevertheless, I end up leaving the study hall feeling changed.

I've been violated. Violated by a linebacker. I had no recourse, and now I have to live with it, when I'm already living with so many things that I could break. I hate myself, and I hate the world.

***

As the bus brings me back to the hell of isolation at home, I think, *I want to be bigger and stronger.* I know the respect I get from that study hall group isn't the best.

A new idea hits me: I may have these problems…but I can make my brother tougher. He will be better than I am. He has to; he's always excelled in sports.

When I get home, my brother Thomas is already downstairs, sitting on his bed. I run into his room and start yelling at him incoherently.

"Why are you yelling at me!?" he cries in shock.

Blinded in the moment, I have no response.

"Mom!"

"Thomas, you need to be strong!" I shout at him.

"Richard!" Mom lets out, from behind me.

I shrink like a dog putting his tail between his legs, looking to hide.

"What are you doing!?" she demands.

I can't talk. I go to my room with her still after me, waiting for Dad to take his turn at yelling at me.

They ground me. The words mean nothing compared to what happens next. The Lord opens my eyes to my shame. I sink lower than I ever have. I may be overrun with problems, yet that doesn't release me from the fact that I was weak. I was weak, and that will forever be mine to carry.

Thomas, I'm sorry.

***

Night falls and brings peace to those who are pure at heart. I lie down to rest, feeling neither at peace nor pure. It's like I'm losing control and being punished at night. Not just with nightmares, but also with something else, something I don't understand. I get attacked and it's real. I try to fight back, but against what?

For example, last night, as I slept, my front teeth were filed down, and people seeing the results think I did it myself. But I was asleep in bed when it happened; I don't remember a thing.

It seems like a lifetime ago that we were at, say, Disneyland, a place where our family always came together and had fun despite all life threw at us. We would run around hitting all the rides, knowing all the back trails to use to beat the crowds. Then would follow a day at the beach where we could boogie-board or just swim in the waves. There were always beautiful things to see, especially in the summer.

So why now – when I'm getting to the age that I should be having the most fun in my life – am I being hurt?

Chapter 7 – No More Fist Fights?

Wednesday: October 21st, 1987 – Age 16

The sound of the alarm is met with swift revenge as I slam it before sliding out of bed. I'm eager to get out of the house as quickly as possible.

I find clothes, dress, and then move out the door almost in one motion, down the hall, into the family room and around the corner. Then I run quietly upstairs. I try to shake the feeling that I'm acting cowardly with so little reason. I see my adorable baby sister, Tiffany, as I head out the door, skipping breakfast.

***

In first period, Mrs Pearce's class, I get caught trying to sneak out and I'm scolded.

Second period finds me mouthing off at Jarvis, who says, "I'm going to get you later."

I have to stay after class, while the teacher lets Jarvis leave. "Stupid Jarvis," I mutter on my way out the door after another tongue lashing, this time from Mr Smith, who is either very concerned or a little hung over.

Third period is naptime – not my best day – but at least I try to pay attention to Mrs Johnson's lecture about sleeping during class.

When I leave her class, I see Jarvis and I know he's coming for me. I remember, *He has a ton of brute strength and he will pound you like a grape.*

I'm a man without fear and this day I'm really mad at the world, so I head right for him. Jarvis has the long hair of a rocker, always wears jeans and uses the F-word for nouns, verbs and anything else he can think of. Jarvis, who is about six-foot-two and fairly well built, is exactly the kind of guy I would look to pick a fight with if I had no other choice but to pick a fight. After all, knock out the big guy and get respect. Knock out a little guy and you were meant to do it anyway.

Jarvis walks up and stares down at me with all the anger he can fire up. I look right back at him and give a little smile.

Jarvis lets out, "What are you smiling about, you little...."

"I'm waiting to see what you're going to do, tough guy." I want to bait him into throwing the first punch.

SLAM! He pushes me into the lockers. I batter my fist into them before bouncing back at him.

That's not good enough.

Then it happens, something I've never seen before. Jarvis closes his eyes and swings at me with an open hand. I stop to watch it come at me in slow motion, with slack-jawed onlookers waiting to see blood.

What is going on here? I've never seen anybody swing so slowly in my life, and why does he have his eyes closed? What would happen if I walked away?

Finally his strike lands on my jaw, moving my head to the left. It feels like he placed his hand on my face and then pushed. I stand, a bit dazed by the odd turn of events.

What just happened?

I don't know what to do and everybody around us is yelling for us to fight.

"Hit him back!"

"Don't be a girl, hit him!"

That must be how he uses his brute strength. I must be immune to it somehow. What am I?

Jarvis, realizing I haven't fallen down, looks to come at me again, but he's interrupted by a teacher pushing through the crowd. I've never seen him before.

"What's going on here?" he demands.

The rules of the playground dictate that you say nothing, and so I do just that.

"Nothing," I say.

The teacher looks at us, unconvinced. "Alright," he says, "you two, split."

Jarvis turns like he's on a stick, shrugs, and bearishly walks away. I look back at the teacher, ignoring what's left of the dispersing crowd.

With a stern look on his face, the teacher says, "You better get to class."

I walk off, trying to forget about Jarvis, who seems to be a real thorn in my side.

I'm now sort of hit by somebody who probably has at least sixty pounds on me, and yet nothing even happened. Nothing. His hand barely moved me, despite his size. That's really weird. I need to learn more about this brute strength.

***

On the bus home, I wonder if Mom knows about the fight. I try to tune out words only I can hear by gazing out the window, longing for a glimpse of what makes other people tick.

These people have normal lives. But how do they get them? I mean, look at them. None of them are perfect. So why is life so easy for them and not me?

When at last the bus arrives at its destination, it's time to go home and hopefully just eat dinner, then sleep. I walk in the door and head for the kitchen.

"Rick, can I talk to you?" Mom stops me.

"Okay."

I follow her down the hall to my parents' master bedroom.

This isn't going to be good.

We walk into the room and sit down on the bed. I listen as Mom talks for about a minute, and I break into uncontrollable tears.

What's happening to me?

"Why are you crying?" Mom has a look I've never seen before on her face, like fear and bewilderment at the same time.

"I don't know." Any answer could not ring truer. I don't know why I'm crying. Fear races up my spine – fear, real fear, is not part of my nature.

I'm falling apart and will never be the same.

Quickly, Mom shuts the door to protect my privacy. She comes back and sits next to me on the bed.

"Calm down, you're not in trouble. I'm just trying to understand what's going on with you. Your grades are going downhill and you're not yourself. Rick, you never cry, even when you're in pain. What's going on? I want to understand so I can help you." She looks as though I've just become either the greatest liar or the greatest mystery on Earth.

I know I need to speak, but at this point, I'm not sure what to say that will convince her I'm not crazy. When the words come, they are nothing grand.

"I don't know. I guess just a lot of different stuff."

I don't want you to put me in the nut house.

I search the vast emptiness in my head.

What's Mom thinking about me?

It becomes impossible to find the words to express myself.

She won't understand anything that's happening to me anyway. How could she?

I don't know...maybe she could.

"What kind of stuff?" Mom continues.

"I don't know."

"You just said that," she says with some frustration. "You don't know what's going on and you don't know why you're crying. What *can* you tell me?"

"Nothing," I say, watching her hands.

"Nothing. Are you saying nothing's going on, or you have nothing to say?" she asks, her worry turning to stress.

"I don't know." I'm at a complete loss for words, still looking anywhere but her eyes.

"Richard, I'm trying to help you. Do you understand that? Are you listening? I can't tell if you're even really listening. Can you look at me?" she pleads.

I look up, and then right back down at the ground.

What's going on? I don't know. Why do we have to talk about all this, anyway?

"Now you're not looking at me anymore. Can you look at me for more than a second? What are you looking at?" She seems completely distraught.

"Nothing."

"Okay." Mom takes a deep breath and tries again. "I'm sorry you seem to be having some problems. However, please understand that I'm trying to help you."

Not even listening, I ask, "Can I get something to eat?"

Mom sighs. "Yes."

***

This rather short talk seems to have resolved nothing for either of us. As I walk to the kitchen, I'm left feeling paranoid about what the other members of the family think of me.

There had to have been talk about me while I was in Mom's room. They'll want to know what happened.

I think it would be better for me not to ask anybody anything, so I wait out the evening. I try to maintain some degree of normal behavior, although, lately, this is easier said than done. I'm becoming more aware of the erratic behavior I've been exhibiting. Still, I'm compelled to act it out, as if by a force of nature.

I can fight this thing. I know I can beat it somehow. I'm Rick and I always win when I need to. I'm getting stronger every day and people are noticing it. Maybe some people will even leave me alone because I'm getting bigger. I guess I'll find out in time.

As water is nature's mirror, my eyes reflect the pain of my soul. I noticed tonight that I can't seem to look people in the eyes very much, even the people I know. It's like I'm getting physically bigger, yet collapsing at the same time. Maybe it's impossible to be too many things at the same time: if my muscles increase, then something else decreases.

Nothing is right. Nothing is right. What do I do?

***

At night, while I sleep, one of the Devil's slashers makes another attempt on my life. It uses my bed as a portal to another world, to bring me in and remove me from this planet. Somebody will open the door the next day to view an empty bed and think I must be out, when really I'm in Hell.

How can something like this happen in a place with so many good people? What does that mean I am? Am I a new target of the underworld? Or did I just stumble across something unknowingly and piss off the Devil?

I know one thing for sure: I want revenge, plain and simple. I want the Devil to face me in the real world. Why all this hiding?

There are so many things I can do, but fighting something that can't be touched isn't one of them. Not yet, anyway.

I'll learn the rules and make it happen.

Chapter 8 – In the Den of Hope

Thursday: October 22nd, 1987 – Age 16

Room 111 may be a den of gambling, but it's where I find hope to make it through the day, because I've seen only the real world in room 111.

What evil lies at the heart of gambling? I don't know; I'm just trying to get more money for lunch.

I look around the table and see players holding their cards close to their chests. The cards round the table and I begin to feel really thirsty. I'm next to Steve, who went out in the hallway earlier and came back with a pop. Well, it never hurts to ask.

"Steve, can I have a swig of your drink?" I ask.

"Sure," he says with a bit of a smile.

Steve gives me his drink and turns back to John to continue their discussion. I take a gulp and there's just something about it, so that gulp leads to another.

"Hey man, that's mine."

Steve grabs it back from me, looking a little put out. He drinks the rest himself and play continues.

"How many cards do you need, Leo?"

"Two."

A round or two goes by, and then I feel a little dizzy and words spill out of my mouth, which isn't good since I'm not in the safest place in the world.

"You know, when I first came into this class I thought you guys looked like something out of *Attack of the Pod People*."

They all look at me like I have bugs crawling out of my eyes. Steve, who is closest to me, says, "Excuse me?"

"You're excused, if I do say so with my bad self."

"What?"

"I think Rick's drunk," says Sam.

A conversation ensues that I can't focus on. I look around, trying to make sense of things.

"It would seem that the world is blurry," are the last words out of my mouth before my head hits the desk.

Some time later, one of the guys decides to act the part of an alarm clock. Wham! I'm awakened by a rather hard shake followed by laughter from the guys, being guys.

"Did I scare the crap out of you?" one asks.

"Yeah," I say, trying to see straight.

"Then you better go change your pants."

I hear their laughter go right out and down the hall. My head really hurts and I think something's wrong. I head to the doorway, feeling like a dope. Lunchtime is here and I'm going to eat.

***

When I get to the lunchroom, I grab a tray. I can smell the so-called food and lumber toward it as the line moves in unison to the beat of the schoolmaster's drum. I sit down in the cafeteria where I can see everybody: Jackman, Borden, Jarvis, John, Pete, Stockman, Tabby, Jessica, Steve, Dave, and a guy whose name I don't know.

I feel like I'm surveying the field of battle while 200 angry students prepare to fight like wild animals. I believe there could be an incident at any moment and somehow it will involve me.

Then again, everybody *seems* like they're okay today. Maybe I'll get away from here without being knifed.

Gazing around at the other students, I think, *I may not be the most popular person in school, but at least I'm not one of those ugly mean girls over there.*

Suddenly, I stop like a dog on a bone.

Wait a damn minute.

I can't believe what I just saw. It's like somebody pulled away the shade and now I can see the true form that lies within those girls…or whatever they are. They look like some sort of demons, or maybe goblins, but for sure they're all bad.

How many of them are like that?

They're actually hissing at Mr Smith.

A second passes, and the veil returns. Now they're smiling at Mr Smith. But they don't fool me.

I've got them now; it's only a matter of time.

I have a new mission, assigned to me by the hairs that run down the back of the neck, the creepy crawlers from the shadows, and, yes, the need to be free.

My mission consists of getting outdoors without anyone seeing me, and leaving this relic that pretends to be a place of learning. I pick a route and make my way out of the lunchroom. I round the first corner that leads me down to the shop classes. Since some of these classes are in session, I must sneak by.

I come to the first door and hear people inside. I lie on the ground and crawl past one door, finally making it to the other side. I hear nothing and see no discernible faces. I'm in a hazy world of darkness, but I see light coming from the doors that lead to the outside world.

I run toward the opening of another door. I do a somersault flip, bouncing up, and I hit the wall, hearing a clang from the embedded lockers. I continue these acrobatics until finally I make it outside to freedom. A blast of cold air cleanses the sweat from my body.

I run for whatever isn't school.

Chapter 9 – The Fear of Hopelessness

Friday: October 23rd, 1987 – Age 16

Linebackers are big strong guys weighing over 200 pounds, who can break people in half. Steve fits the bill of linebacker nicely. I weigh 125 of the toughest pounds you could ever see, at least according to those who know me. Steve, on the other hand, is around 260, much of it owing to the steroids I think he must take.

Right now, my 125 pounds are in study hall awaiting the game. When Steve comes in, he's practically foaming at the mouth with rage that I sense is directed at me. Steve hooked up with Jessica, a brunette goddess from math I used to love. Despite the fact that the only moves I've ever made toward Jessica have gone unanswered, I'm convinced Steve's rage is somehow related to my feelings for her. I can see this in his eyes. Not knowing what to do, I sit and wait.

Beside me is a large clearing left by the desks pushed into the regular poker circle. Steve rushes over and grabs me from my seat. He spins me over his head and throws me at the wall like a rag doll.

I need to move fast and calm him down. My reflexes kick into gear, adrenaline surging through my body. Like something out of a comic book, instincts in control, I flip over, hitting the wall with my feet, and jump right back at him.

I have to break off the fight with humor or I could be in serious trouble; the other guys are on his side.

Steve takes a step or two back from the throw, regaining composure. I stretch out my body as hard as I can and go into somersault mode. I place my hands on the floor as far out from the wall as I can, tucking under my shoulders as I hit the floor and stop almost under him.

I lie on my back, my leg cocked and ready to kick him in the balls, and I say, "Should we call it a draw?"

Steve laughs and, with that, the fight is over. I have no reason to fight anyway, and it's kind of funny, so what else can I do but laugh? Steve offers a hand and helps me to my feet.

"Nice throw," I say with a smile.

"Thanks man, how much do you weigh?" he asks.

"About 125."

"I guess that's about right?"

"Well, just good the wall wasn't closer."

"Yeah, I guess."

The other guys in the room are talking about what they just witnessed, not something you see every day, and I'm proud of myself for the cool stunt. Yet the bigger part of me has to wonder what set Steve off like that.

It could be steroids. That would explain some of the rage. But somebody must have told him a whopper of a lie. I mean, all things aside, I think Steve really likes me, and that was more than just anger going on there. If he were calm, I don't think he could throw me that hard, but you never know. It must be Jessica.

Before long, we're playing cards like nothing happened; and not long after that, class is over.

At lunch, I go walking but don't eat, because now I have a new critter crawling around on my back, whispering in my ear.

I need verification that it was Jessica who lit the fuse.

Even though part of me still wants her, another part builds her up as a creature worse than the Devil.

Jessica has something inside her, something that's being overshadowed. I know she does. I can help her. I know I can, whatever it takes, even doing the impossible. Then somehow that goodness inside her will come out. Then Jessica can shine inside and out. Am I wrong? I don't know.

"I see you, Rick. I see that you're somebody Jessica would want to be with if she had the chance," says the Unknown.

Then why does she hate me? I don't have a million pictures of her in my locker or at home. I don't follow her around when I have other classes or places to be. I just want her to notice me. I'm a person. I could be there for her, and then maybe I could ask her out or something.

"Rick, you think because you can change yourself, you can change others. You're wrong and you will pay a price in time," the Unknown tells me.

"I can't see you, but I know you're lying," I reply.

A dark cloudy image with piercing eyes materializes before me.

"Do you see me now?" it says.

"Yes," I say.

And then nothing.

I continue my walk. I'm a kid like the other kids. I want to fit in, and with the guys in study hall, I seem to. But I also want a girlfriend, and I can't seem to make that happen.

I don't want to see things that others don't see. I try to understand the tests I've had flung my way, but at this point it's no easier than trying to figure out why this is all happening in the first place.

What do I do if the walls crumble down? Why do all roads point to pain and death? Why is my life so important that Satan wants it to end so badly? How many times do I have to bounce back before he faces me like a man? I know his power is great, but so is my willpower and he can't win unless I let him.

That must be it. That must be why he won't face me. He can bring me to the edge of death, but he can't kill me. Only I can do that, and that's exactly what he wants me to do.

I need a way to show him I'm not afraid to die. I'll show him even if it gives him the chance to take me. Then we'll see what happens.

***

Later that night I sit against the wall in my room, staring at my bed. It's time to try my plan and see if I can get a reaction from the snake. I crawl to the bed. I open the cabinet and take out all my clothes, comics, magazines and everything else I keep in there.

Once everything is out, I move into the tiny space. It takes some time to get in and then make adjustment after adjustment so I can fling the door closed with a hanger. In that little dark space, I lie quietly and look around. The only light shines through a crack where the door isn't completely closed. I hear silence, but I pick up a smell that says I'm not alone.

I'm not sure how he's here, but this needs to end, one way or another.

I want to know more. I get ready to take the next step. This is it. I'll either be attacked or left alone, but I'll find out now.

In a calm and steady voice surrounded by wood and darkness, I say, "I'm dead."

***

I'm in a mist of dreams. Leash in hand, I'm pulled on my skateboard by Badger, who is running as fast as he can when...crash! I look around, only to witness the walls fading away.

I find myself surrounded by intense heat and rising smoke. I'm looking into Hell. Sounds of moaning and wailing come from caverns that look like they're made of blood-red sandstone, moving as liquid mountains.

Then I see him. He's coming for me and I want my revenge.

It's the Devil incarnate. Not a red demon with a tail, but a rather handsome-looking man, a wolf in sheep's clothing. This man, this Devil, who thrives on the pain of others and lives in a world unseen, has forged a game that has been raised to a level of carnage. The smell of blood is in the air and I'm filled with rage like never before. My only desire is to destroy him, no matter the sacrifice.

Without a discernible movement, he's upon me. I pull, but can't get away.

I can't allow myself to be bound. Even if I rip every muscle in my body, I have to get him.

He takes my arm with a vice-like grip, palm up, and carves into my flesh. He brands it, as a white-hot iron would sear cattle. The carving resembles a knife. Once he finishes, he speaks.

"NOW YOU CARRY MY MARK!"

Then he dissolves backward into a cloud of darkness and smoke. I try and try to see where he's going, but I can't.

I land on the floor, covered in sweat and defeated, looking for a trace of what just happened. None remains. It's like somebody pulled the cable and no more TV. But this wasn't TV; this was pain, wrenched muscles, and somebody you're not supposed to meet in this life.

My arm still burns. I inspect the mark, but there's no wound. I've gone through something I can't explain and I have no proof.

Where's the scar?

No blood or anything. It's just gone – nothing left but pain. I would rather carry a scar and be able to explain what happened.

It must still be there. It just can't be seen, that has to be it. It hurts too much not to be there.

Exhaustion finds me.

Next time, I'll be prepared to meet anything that comes for me. I need some protective circles.

I've seen these circles work in the movies and have used them in games.

There has to be truth to them. After all, I've always been told the Adversary works in half-truths and lies. It would make perfect sense for this to be one of those half-truths.

I curl up on the floor, trying to forget the pain. I want peace of mind. I want to live and feel like everybody else seems to, like my brother Thomas. But I know I've entered something far from ordinary. It's something with no real beginning, and it feels like there will be no end to the torment. I live only for the moment, trying to find the light. I know I can fight. But when I can't see my attacker, that fight is made impossible. I can't even run, because I don't know what I'm running *from*.

I look up, as if I can see the heavens through the ceiling. I search for some small sign that my life is mine and I'll be okay. I want to believe God will answer my prayers, but I don't see any of the results.

Where will I be in a year, if this continues? How do I speak to those around me when I'm not sure they care? Help me, somebody. Please.

Memories haunt me until it seems my past is coming to life. I see it blend with the future, and I know something is coming – something big – and I don't think I can stop it. Trying to turn from it won't help. I'm going to be punished.

That has to be why all this is happening: it's punishment…but for what?

Struggling amongst the wolves
And the waves of the seas.
Trying to find rest among my dreams.
Living, but not in love; only in agony.

My heart doesn't sing a name;
It only cries to express my pain.
As I rise to meet the day,
It seems the more who know my name.
Why would so many come out to see one
Who lives like a mouse until the lion is called?

Still I beg all those above that as I run,
My pain will melt, so I can be free like the dove,
My heart steadfast to stem the tide, as I know
Nothing of love, of victory, of pride.

You hear tales that always begin and end the same,
Where some brave knight will save the maiden.
I have no sword or armor to wear;
I stand as if naked, for all to mock.

Please, God, strengthen me now,
Or release me from my shame,
Because I know not death, but I'm in pain.
As Samson of old, I need to tear down my troubles
And set things right before I take my last bow.

When at last the beast comes out to play,
I'll be ready and he will that day pay –
For wounded heart and broken back
And all those he set to trap.
There's nothing he can do to stop my will.
He may crush, break, or burn me,
But never will I say I am defeated.
I'll come to fight until the very end.

And when all is done,
Justice will sound in every horn,
Throughout every land,
With every tongue.

Beating the Adversary

You think because this day you have won,
I'll give up and turn and run.
I don't fear you and can take the pain,
And want you to know
In the end, you will know my name.
Don't try to hide in the shadows of night.
Come out and face me, for I will fight.

Do you fear me?
Can you not fight a man face-to-face
Without powers to aid?
Do you run and fear
That all will know your real name –
A name that shows nothing
But misery and shame?
Can you see me? Because I know your name.

Remember me now and forever more.
I'm coming for you, in deed and verse.
I know you think I'm just a man, but
I know I can do much more than you think I can.

I'm not the first and may not be the last,
But your day will come
And you will then only be in my past.

I'll move on to mend my wounds,
To find a love, and know the truth.
I know you're not alone here on this Earth,
But that doesn't matter,
For there are many of us
Who have been trained since birth.

I look for you and I can't see.
I look for you and you're quick to hide from me.
Fear or courage, it doesn't matter why,
For I believe in the end only one will die.

Chapter 10 – Sergeant of Pain

Monday: October 26th, 1987 – Age 16

The bell signals the end of yet another class in this vortex of mysteries. I wait in study hall for the other guys. Steve hurries into class and walks over to me.

Sitting down, he tells me, "I'm going for my 'Sergeant of Pain' Ranking tonight."

"That's cool. What exactly does that mean?" I say, not really thinking it's cool, but definitely wondering what he's talking about.

Steve explains with a gleam in his eye, "'Sergeant of Pain' is a safe spot in the Rankings of Hell, because you don't have to worry about being punished if you reach that rank. There are other ranks that are higher, but this is the one I've been after for some time."

"What do you have to do to get it?" I ask, thinking he must be losing it.

"I just have to beat somebody in a fight. I have no idea who it will be yet. But I hear they're very interested in you."

"Me? Why?"

"Your potential rating is through the roof," Steve says excitedly. "Do you want me to enter you?"

"No. I'm doing okay. Besides, I've already made some plans of my own." I wonder if Steve is okay, though. This just doesn't sound good, to me.

The door opens again and some of the other guys filter in, so we can play. The rounds blur and I'm losing money. Perhaps bad luck. Or maybe it's worry.

***

8:30 PM

My worry is overtaken by fear. Not for myself, but for Steve, whom I've come to respect in an odd way.

Not sure where or when he'll be tested, but I hear people have been killed. I guess only time will tell.

I need to run and clear my head. I bolt for the front door and blast through it like a man in flames. I race to the elementary school, completely out of my mind. I circle the school, over and over. Thoughts swarm in my head, devouring any hope of logic.

I drop to my knees, on fire emotionally, and then scream my pain into the night. I hear my voice echo all around. I've found a release for the moment, giving me the kind of pride you feel when you beat something that's attempting to take you down.

I slowly get back to my feet.

I feel better now. I guess I'll go home.

I return home, sore throat and all. I open the door and see a very concerned Mom.

"Was that you?" she asks.

I don't know how to explain myself. All I can say is, "I guess that was pretty loud."

"Don't do that again," she tells me. "You scared me to death. You probably scared the whole neighborhood. If you need to yell like that again, fly into space to do it. Just don't do it here."

"Okay, I won't."

After, in my room, a thought strikes.

Where did I hear something like that before? "If you need to yell like that again, fly into space to do it." It was in one of my comics.

This happens to me sometimes. I'll look around and see or hear something that reminds me of a certain movie, and I call that a "shot". Maybe the movie was six months ago…but it could be years down the road. When I later see that movie, it will turn me back to the "shot" I witnessed, and I seem to know what's going to happen next, based on random events that have almost no connection. Like precognition or something.

I rush to get out a certain box so I can examine the comic and double-check the issue for myself. I turn the pages.

Aahhh, there it is. I'm right.

It's hard to focus on anything. I need the pain to stop. It has to stop.

***

Tuesday: October 27th, 1987 – Age 16

I await the day's game in study hall. There's no class prior, so I'm in the room first. It soon gets late for class to start, though, and I'm left wondering where everybody is. Then Brent comes in and it seems my time for reflection has run out.

"Coach is really mad at you," he tells me. "You're supposed to be in the weight room, lifting weights with us. Everybody from study hall is supposed to be lifting now." He's a little cocky about the whole thing.

"When did that start?" I ask, wondering why nobody told me before.

"Yesterday."

I get up and follow Brent, but by the time I reach the door, he's gone.

How did I miss him? Well, whatever. I'll just go change and then lift weights, like he said.

Fifteen minutes later, I'm in the weight room. I stick out like a toddler playing in the NBA; I'm the smallest person amongst a bunch of football players, each giving their own brand of advice on what to do or which machine to try. Most of the players know very little about the proper way to lift and try to grunt their way to bigger muscles.

The strange thing is I don't see Brent here.

Oh well.

Something catches my ear that's of great interest to me.

"Did you hear that guy screaming last night?" someone asks.

"Yeah, I did. It was weird," comes the response.

I listen to them discuss who it might have been, and a smile comes over me.

Wow. That's pretty impressive. Our school boundaries are pretty big. I wonder where they heard it.

Neither of the guys gives their name, rank, or address, so there's no telling how far away my cry was heard.

Even so, I get some sense of pride from this. It makes me feel like a lion, though I don't sound like one today. A horse would be more like it, and I feel like somebody rubbed my throat with sandpaper.

However, I'm getting a good workout and feel good about myself, if only for the moment. Sometimes catching the relief from one moment is all it takes to last for the day.

Chapter 11 – Zombies

Wednesday: October 28th, 1987 – Age 16

Daybreak ends the battle of nightmares and brings another school day. But school doesn't seem like the thing for me to do today.

Mom is substitute teaching today, so she won't be here. I'm going to get more sleep.

I roll back into bed for a few minutes, and then crack open my eyes to see the clock read 2:30pm. It's suddenly almost time for everybody to start coming home. That wasn't exactly a funfest of a day, but sleep is becoming harder at night. I wish I had a TV in my room, so I could turn it on and have time to turn it off if somebody opened the front door to come in.

I lie there thinking, and my mind drifts to the Rankings.

Sometimes the connections to these things are hard to figure out. I'll bet the people who get wrapped up in the Rankings don't really know what's going on. How could anybody who doesn't believe in greater powers understand something completely about them?

The meek will inherit the Earth, the scriptures say. This whole thing has to be, at least in part, a way to filter out the meek...or the weak, as they may say. They like potential, but not if you stay in potential mode once you've become an entity, or what some may call part of the "in-crowd". You're not as hard to shake, because all the buttons are easy to find, like wearing your emotions on your sleeve.

There's no telling how far up this thing goes. There has to be somebody else out there who's seen what I've been seeing and is on my side. I wonder how much will happen before the government send in the army to police the situation. I mean, what if I start seeing dead bodies all over the place? What am I supposed to do? I need to get more insight into everything.

Cops must feel the same way sometimes. Dealing with criminals all the time, you might start seeing a criminal in everybody. My reality has become thinking everyone is out to get me.

How is it that everything is happening all around me, but I don't understand enough to help resolve it?

***

In the middle of the night, I decide it's time to make a protection circle. If anything, it might help me get some real sleep. I lurk upstairs to acquire something to make the circle.

In the dining room I hear noises coming from outside the sliding glass door. I grasp the saltshaker, yank it off the table, and start making a circle of salt around the table.

The noise, which is gaining in volume, drives the question:

Should I look?

I look through the blinds covering the glass door and see the dead literally clawing over each other to get in and draw blood.

I lock eyes with a large male, whose noise turns into shrieking and wailing. Things are becoming worse by the second, and yet nobody in the house comes running. I'm not sure what's going on here. The glass door is taking a beating. I've made the circle, but it doesn't seem to help; the zombies are still outside.

Wonder is, of course, overpowered by fear. The noise is now very loud. I close the blinds and lie back against the big solid oak table leg coming down from the center of the table.

I listen to the scratching and moaning from outside and note it has calmed down a bit, now that I can no longer be seen. I can't leave the door or someone else may stumble into danger. Yet I'm tired, and my heavy eyelids close so easily.

Should I go to sleep for a minute? After all, if the glass breaks, I'll hear it – or maybe I'm getting too used to this kind of stuff, lifeless bodies scratching the door and wailing into the night.

My eyes remain closed, maybe as an act of courage. Or maybe it's just the exhaustion that has been stalking me for some time.

The next sound I hear is an alarm clock coming from down the hall.

Man, I better hurry downstairs. I don't want to be found under the table like this. I'd have to explain what happened last night, and Mom would freak out if she knew zombies were trying to get in her house.

Down the stairs I head, quietly slipping past Mary Ann when she steps into the inner bathroom for a shower, and I dart into my room.

I have to figure out what happened tonight. If I can just think for a while, I might be able to figure this out. At least I'm still alive.

Evil is bounding at my door and I have no way to defend my house or family from continued attacks.

I'll need to make sure they only come after me. *That way, I can keep my loved ones safe. I'm the target. I just have to stay away from the others and they'll be okay...and the Unknown will have to come directly after me.*

Chapter 12 – The Offering

Thursday: October 29th, 1987 – Age 16

I literally fall into bed, with my alarm clock set as late as possible. But mothers worry about things and like to make school a priority. Sure enough, Mom knocks at the door and opens it slightly.

"Rick, let's go. I have some things to do today and you've overslept." Her voice is friendly.

"Okay, Mom," I reply, half-asleep.

"Get up, please."

"I'm up."

"Then get out of bed."

I make my way to the car, not knowing what to expect at school. I'm certainly not going to say anything to Mom about all the strange things happening to me. All I know is I'm going back to a place I've come to hate, simply because it's the right thing to do.

What I don't know is Mom has already made an appointment for me to see a psychologist in the near future. If I knew what she had planned, I wouldn't be happy. I would be freaking out.

Why?

Because all the movies about mental illness take great care to show these kinds of people mutilating others for the pure thrill of gaining a reputation by body count, and that's just not me.

Mom bounces questions off me, like, "How are your classes going? Do you like your teachers?"

I avoid answering, or at least I don't give much explanation. I am, after all, living in a different world now, a world I don't think any normal person should know about. It would just freak Mom out, and I don't know what I can do to get out of it.

When we arrive at school and exchange goodbyes, I head into the building and then out the back. I don't want to go to a class that's already started. By the time I head back inside, second period is close to ending. I've become accustomed to walking the halls as if I'm supposed to be out of class.

Something is going on in the gym. I'm not sure what, but I feel a presence emerge from the building. My body tenses as I walk past, and I decide to head to class where I can sit and think about it. I feel a darkness fall upon my back as I walk away from the gym.

If I'm to fight, I want to do it from the safest place possible. After all, I'm the underdog in something that's not exactly David and Goliath. It's more like David and the mountain falling from the sky, get ready to catch it.

I find a seat in class and wait for the teacher to begin. I look for a sign of the Unknown. There's nothing worse than what you don't know.

I wonder what the other guys are doing. I don't have a single class with anyone I know. It's like they made sure they wouldn't have class with me. One of two things is happening: either Ranking is spreading more than I thought, or they hate me more than I imagined.

Watching my fellow students, I spot one of those demon girls. I never noticed this girl's true face before; I'll have to keep her in mind. They're growing in number, and showing their faces more and more. It's like they're becoming braver. Maybe it's the upcoming Awakening of all the Ranking's sleepers that's brought it on – or it could be the upcoming "Offering", as the Ranking's people call it: the sacrifice of a virgin.

When the bell rings, I'm out of my seat, all too happy to be moving on, with thoughts of the Offering in my head.

That could be why so many girls are trying to lose their virginity right now. It seems like I hear that all the time. "He was my first" or "We're planning". Does that even make sense? I'm not sure who I could do it with at this point, myself. Most of the girls won't even look at me and so many more have been demonized.

The world is going to Hell and there's nothing I can do to stop it. How can I get people to see what I see? If I draw it, is that enough? Or maybe just write it down?

No. I can't write it down. The Unknown or the Adversary would recover it. I have to keep it all in my head. I can't let them see it.

Why is all this pain and misery focused on me? What have I done to deserve this?

I want things to be normal, the way they used to be before my world started to turn. Normal like you can see on TV when everything's fine and the problems never seem that big.

The world I live in continues to change almost by the second and that makes things very hard to deal with. High school is tough enough on its own, without all this.

Something or someone is going to try to kill me. I need to get ready for that. I can't just hope for the best. I need to run or exercise or something.

I make my way to the door and run, which always helps me feel better. I get more than twenty minutes in; time seems to vanish.

It would be nice to have somebody to run with. But with the state I'm in, that's not possible, because I can't stay focused long enough to get through a conversation.

Chapter 13 – A Lamb to the Slaughter

Wednesday: November 4th, 1987 – Age 16

The words of the teacher bounce off me and fade into isolation. In a room of students filled with raging hormones, thoughts of that next big school dance compete with the day's assignments (or any other normal teenage function, for that matter).

The sound of another period ending breaks the silence, and I head for the door in a crowd of nameless faces. A call beckons to me from the bowels of the gym. A journey begins – not a journey of body or spirit, but of mind. Some would call it a "rite of passage".

My darkness calls it, **"**Calling a lamb to the slaughter.**"**

I open the first set of gym doors and step into the courtyard, cold air nipping my body. I'm being watched by one, but overlooked by many. I hurry through the courtyard and reach the doors on the other side. I pass under the doorframe to leave the courtyard as if for the last time, a figure shrouded with confusion and encased in loneliness. I walk up the small flight of stairs and turn right at the corner.

A familiar voice cries out over the sound of basketballs and cursing.

"Rick, come in here for a minute!"

I see Brent from study hall wave me into his class. It's one of only two classrooms in the building.

I follow his direction into the class, where I find an empty seat next to him and sit down to talk. Brent starts in on something and I notice Abby, whom I call Tabby, because that's the way I heard it the first time and I haven't gotten it out of my head. This girl is Head Cheerleader and considered one of the best-looking girls in the school.

Brent says, "Rick, you're not taking school seriously enough."

"What do you mean?" *When did I get another parent?*

Brent continues, "Well, you're out of class right now, aren't you? I know you are, because I've never seen you over here before."

Tabby looks at me like I'm a piece of meat and she has to butt in, saying, "I love your facial bone structure and eyes. I bet you were a beautiful baby. I'd love to have a beautiful baby."

"Thanks."

She wants me because she thinks I'll produce beautiful children. That's weird.

My eye is suddenly arrested by a blond now sitting in the other seat next to Brent, wearing a button-down shirt and a skirt, with heels.

"Rick, this is serious," Brent goes on. "Are you listening to me at all? I think something may be wrong with you and you're going to stay with me for the rest of the day."

"What?"

"Yep, you're not leaving my side."

"Okay," I reply, looking at the blond and wanting very much for her shirt to open just one button lower.

"That's Celeste," Brent tells me.

I look back at Brent. The words don't come out of my mouth, just, "Ohhh."

I've never really liked blonds much before, but there's something about this one. I concentrate on that button. What seems like an intense force comes out of me, and then the button pops off, revealing part of a white lace bra.

Celeste says, "Boy, you must have really wanted that button to come off."

I distance myself a bit in my seat as she speaks to me, and the eyes around me grow bigger as the button comes to a stop on the floor. Brent reaches down, picks up the button and hands it to Celeste. She inspects it for a moment and then puts it in her pocket.

"Thank you," she says.

"Who do you think is better looking, me or Celeste?" Abby asks with a grin.

Abby is Head Cheerleader, so the odds are probably on her. But I have to go the other way.

"I think it's her." I point to Celeste.

"What?" says Abby.

Abby sparks something inside me, urging me to continue. "She has toned legs and your legs are just kinda there. Her hair picks up the light and it's the perfect length, and yours just kinda flops around. And her eyes are much prettier. Not to mention the other things."

"You're horrible!"

"You asked. I don't understand. If you didn't want to know, why did you ask?"

Abby turns in her seat, wanting nothing more to do with me.

Girls. I don't get it. She must have thought I'd say of course, it's you, Tabby, there's nobody better looking than you.

Celeste breaks my train of thought. "Would you like to smell my perfume?"

I don't like the sound of that one bit. I start to stand, but Brent grabs me by the shirt with his left hand, forcing me back down. I feel the weight of staring eyes. I press my wrist to the back of his hand and grab his thumb, turning his hand down and away from my body with my right hand, putting my left hand into his elbow. From this position I could easily hold off the much stronger Brent all day – but this isn't karate class and he's now very mad at me.

"Rick, you bastard, let go and maybe I'll let you live."

It's time to regroup and let Brent save face. I let go, saying, "You're actually much stronger than my karate teacher."

"Are you saying you know karate?" Brent has so much doubt in his voice that it would take a saw to cut through it.

"Yes. I've taken some karate."

Abby says, "Can you teach us how to do that?"

"Yes, it's easy."

After some instruction on self-defense and a few well-placed jokes, all is well with Brent again. But I'm still in the room. I need to get out of here. It's like I'm trapped in some weird mind game.

What does Brent really want from me anyway? At least that Celeste is pretty. Except...what is she doing?

Celeste reaches down and takes a bottle of perfume out of her bag.

It's probably cheap perfume, too, which will be a problem...but on the bright side, maybe it will get me out of the room.

As if reading from a script, Celeste inquires again, "Did you want to smell it?"

Without waiting for a response, she sprays it right at me. The sneezing hits. Then my lungs start to restrict my breathing and puffiness sets in.

I could be in real trouble here.

"Brent, I need to go. I'm having an allergic reaction."

Brent points to the windows in response. "Somebody open a couple of those windows. You're staying right here, Rick. I'm not done with you."

"Fine."

I ponder how to escape and look around the room in discomfort.

Then I hear, "Brent, please come up here for a moment."

He glares at me. "Don't move, Rick."

"Okay."

Brent heads for the front of the class and I head out the door as quickly as I can without drawing attention to myself. The last thing I need is for Brent to come running after me and put me in a headlock or something. I have no idea why he even cares about me. Nobody else seems to, and he doesn't really know me.

I burst back across the hall to the gym, making sure to get out of Brent's line of sight, still having trouble breathing. The gym doesn't have many people in it, and only one near me. I walk over to him.

I better look like I belong here.

He's tall, maybe six-foot-six, and looks to be around 240 lbs with well-defined muscles. He's dressed for basketball, limbs exposed, making it very easy to see his fake tan and blond hair. I get close enough to see he has blue eyes.

"Hi, my name's Rick. How you doing?" I ask. I don't actually care; I just want to stay out of the hallway.

"I'm good. My name's Dirk," he says with a pretty-boy smile.

That name again.

"Are you on the basketball team?"

"Yes," he says like I should already know that.

"So you probably know the cheerleaders," I realize.

"Yeah, I know some of them." Dirk passes me the ball to shoot as we talk.

"That's cool. I only know Tabby."

"I don't know her," Dirk responds.

"She's pretty, but kind of a tramp." I almost laugh, though it wasn't funny.

"I was raised to see beauty in everybody. But like I said, I don't know her," Dirk answers, now watching my behavior a little more closely.

"Yeah, I think that's good," I reply, but most likely we're not on the same page.

"You know what's fun to do to the cheerleaders?" he suddenly asks.

"What?"

"When I'm in a game and I need to get the ball out of bounds, I'll throw it off one of the other team members and ricochet it into a cheerleader from the other team, if possible. Then guess the best part."

"I don't know," I say, having no idea what he's talking about.

"I can tell her sorry the ball hit her and ask her out," Dirk finishes with a grin that would light up a prison cell.

This guy is mean. "Well, I guess that's one way to do it."

"What grade are you in?"

"I'm a junior."

"You dribble the ball very well, and if you can pass just as good, I bet I can get you on the team next year."

"Wow. That would be awesome." I look over at the doorway and see Clint walk by. Believing he may be able to help me make an exit, I say, "There's my friend. I'll see you later."

"Okay, catch you later, man."

I'm lucky to have seen Clint. Clint is an old friend, who has black hair and blue eyes. He reminds me of Joseph Smith, because he has a big nose and, more importantly, is large in stature. In fact, Clint and Joseph Smith are the root of my big nose theory: the belief that God favors those with big noses.

Clint sits on the stairs at the south end of the building, a book in his hand. I head over and sit next to him. I need to let go emotionally, which is unlucky for Clint, who is most likely having a normal day.

"Man, I'm glad to be out of that class," I say. Somewhere inside, I believe Clint will understand me.

Clint looks down the hall and then back at me. "What class are you out of?" he asks.

"I was just in class with Brent and Tabby."

"Who?" Clint squints his eyes in question.

"You know, the head cheerleader, Tabby."

"Oh. Her name is Abby."

"Did you know she has a penis-vagina?" I ask as a matter of fact.

"What are you talking about?"

"She has a penis-vagina," I repeat, fully confident in the statement.

Clint looks worried. “Are you saying she’s a hermaphrodite?”

“What’s that?” Now I’m the confused one.

“It’s somebody who has both male and female sexual organs.”

“Well, I don’t know about that, but she does have a penis-vagina. She has to take the penis and push it up inside her. That’s why she needs pudding to have sex.”

“Rick, I have no idea what you’re talking about now. Biologically speaking, that’s impossible. And why would she need pudding?”

“To stick it up the hole. Her boyfriend is a little off, you know.”

“Okay.”

“Do you think you can get sick and end up with a penis-vagina? Because I don’t want one, but I have a space.”

“I’m afraid to ask. What space are you talking about?” Clint looks at me with deep worry.

“Feel right here next to my penis, there’s a space. I think I’m in trouble. Plus I keep having periods out of my nose.”

He backs away. “Okay, calm down, you’re not in trouble. I’m not going to feel your space. I think you need to talk to somebody who can help you get through this. Let me go call someone and I’ll find out who you should see.”

“Okay.” I realize that, for the moment, someone is looking out for me. But how long I’ll be able to concentrate on the moment is unknown.

“You stay right there,” he tells me.

***

Some time goes by and Clint hasn’t returned, and I’m feeling very thirsty. I get up and sneak northward to the fountain, and then leave the building. The sound of basketballs comes from the court, but for the moment I don’t see anybody in the hallway, so I head back where I came from and turn right to leave the building.

I look up and see Jessica with her two friends. Anger flows from her – blinding anger.

"What are you doing here?!" Jessica yells as if she owns the school.

"Just walking." The battle begins and she goes for the next strike.

"Look, you crazy psycho, stay away from me."

"You think I'm psycho? Then you're the crazy one," I say boldly.

"What?"

"You don't call somebody you think is a psycho 'psycho'. Unless you're stupid or want to get shot or something."

Laughter fills the hallway and a look of frustration comes over Jessica's face. Jessica's two friends whisper something in her ear. My guess is they're explaining my quip. She's not the brightest light bulb in the lot.

"You're such a loser, I could kill you and nobody would care," she shouts at me.

I know things are in my favor when insults turn to death threats.

More of a crowd has gathered by now, and I say, "You're not very smart, are you?"

Jessica starts to speak when I feel a presence beside me. It's a new face, and he seems to want me to say something. So I do:

"Maybe she has a penis-vagina."

He laughs loudly and says, "That's the funniest thing I've ever heard in my life."

"Thanks, man. Maybe she's mad because she can't be one of Satan's sluts."

"What is that, like a motorcycle thing?" my new stranger asks.

"*No.* It's like a real thing. Where have you been? Girls can either be virgins or allow themselves to be taken as sluts. The sluts try to get a gang to fight for them, but the real power is in being a virgin. I mean, virgins can get wings to appear and disappear on their backs – wouldn't that be the best?" I ask, expecting a serious answer back.

His jaw hangs open. "I guess," is his response.

My sudden friend disappears almost as soon as he appeared. I have no idea where he went or why. Time seems to spin.

Next thing I know, I'm attacked from behind by what might be five or six guys I believe are after their Rankings. And they don't just want to hold or pound me; they want to humiliate me. I fight back with the odds stacked against me. What's worse is I'm not certain anybody else can see what's happening.

Why am I being punished...for being different? Do I deserve this?

My only answer would be, *No.*

Holy crap, those voices – those voices sound familiar.

I twist and turn, trying to gain a footing I can use to my advantage.

I may have been occasionally annoying, maybe even vulgar, but I'm not a stalker or some kind of criminal.

Yet blow after blow strikes my body. I'm forced to the ground and I feel my pants coming down.

Oh no! No, please not that. I can't take the humiliation. I'd rather die.

My knees hit the ground and, for the first time in a long time, I offer prayer: "Oh, God."

He hears me. I feel my body fill with strength, like I could lift a hundred men.

Freedom!

As I launch myself upward, I fling my arms back over my head and hear bodies hit the ground. Before I bother to look, I hear them running...but it's not over yet.

It's Satan's turn, and he wants to take his best shot at me.

I've freed myself. God has given me the strength to free myself.

I should probably get out of here before something else happens.

A shroud of darkness surrounds me, transporting me to a world full of pain, misery, weeping, wailing, and gnashing of teeth all coming from a place called HELL. A chain with a hook on the end flies out of the darkness and plunges into my flesh. The blood from the hook speaks of entrapment and pain as it pulls out and drops to the floor. Quickly from the other side comes another and another, back and forth until I'm completely restrained by hooks, my blood spilling and flesh tearing painfully away from my body.

My blood. Blood screaming the tormented cry of innocence being taken away.

A dark voice comes from everywhere and nowhere: **"Yield to me."**

"No. I will not!" I respond with raw, untamed rage.

"We shall see."

My arms are the first point of attack and mutilation. Hooks cut into my flesh, forcing my body into a cross.

What the hell?

I strain to force my arms inward, ripping out some of the hooks that are badly placed, only to have more sink in, stretching me back.

I have to get them out. I can't die here.

I advance a step and continue to press with my arms. My muscles wrench to the point of ripping. I grab at the chains that bind me, tearing the hooks out of my body. I ignore the anguish, as it's the price of freedom.

"Would you rather die than follow me?" bellows the Adversary.

"Why are you doing this? I've done nothing!"

"No. You agreed to let me enter your life."

I wonder what he means.

During the argument, I said yes to something. What was it? I have to remember, but it's so hard to concentrate. I can't give up. It won't end for me like this. Not like this.

I hear other voices:

"All you have to do is take a position as a Sergeant of Pain and the pain will stop. It will all stop."

It's like a tornado of fire surrounding me, cutting away at me in waves. Visions flood into my head so quickly, I can't focus on them. It's hard to think with all the pain, but I must try to focus on life. There's hardly anything left of me; it's spirit versus demons.

I remember the one person who can help me – our Heavenly Father – and the insanity fades away, dropping me back in the school.

Somehow I'm in front of the school trophy case. I check my reflection in the glass. The young man who looks back has no flesh left on his body and his head is badly torn up.

My flesh.

Startled, I blink, and in that blink I'm back without a scratch, despite just experiencing more pain than I could have imagined possible.

Not one scratch.

I'm not really one to seek attention, but the thought races through my mind: *Nobody will ever believe me now. How can I talk about this without proof that it happened?*

Somebody says, "Where'd you go?"

"What? I've been here the whole time."

"No, you haven't."

I've heard enough. The next distraction and I head out the door.

I'm going home.

Although I don't know how long I'll be there, since I've just been through something that must be the death reserved for those destined for Hell. I can't believe what just happened to me. Am I already such a threat to Satan that he has to kill me before I have a chance to stop him or perform some kind of mission?

My mission…could it be about my mission? Is the Adversary trying to keep me from going on my two-year mission to serve the church and the Lord?

No. No, that can't be it. Because it seems like I'm attacked whenever I talk to a girl. The Adversary would want to keep me from my mission, so he would want me to have a girlfriend. Whatever the reason, things will never be the same for me, from this day.

***

I walk into my house, completely numb. I go downstairs and get my electric shaver from under the sink before going into the bathroom. I shut the door behind me. I open the side-burn trimmer on the razor and shave down the sides of my face. I hear Mary Ann go to get our mom as I start on the back of my head. It doesn't go smoothly; the razor grabs at my hair occasionally. My mom comes downstairs and knocks at the door.

"Richard, open the door. Open the door, I need you to come out here."

I open the door, looking like I went to the butcher for a haircut. In the mirror I see tears in the eyes of Mary Ann and my mom. A sense of guilt comes over me, but I'm not sure why.

Mom takes me into my room and asks questions I can't answer in words, because I have no more words.

“What’s wrong? What happened to you?”

These questions go unanswered. If I did say something, there’s no way she would comprehend.

I know she’s been there for me, as she tries to be there for all the kids, but this is beyond anything she’s dealt with before. It’s like a horror movie came to life and attacked me. How can so much evil be understood by someone who hasn’t been to Hell the way I have?

I wonder what Mom thinks of me.

She probably thinks I'm crazy, but she'll go away soon enough. She has to go to bed sometime. I want to be alone. I need to think. Try to think. Why would something like that happen? How *could something like that happen? Why is it so hard to think?*

When at last she leaves, I lie in bed trying to sleep – and wondering what sleep will bring me.

Chapter 14 – Get Up or Stay Down

Thursday: November 5th, 1987 – Age 16

"Breakfast is ready." This comes from Mom, who stands in the open doorway.

I lean forward to get out of bed and say, "Okay."

I take the time to put on a shirt. I head upstairs to eat my breakfast and see what's going on today. French toast is for breakfast. *I love French toast.* My mother waits for me to finish, even giving me seconds so I'm full. *I love seconds.*

Then she says, "Go and get ready. We'll go on a drive. Don't worry, you won't have to go to school today."

"Really?" I say, thrilled and not catching the implications.

"Yes, really. Now go get ready and come back up here when you're done," Mom says with a smile.

"Okay."

I hurry downstairs to put on some proper clothes, excited. Then I head back upstairs.

"Let's go," says Mom. "We'll talk in the car."

She heads for the garage with keys in hand and I follow outside. We each get into the car on our respective sides. She backs out of the driveway and flips the car into drive.

Then she tells me, "I'm very worried about you. So we're going to a place I found that may be able to help you."

"Okay."

"We need to take you to a hospital that will be able to help you."

"Okay."

I'm fine with her choice, because while I haven't yet put the pieces together, I know something's wrong with me.

"You'll be staying there a while, like you might in a regular hospital if you were sick."

"How long will I be there?" I ask, wondering if she means weeks or months.

"Well, I'm not really sure. We can find out more information when we get there."

"Okay."

The drive to the hospital isn't filled with conversation or wild hopes of magic things that will stem the tide. It's just a drive like many other drives, only with a little hope that things will be different. A mother hoping things will be better for her son and a son hoping this means the nightmare will end.

No matter what happens, this is the end of one chapter in my life –

and a new chapter is about to begin.

PART 2:
The Hospital

Chapter 15 – Attacking the Problem

Thursday: November 5th, 1987 – Age 16

I walk into the building and sanitized air sprays my face. Little do I know it will be my last breath of freedom for a while. Among other things (the names of which I won't learn for a long time), I'm going to be treated for depression. Mom fills out paperwork for assignment, while I sit awaiting my isolation orders. It's procedure.

I look around for signs of life, but don't see any aside from the paperwork lady, who looks like Grace from *Ferris Bueller's Day Off*. Mom works on the papers with a look that I know. She's trying to make sure they're completed correctly. When she finishes, she returns them to the lady, who in turn sends them to somebody else, and the detention request is complete. I know it's going to help me, but there's also that away-from-home feeling.

A door opens to our left and we're flagged. We follow Paperwork Lady into another room, where once again all I get is a seat. They should really give out prizes; even the dentist does that.

This room looks like any other doctor's office; everything is sterile but the emotions. When the door next opens, it's by a man who looks to me like he abuses children. I'm probably just being paranoid, but that wanting-to-be-here-for-my-own-good feeling vanishes.

"Hello, I'm Doctor Aiton," he introduces himself in a very effeminate French accent. "I'll be giving you a brief physical examination.

The so-called doctor centers himself in the room and gives me a real gander. His hair is greasy and he generally seems unfinished in a way one wouldn't expect from a doctor; plus, he stinks. He just doesn't look trustworthy. I'll never say it out loud, but I don't like him.

He sits down to take my medical history.

"It looks like you had some troubles as a child, no?"

Are you stupid or something?

Mom answers for me. "Yes. He was born without an esophagus and was fed through a tube for about eighteen months. Then he had an intracolonic disposition. Not long after that, he was trying to get into his walker and fell, splitting his nose open. But what I'm worried about now is the head injury he had when he was about three and fell off a chair he climbed onto when I went to care for his little brother."

"Sounds like you had a very busy childhood," notes the doctor.

"Yes, he went through the ringer," Mom replies, doing her best in a situation that has gotten really ugly for me.

I want to put the doctor through the wall. However, that's the kind of statement that would keep a person in a place like this for a very long time. The rules must be obeyed, and yes, if I have to get to know him, he might turn out to be an awesome guy. But it isn't his day, because I'm having a bad day, after the nightmare of a yesterday.

Doctor Aiton looks at me as seriously as I think he can and says, "I have some questions and I need you to answer honestly." He pauses as if I have a choice about any of this, and then asks, "Are you using any drugs?"

There's no hesitation in my honest response: "No."

"Do you smoke?"

Again without hesitation, my upstanding answer: "No."

"Do you use alcohol?"

Once more with the honesty of a child, I reply, "Well, I had some on accident."

"How do you drink alcohol by accident?" he asks, looking rather disgusted that I would dare to use the word "accident".

A little put off by his tone, I say, "Well, my friend put some in his pop and I asked for a drink without knowing it was there and then I started acting really weird."

"So you're trying to tell me you got drunk from a little alcohol in a pop can?" Doctor Aiton quips with a smirk on his face.

"I guess." *Why is that a big deal?*

"Maybe the alcohol acted like a catalyst for your depression. Tell the other doctors about it when you see them."

"Okay." *Whatever.*

"It's time we do the check-up," he says. "Mom, you can wait outside and I'll let you back in for another minute when we're done."

Mom gets up from her seat. "That would be fine," she replies.

When I'm isolated, the doctor turns to me. "Alright, I'd like you to hop up onto the table and take off your shirt and I'll listen to your breathing."

I place a hand on the table and jump onto it.

Why does he want my shirt off just to check breathing? Well, if worse comes to worst I'll just beat him senseless.

I take off my shirt, bringing the weight of his eyes on my body.

"Okay, please take some deep breaths for me."

I do as he instructs and begin breathing so he can listen clearly, to get it over with.

"That's good. Again."

This repeats a couple more times.

"That sounds good. Let's check your reflexes."

Doctor Aiton grabs his little hammer and proceeds to whack my knees to make sure they will kick.

"Okay, good, that looks good. Please get down and drop your pants, putting your hands on the table."

I guess I better do it if I hope to get out of this place.

I get down and do as he says, and he checks to see that everything is okay. Then, almost as the humiliation of the moment grows too much, it's over and there's nothing that can be done but crack jokes to deal with it.

"Get dressed and I'll get your mom," he instructs.

I quickly pull up my pants as he opens the door. Of course I check out fine, which is what he tells my mom when she comes back into the room.

I'm healthy, strong as a horse, so the reason for the check-up puzzles me.

Then the so-called doctor says, "Your mom is going to have to leave soon." He glances at a chart. "Rick, do you understand what's happening?"

The not-so-funny joke is that I'm going to be staying here for a little while – in this place that's like something out of a movie, and what I've seen in the movies has been all bad.

But what comes out is, "Do you have a weight room or a basketball court?"

"Yes. We have both." The so-called doctor shifts in his chair. "Do you have any other questions?"

My mind is about as blank as it can be, so I just say, "No."

"Okay, then it's time to say goodbye to your mom."

We rise to our feet as if somebody rang a dinner bell. Mom gives me a hug and I hug her back. Then she's shown out of the room and the door shuts.

I sit again, now alone in a room in a strange building with locks on every drawer and cupboard. It feels there are eyes in the walls, watching even my smallest movements. I believe buildings eventually gain a spiritual attitude from those who dwell within their walls, for better or worse. There's something very disturbing about this building. It doesn't help that I had a physical exam that made me feel ill. And that doctor….

I'd like to hurt him.

I hear a noise on the other side of the door. The knob turns. I know I'm not the biggest guy on the planet, but one-on-one I can certainly hold my own. With more than one attacker, I've learned it's in the hands of God: if I'm doing the right thing, he will help me, just like Nephi from the Book of Mormon.

The door opens and I see a dreadfully ugly woman who speaks in a voice that sounds like the albino from *The Princess Bride*, before he clears his throat.

"My name is Marta," she says. "Come with me."

I'm led down a hallway and through a pretty tough-looking door. I walk inside and find myself in a room that's very open, a dream come true for SWAT. There are some old couches, chairs and a very old TV. Along the east wall are the boys' rooms, while the girls' rooms line the south. There are fewer girls' rooms. On the west side is (I learn later) the door to the padded room, and south of that are conference rooms for family visits and counseling. Beside me is the door to the kitchen. Through it, I can see the cafeteria-style tables and chairs. The smell of burnt offerings wafts my way.

Everyone stops to check out the new guy – me. I see three adults. One of them is a colossus standing about six-foot-eight, who is easily over 300 pounds. He's the biggest man I've ever seen in real life; his calves look bigger than my thighs. He must be security.

I'm introduced to the half a dozen other teenagers already there. There are two girls, Bethany and Samantha, who look like cheerleaders for depression: very cute, but no smiles. Then there's Josh, Mark, and Steven. I don't know it, but clinically speaking, I'm by far the worst off of us all.

Marta flares her nostrils and says, "Josh, come over here and meet your new roommate, Rick."

Josh is about my height, with blond hair, and a little on the chunky side. He walks over to me and says, "Hi."

Not a big talker. I like that.

Something about Josh's tone reminds me of Eeyore.

"Josh, take Rick and show him to your room," Marta orders.

I'll bet Josh just doesn't like to talk in front of the staff. I really don't blame him.

Josh walks me to our room and sits on his bed, leaving me to figure out the rest. I will be on the other side of the room, which is divided by a wardrobe set for each of us, facing our respective beds.

Straight across from the entrance is the door to the bathroom. I walk into it and look in the mirror. What I see is a blurry version of myself looking back. In fact, the mirror has no glass in it and the entire bathroom looks like they did their best to please the insurance company. The shower curtain rod is sawed partway through so no one can hang himself on it. It looks like it would fall if you threw an extra towel on it.

I look back at Josh, still on his bed, and go over to make small talk, but the look on his face says, *Please leave me alone. Isolation is my friend.*

Conversation with the others is like a beautiful, silver platter serving up dung, so I wait for dinner call. When it comes, I make my way to the line. I'm then pulled aside to talk to a doctor. He's wearing a t-shirt, shorts, flip-flops, and his hair screams California. *Maybe he's Dr Surfer Dude.*

The doctor walks me down the hall to speak to me.

"Rick, I believe you're suffering from a chemical imbalance in your head. You're going to be seen by myself and some other doctors while you're here, to try to find an exact diagnosis. However, it's important that we start you on something right away, and I'm not going to be here today much longer. So I'm going to start you on Hydrocodone, which should help you make sense of things. Do you have any questions about the medication?"

"No." *Like I have a choice.*

"Okay, then if you're sure, the nurse here will give you your dose; follow her."

"Okay." *Can I go eat now?*

She leads me to a tray that has my cup with Hydrocodone in it and a cup of water next to it, which I use to down the pill, hoping the medicine will help. She checks under my tongue, to make sure I swallowed the pill. Then I go off to feed my face, cafeteria-style. We eat a culinary delight the likes of macaroni and cheese.

Not long after dinner, we have to be in bed. I'm given my bags, which my mother brought back for me by way of the charge nurse. I take them into my new room and unpack.

What a wonderful day. I'm now in the nut farm and I don't even know for how long.

The light in the room seems to get darker and the sounds of slumber fill the air. The day ends with the sound of a fly heading out our door into the darkness.

Chapter 16 – Kindness

Friday: November 6th, 1987 – Age 16

The hospital has a schedule to keep; rolling through eventide brings busy hands of pancake-makers and dishwashers. There's a time to wake up, a time to eat, a time for each of us to see the doctor, and a time to go back to bed. Let's not forget the medicine at breakfast, lunch for some, and dinner. Somebody comes out with pills assigned to little cups upon plastic trays. Each pill-taker swallows the pills, and then it's tongue-check time. It's like a scene from a TV show; but since life is easier than it has been in a long time, I'll take the TV show.

After breakfast, I eavesdrop on the others. What I hear isn't poetry. My eyes open to a whole other world – a world I could have gone my whole life without finding in such an in-your-face way. The first thing I hear when I sit down is one girl telling the other, "My dad would hit me; and if he got drunk, he would do worse."

I'm struck with the feeling that she means *sexually*, and I want to kill a man I've never met.

The other girl replies, "I know. My step-dad would try to have me every time my stupid mom left the house. I wish somebody would cut his pecker off and let him bleed to death."

No doubt.

I already feel sorry for them. I've found out they're here not just as a result of depression (like I've been told I am), but because of family. "Family" has always been a safe word to me, but for these kids it means something very different.

Steven tells me, "If you can get into the girls' room at night, they'll do it with you."

This isn't something I'm about to try to confirm, but in my current state I take it as a fact.

It takes little work on my part to find out people's darkest secrets. In an effort to fight the unreal world, I feel like I've fallen into another one. Except this isn't just something in my head. Now I must process a world of very real abuse from very real people. It leaves me feeling overwhelmed. And yet at the same time, I find a certain amount of peace in knowing I'll go home to those who, in my heart, I know are good people, even when my head is going north and south.

***

Something I don't expect is that I'm on my way to becoming the group leader, chosen by natural selection if you like, like the alpha male in a wolf pack. Though at the same time, I'm still a loner without a cause, only wishing to give service.

Despite all I've been through, I like myself and I'm glad to be alive. I just don't know what life is. The other kids here don't like themselves, and so they hurt themselves or find other ways to push abuse like a drug. It leaves the air thick with negative energy. It feels strange, like a blanket that just won't keep all of me warm. No matter how I pull or push it around, there's still some part of me that's cold. I wish I could switch on a light for all the others and we could find a way to be at least content, if not happy. But everybody has to find their own light, their own happiness. I'm just a watcher in a world of hopelessness and I'm not sure what to do about it.

Perhaps in time I will learn the answers to life's great questions, but for now I need to concentrate on myself, and get ready for whatever lies around the corner in my life. I know a few things for sure. One is that my world was recently shattered and I'm now in a place that feels so different from the outside world that I will be okay for at least a little while. Second, I know that no matter what anybody says about me, no matter how insulting or foul, I've survived. And third, I will find a way to take revenge on the Adversary.

It's hard even for me to imagine how I, a person of flesh and blood, will take revenge on something so powerful that even God Himself can't banish it. The great serpent of lies, the spark behind each flame of anger, the builder of wars and rumors of wars – the Devil.

There really is no greater mask than the mask of the Unknown, and the Devil wears it proudly. Had I known exactly how powerful the Devil was when this all started, would I have given up?

No.

How do I explain what I don't fully understand? How can I beat the Devil if I can't control my own actions?

***

This hospital has its own way of showing kindness. Kindness here is making sure everybody is healthy, not happy. They will go to extremes to ensure that health is maintained – the room with all the pads on the walls is not a joke.

I look around; it feels safer to know what surrounds me. I know there are only a handful of people here, and none of these kids are football players or weightlifters or anything. But I'm so emotionally scarred by my recent experiences that I'm frightened of my companions, all the same.

The Heavenly Father filled me with strength when I needed it, so I'm sure He must have been close. But I couldn't feel Him there when things got worse – when the hooks dug into my flesh. Why would such a horrible thing happen to me right in front of Him? Why couldn't He stop it?

I try to get a grip on the events of my past as this strange place shows me new things about the world I live in – the real world in all its misery. There will come a time when all questions will be answered and the misery will end. But for now I only know what is right in front of me.

Chapter 17 – Yoga and Life

Saturday: November 7th, 1987 – Age 16

"Everybody come over here," calls out a blond lady standing under the basketball hoop in the hospital gym. "We're going to do some breathing exercises."

I don't take this news well. I just started lifting weights and don't want to stop.

"Hurry, please, we have a lot to do and not a lot of time."

Man, I thought this was going to be cool for once. Breathing exercises sound lame.

"What I'm going to teach you today will help you relax and clear your minds," she assures us.

I move up, along with the rest of the group, and I see that the instructor is stunning. She has long blond hair and blue eyes and her body is a work of art. She doesn't say her name, most likely on purpose.

"Alright, let's get started. We'll start with our stretching."

It's really hard to concentrate when there's a beautiful woman stretching in front of you. That's the first thing I learn. I wonder how she came to be here. Maybe she felt it was a good cause. Maybe it's for school credit. Or maybe she just likes being in the nut house. I can't figure it out, and maybe it doesn't need to be figured out.

I try to get into it, but I quickly realize something is wrong.

Man, I have no flexibility at all. This really sucks. No weight lifting and I can't even do this.

Then we have phase two of the hot instructor's plan: doing what she calls meditation, which is breathing and thinking at the same time. It's a real double threat.

The purpose behind yoga, or meditation in general, is that it's good for relaxing the body and mind. If I could only read the fine print, I might understand that this yoga thing will, by itself, do nothing for me now. Then I may be able to get past it and consider the real reason we're doing it, as it's a puzzle worth looking into. If I could, I would discover it's not supposed to be the whole, but only part of a different lifestyle – a lifestyle that allows for emotions, but demands that each person rein in those emotions.

I won't get to this conclusion anytime soon, though, because I'm too focused on myself. I don't completely have the "me first" attitude and I'm certainly not a narcissist. However, I'm trapped in a world that revolves mostly around me. The very word "me" is a trap and if I want to solve all my puzzles, I need to view the world from outside my little box.

I haven't heard of anybody else having my problem. If I did, it's not like I would start a support group in my current state. All the same, it would be nice to have someone to reach out to or something to read or…just something. Having to figure everything out for myself, by myself, is hard, to say the least, and I've only started to scratch the surface.

At this point, the only major difference in me is that I've stopped cursing so much since coming to the hospital and getting on my medication.

***

When our yoga class ends, it's a sad moment.

Who knows when they'll next let us visit the gym? It's like being in prison.

The walk back to the hospital is not a fun walk. When the door closes behind us, the day passes; meals and TV fill the time. It almost feels normal until "lights out" draws near and I walk into our room to see Josh trying to cut himself open.

Steven said to me earlier, "Josh's family came when yours was here." I heard something about him not liking his family.

I rush to the door and yell, "Help! Something's wrong!"

I see a staff member hit an alarm, and then, from a secured door, some people I've never seen before appear in a flash. They pounce on Josh like he just shot at the President or something. They hog-tie him into a straitjacket and have him out the door so fast, he barely has time to scream. The door to the padded room opens and Josh is strapped down to the table.

This isn't what I wanted when I called for help. I didn't know they would do that, or I would have tried to stop him myself. I can't begin to imagine the damage that could come from spending the night in a box like that. The others mentioned the adults holding the padded room over the heads of the patients. When I heard this, it didn't bother me, because I knew I wouldn't be going in there. I didn't think of anyone else going in.

Marta looks me in the eyes and says, "He wanted attention and now he's gotten it."

"He didn't want *that*," I'm quick to reply. Josh doesn't love any of us, after all, so why would he seek our attention?

"You just watch yourself, or you could be in there too," Marta says sharply.

"Whatever." I roll my eyes in defiance as Marta walks away.

Falling asleep means getting rid of the vision of a strapped-down Josh alone in a dark padded room. The thought is like a bag over the head: trying to breathe, but only gasping bag air, again and again.

I have to forgive myself. After all, I didn't know they would take it so far so quickly and I can't control Josh. I can only try to help him when I can help.

Why should I care this much for somebody I just met? Maybe I'm becoming weak. Or maybe it's just the right thing to do. I would have liked someone to help me when I needed it most. I guess Josh is seeking attention where I didn't want any.

Maybe that shows my strength. Maybe being stronger means sticking up for those who can't stick up for themselves.

My heart breaks a little for Josh, who must be afraid. I'll never know what might have been if I had turned a blind eye, but for the first time in my life I feel I've discovered what it means to be a parent by making a tough choice and having to live with the consequences.

***

The following morning, I lunge up in bed, sweaty and out of breath from the jarring wake-up call after an almost sleepless night.

Is Josh okay? He must be, since there was no noise last night. I hope I see him by breakfast. I wish they'd just given him a shot and let him sleep it off.

It hits me that it's Sunday, but it doesn't feel like it. No church or family dinner. My confinement just slapped me in the face. I've gone from a rock to a hard place.

I'm just here for testing and when they think they have something that works for me, I can go home, I remind myself.

They ask a lot of questions, and getting out of here depends a great deal on my answers. *Are you hearing things? How many fingers?* Or whatever lame thing comes out at the time, like, *Do you want to get better?*

No, I feel like saying. *I want to stay like this, you idiot. Get real.*

Of course I keep it all inside, because I don't want to rock the boat.

I've known for some time now that I have something seriously wrong with me, or being done to me, and I want to be back to myself and have my old life again. I want to start doing normal things.

Something comes over me. You could say a light turns on. Perhaps it's the medication starting to work, because something the doctor recently told me suddenly clicks:

It's not a matter of being crazy or having somebody try to ruin me, though I know the Adversary took advantage all he could. The chemicals in my head simply became imbalanced, most likely because of my head injury.

But how could I *imagine* something so painful that it could only be the death of the damned? How could that not have been *real?*

***

Josh is let out to rejoin the group and I feel terrible about the way things were handled. He may be a risk to himself, but nobody even stopped to talk to him. They have much to learn about the teenage mind.

I mean, couldn't they take the thing away from him and ask him something? He wasn't crazed; he was just upset about something. Man, I just didn't want him to hurt himself in a serious way.

Now that I've had the night to think about it, I know that yes, he probably had to go in the room. But he didn't have a single moment for repentance of any kind.

I walk over to Steven, who doesn't seem to want to look at me, but he does say to me rather sheepishly, "You ratted him out."

"That's not what I meant to do. I only wanted to get him help." I turn and Josh is alone, so I head over to him.

"Josh. I didn't mean for that to happen. I'm sorry. Are you okay?"

Josh looks at the ground. "Yeah. I'm okay. Don't worry about it."

"Josh, if you want to talk about anything, let me know. I won't tell anyone. I just don't want you to hurt yourself." I try to look him in the eyes, but he won't look up at me.

Josh seems to drift into space for a second, but then pulls back and replies, "Okay."

Not completely sure what that means, but I guess time will tell.

The day starts to go by slowly. I find out it's a light staff day, meaning the doctors are on call and no visitors are allowed. Mom said she would be here on Monday, and I'll ask her when I can go home. Meanwhile, it could be worse here. There could be nothing to look at, but Bethany and Samantha are kind of pretty girls.

As my head continues to clear, and because I have nothing to do, I pick up on the quirks and tells of others. For example, Bethany and Samantha both give off the vibe of girls who are easy, but I already discovered the reason for that, and the people who hurt them were probably much closer than I would want to consider. Josh, the recluse, is a "no brainer", hurt so much that he would rather live in his Hell than risk himself at any level. Steven likes to put on a big front, but quickly backs down, most likely due to having a poor male influence in his life. Everybody has something – like me, and the way I'm always giving people the once-over. Like I'm doing now.

There are two other guys I have nothing to do with yet, and there's Jaffa, big bad Jaffa.

Why is somebody that big working in a place like this? He looks like he could smash through any line in the NFL. So why work some job that probably pays eight dollars an hour?

The reality of being caged sinks in, but I try to avoid the idea that this cage makes me an animal – because something inside me knows I could come back.

Chapter 18 – Hoping for Home

Monday: November 9th, 1987 – Age 16

When Monday comes calling like a horse with a dead rider, I know in my heart that I won't be going home any time soon.

I bet my friends hardly even know I'm gone.

Mom will be here before too long. I walk out of my room to see what the others are doing and try to have a "normal" morning. It's not that simple, since there's no normal, but I try to find it anyway. The phantoms of depression cross over me as the gears in my head change to that of paranoia.

I wonder what people will think of me. I should tell Mom and Dad to tell the truth if anybody asks...but only if anybody asks. I have four sisters and they all have friends and, well, I'm sure they'll get asked. I have to try not to let it bother me. It's just hard to know how to feel when I can't see any of the faces of the people who may be talking about me. I've been watching people for so long, I never really thought about not being able to see their faces.

I know what you're thinking: Mom is going to show up and find her son in great despair. But when she arrives, there's a light on in her son's head. It may be a dim light, but it's light. It's like I was part of an elaborate vanishing act and it's over now. I've never seen Mom so happy, and I'm happy to see her too. I hurry over and give her a hug.

"Mom, can I go home now?" I ask, hoping to get back some of the life I knew.

"I'll find out what they have in mind for you before I go," she tells me. "I had to get special permission to be here today, so I don't have a lot of time."

"Okay." *What's wrong?*

"How are you doing?" she wonders.

"I'm fine. I think I'm better now."

"Why do you say that?" She examines me and adds, "It does actually look like some of the life is back in your eyes; that's a good sign."

"I can think better now. There aren't so many distractions around me anymore," I explain, knowing the noise around me is going away.

"That's wonderful!" she says. "I'm so glad to hear things are going better for you. Your father and I have been so worried since I checked you in. I was hoping I did the right thing."

I don't know what to say to this, so I change the subject. "They said on Wednesday that we get to go see a movie, and next week we get to go to the zoo, so at least we get to do a few things."

Mom nods. Then she says, "They told me on the way in that one of the things we have to do in order for you to go home is have a family counseling session."

"What does that mean?" I ask.

"That means we all come in and talk to a doctor together. They probably want to see how we interact together."

"Oh, okay." *Well, I don't see why I have to do that.*

"The kids want me to say hi, and we'll tell people whatever you want us to tell them. We could say you're visiting your aunt or uncle."

"I guess just tell them the truth if they ask," I say. "But just if somebody asks, since I'm hoping not to be in here very long."

She looks at me. "Are you sure? We don't mind covering for you."

"No, it's okay. I'm sure people already figured out something was wrong with me."

"Okay, then that's what we'll do. We already told Bishop Cook, but of course he won't tell anybody. He wanted to come see you, but the policy is family only."

"That's okay."

We hold each other's eyes, neither of us speaking. Then Mom takes a breath and says, "I'd better go see about how long they think you'll be here."

I nod. "Okay."

I watch as Mom goes to find a doctor or somebody else of importance. When she returns, she tells me, "He said they couldn't really put a timetable on it because it's different for everybody. He said most of it depends on you, and good behavior will go a long way for you."

"I've been trying to be good," I say, meeting her eyes.

"Alright, then. They didn't want me to stay very long, so I better get going. Give me a hug." She has a look of hurt on her face that I've never seen before.

"Okay."

After giving hugs, I say, "Goodbye."

"Bye. We'll all be here soon."

"Okay."

I watch as Mom is led through the door. Then it's back to hospital life and everything that goes along with it.

***

Josh sits on the couch. With nothing left to do, I slouch on the other side of the couch. He doesn't look at me and I don't look at him. I think what I can say. In the end, I guess the simplest way to start any conversation is with some form of hello.

"Hey, Josh, how are you doing?" I ask.

"I'm okay, I guess," he replies in typical Eeyore style.

"That's really good to hear," I say, trying for enthusiasm. I remember seeing Josh with a woman earlier and ask, "Who was that you were talking to?"

Josh looks at the ground. "That was my Mom. She promised to come visit me. She said the whole family has to come in for counseling. I'm not really sure I like that idea."

"Why not?" I ask, thinking of my own situation.

"I don't like my dad," Josh answers with anguish on his face.

"I'm sorry you have troubles with him," I say, trying to show sympathy

"He's never liked me!" Josh says in the loudest voice I've ever heard from him, but still it's barely at a normal level.

"Oh." I'm rather shocked, because I can't relate to the statement.

"Yeah, he's always yelling," says Josh. He looks like maybe he wishes he hadn't said it. Then he stands up and walks away.

I try to compare what he said to what I've experienced from my own father, and I just can't do it. So I try to see with Josh's eyes and feel Josh's pain from his point of view.

Yelling may really mean hitting, or he could be confusing his dad's intentions.

Trying to think and feel like this in the true sense of the word is new to me, so it's going to take concentration and time.

I find comfort in trying to help my new friends, but in my heart I know each person must be accountable for himself or herself in order to make a difference in their own life. It's a lesson I learned somewhere along the way and have tried to live up to – although when the real world falls apart and the demons come crashing down like waves of the ocean, it can be impossible just to breath, let alone make the right decisions.

Forgetting myself in the service of others brings a little light to my soul. It's like home – at least, the way home used to feel, before the confusion took over my life.

Confusion. The doctors call it depression.

Well, whatever it's called, it feels like tar flowing through my head. When things get really bad, it's like the tar pours over my whole body, just waiting for people to tack feathers on me.

I am not a puppet to be controlled. I will fight back, and in time I will….

I will win.
I just hope the others here do, too.

Chapter 19 – Movie Madness

Wednesday: November 11th, 1987 – Age 16

We are at the Valley Fair Mall, about to see a movie. There's an escort at each end of the row and several behind us. Escaping the staff isn't on my mind, since Dad passed the movie gene on to me; to be able to get lost in something, if only for a couple hours, is a sacred release from the pressures of life. I believe that's why the hope that the movie will be good runs so high. We are seeing *Adventures in Babysitting,* starring Thor, one of my favorite guys. I have to admit this isn't that good a movie, but at least it's a movie.

Before I'm ready, the movie is over, bringing that all too familiar feeling that somebody is encroaching on my space – this time because somebody really is.

"Stay in your seats until everyone leaves," says Marta, demonstrating her authority over us. She has to be one of the meanest people I've ever known.

"Okay," we answer in unison. We not only have to wait for everyone to leave, but we have to remain seated as they go.

Every single person looks at us like we're a chain gang surrounded by these hulking guys and Marta. Then I notice a rather big man, not extremely packed with muscle since his gut accounts for much of the weight and his long hair and beard would be the rest of it. But he seems like the kind of guy who can handle things, and he's staring at Bethany in a rather creepy way. It's not the undressing with the eyes look; it's much worse. Plus, this guy is probably in his forties and Bethany is a teenager.

I'm only too glad when this guy passes by. All the same, my instincts kick into gear. It's time to stay close to Bethany. Since there's only Samantha seated between us, that shouldn't be a problem.

Time comes to go, so we file out. I keep an eye out and everything seems to be going fine as we head out of the mall to where the van is supposed to be, to pick us up. However, the van isn't there and what's worse, there's Mister Heavyweight Creepy in the shadows.

The escorts are distracted by the fact that the ride is late, and Creepy is now right in front of Bethany, with me at her side. Then it starts.

"Hey, little momma, why don't you come with me and I'll #%@$ you real good."

"What did you just say to her!?" I let fly as I feel myself setting on fire.

The next thing I realize, Marta has me by the arm and we're all running. Marta is certainly not in great shape, but she's still running.

"Are you crazy?" she shouts at me. "Do you know what you've done? You flattened that guy! We could lose our license for you fighting like that – you could go to jail!"

"What are you talking about?" I ask.

"Don't play dumb with me! You'll be in your room all night!" Marta shrieks like a witch with frostbite.

I look in her eyes, knowing I need a sound defense that could hold up in court. But all I say is, "What?"

I'm totally and completely confused. As much as I would love to see myself beat Creepy down, I can't remember a thing. One minute I'm standing up for Bethany and the next thing I know, I'm running to stay out of jail, according to Marta.

I guess my head got overloaded or something.

The medication. I guess I'm still adjusting to the medication.

But it's working and I'm not going to stop it now. The doctor said some results would take longer to be seen fully.

I guess I'm either in my room or in the hole for the night. But the girls are looking at me like I'm a hero and I would really like to talk to a friendly girl for a change.

Man, when I was little and in the hospital all the time, those nurses must have spoiled me, because I remember thinking girls didn't even get mad. Like they were angels sent to care for the sick. Now I'm not really sure what girls are.

Life finds a way to throw curve balls and I just received a whopper. Yet another event has taken place, where I don't know if it was real or what to do to make sure it doesn't happen again. I'm only convinced of the medication's ability to help me to a point.

But there's hope on the horizon, even if I'm not yet aware of it. The method will be self-evaluation – in this case, learning to recognize emotions are building, and controlling them before they control me.

***

Friday: November 13th, 1987 – Age 16

Our leftovers find their way back to a laboratory, to get ground into another food source. Bethany has retreated to the TV area and since I need practice talking to girls, I force myself to go talk her.

I sit in the chair next to hers, hoping I can communicate in a language she understands. Everybody seems to have their own language here. Bethany looks discouraged, like she got a bad ending in the TV show of life. I glance at the actual TV and then back at her, thinking I can start with the TV and move on from there, and hopefully something like a conversation might occur.

"Hey, Bethany, what are you watching?" I ask.

"Nothing special, it was just on," she says, in a bit of a snit.

"Oh. Well, you look a little down. Are you sick?" I ask, trying to show respect.

“I think I might have a bit of a cold,” she replies, looking happier with me for noticing.

“Oh, well that doesn’t sound too bad.”

“Yeah, I guess.” Bethany rolls her eyes, but continues, “I found out Samantha is going home soon.”

“How soon?” I think this is the real reason she’s down.

“She doesn’t know yet, but once they tell you it’s usually not long, like a couple days or something.” She speaks like some sort of impending doom is on its way to our little corner of the world.

“I’m sorry about that. I’m nervous myself right now, because my family is coming and I’m not sure how everybody will be.” I hope she can relate to my feelings.

“Is your family mean?”

“No, but I don’t like my brother very much,” I say, feeling overwhelmed by how well Thomas, in particular, is doing in life while I’m in here.

“I’m sure things will be fine. How many people are in your family?”

“My mom and dad, plus six kids including me.”

“That’s a lot. My parents are divorced and I only have one brother,” Bethany responds.

“So do you get to see both your parents?” I ask. This concept is still new to me. I’ve lived in my own world all my life.

“I never see my dad.” She looks rather grim.

“Sorry about that, Bethany,” I say sincerely.

“Thank you,” she says in a soft tone.

“Rick, come over here. Your family is being brought in now,” Jaffa says in what you could call a nice tone, but when the voice is as deep as Jaffa’s it’s hard to tell.

“Okay,” I call back. “I have to go, Bethany.”

“Bye.”

I stand up and walk toward Jaffa, who leads me to one of the offices.

It's so weird that he's gay. I always thought gay guys were little or at least more like normal, and Jaffa is so freaking big. When he told me, I didn't believe it. Then they took us to a basketball game at the YMCA and his boyfriend was there. *Holy cow, and that guy was just as big. Talk about an eye opener. I guess I'm learning a lot about people in this place.*

"Rick."

I give no reply.

"Rick, pay attention," Jaffa says. "It's time for your session."

This time, I look up and take notice. "Okay."

Jaffa points into a room that looks pretty big. "Wait in there," he says, with a look of compassion. "The doctor will be here in a couple minutes with your family."

"Okay." I reply. My only concern is my family's reaction when they see me.

Inside the room I see a desk on the opposite wall, a table in the middle, and chairs lining the walls. I choose a chair toward the middle of the room and wait for my audience, my family, to come for my inspection.

Before long, a man opens the door and comes inside. He's a rather tall, thinning blond wearing a freaky weird tie like some kind of Rorshach inkblot test. My family are with him. I can't see them all yet through the glass window in the door, but I can see my dad.

Well, ready or not, they're here.

Hugs are exchanged as my family comes in and my nervousness fades, but other emotions surface. The doctor begins to talk and I feel pressured, as I know the focus of the meeting is on me and some of my siblings may not be very understanding at this point. I can't blame them either, because I know full well that I haven't been myself. I got to the point where I was losing control over myself and emotions were spilling out.

The doctor calls order, as he has a schedule to keep (and hopefully a new tie to buy).

"Alright, everybody," he says. "Let's take a seat so we can get started."

We listen to the doctor and sit down. Dad is closest to the doctor, with my mother next to him, and I'm seated next to her. Mary Ann sits next to me and Thomas, Katie, Melissa and Tiffany are seated across from us. Not sure we make the Cleavers, but everybody seems agreeable so far.

The doctor begins again:

"Okay, thanks. Now, the purpose of meeting here today is not to point fingers at each other, but simply to give us an idea of how the family interact together. This tells us where we should put focus when it's time for Richard to leave us. For example, if we need to have another family meeting before Richard leaves us here, or if we feel the focus should remain on him for the rest of his stay."

My dad speaks on behalf of the family. "That sounds good; we'll do whatever's needed. Can you also give us an idea about what's going on with Richard?"

The doctor smiles. "Yes, why don't I start with that? Richard is unique in that we feel what's happened to him was largely caused by the head injury he sustained as a child. However, one of his biggest challenges right now is depression. Keep in mind that this often runs in families, and your paperwork indicates you, indeed, have a family history of depression. So we can't rule out the possibility that Richard inherited his condition. Still, in Richard's case, we feel the head injury triggered a chemical imbalance in his head, which really started to present itself when he hit puberty.

"As for a firm diagnosis, at the moment it looks like Richard fits mostly as bipolar. However, from the information we've gathered, he's doesn't fit into bipolar exactly. So we're continuing to gather information. It would help if Richard were a little more forthcoming. We know he has trouble falling asleep and getting up in the morning; this could be attributed to depression. We also know sometimes he hears things, which can be a sign of mania. There have also been concentration problems at school and home."

We all stare at him, overwhelmed by this explanation.

The doctor moves swiftly on. "Now, let me see if I have all your names right. It says the father is David and mother is Mar-ci-a."

"That's Marsha spelled m-a-r-c-i-a. It's a little different that way," Mom says with a smile. She shifts in her chair to face the doctor better.

"Thank you for that. Now you must be Thomas," he says, pointing to my brother.

"I hate him!" I find myself blurting out. It's received by wide eyes.

The room draws quiet. "Can you tell me why?" the doctor replies.

"No," I say, looking at the ground. My tongue feels like it's caught in a bear trap.

"Why can't you tell me?" he asks.

"I don't know."

The doctor looks around, seeing how uncomfortable the statement has made everybody, but decides to continue.

"Okay, let's move on. It just lists the names of the sisters here, so I'm going to have to do my best with remembering who's who."

Mary Ann volunteers to give the rundown. "I'm Mary Ann and this is Katie, Melissa and Tiffany." She points to each of the girls as she goes.

"Thank you very much for that. As I said, I'll do my best to remember all the right names with the right faces. Please feel free to raise your hand if you have a question and I'll be sure to get to everybody. That way, I can hear each person and address the questions with the respect they deserve. Now, are there any other questions before I start with some of my own?"

He pauses, but no one speaks.

"No?" He nods like he expected this. "That's okay. Like I said, just let me know."

This guy doesn't seem so bad, I realize. In fact, the hospital isn't as bad as I expected. When they explain things, I can see how it all fits. One thing triggers another and before you know it, you have a giant snowball rolling down the hill.

The doctor swivels his chair and opens a desk drawer to take something out. He turns back toward us and I see it's a box of crayons – not exactly a smoking gun. He leans forward with one of those "I know everything" looks on his face.

"Okay, guys, here's what we're going to do. I'm going to give each of you one crayon. That will be your color for the exercise. You can either draw your own picture or you can draw on somebody else's picture; it's completely up to you. Alright, so let me hand these out."

With that, the good doctor hands out the crayons, wanting to see who will interact with whom. It makes the exercise simple and shows the doctor the dynamics he's looking for.

He gives Dad blue, while Mom gets the green crayon. He continues handing out the crayons. Soon, each of us has a crayon and a piece of paper.

It doesn't take long to see that Mom has colored on her picture, my picture, and will probably hit everybody else's picture. Dad is content on drawing away – he's an artist, after all – but he manages to draw a bit of something on my paper, as each of my siblings does as well. I'm the only one not to draw on another picture.

By the end of the exercise, green crayon is on each picture. The doctor collects our pictures for the file and issues the two-minute warning for goodbyes. Before long, my family has left the building, leaving me in the hospital.

***

I head back to my room and find Josh sitting on his bed, something he does a great deal of.

"Hey Josh, what's up?" I ask like we're not in a hospital.

"Nothing," Josh takes my standard line.

"My family just left. We had to draw pictures. It was kind of weird," I say, wondering if he had to do the same thing.

"Yeah, I did that." Josh looks almost relieved.

"How long have you been here?" I ask, referring to the hospital.

"For a while, but I've been here before," he says, looking like he wants to be alone.

Turning from Josh, I reflect on the events of the day, not knowing that at home those who love me are doing the same. I'm concerned only with me and how I did, whether I should have done something different. In time, I'll learn my mother spent the day worrying about treating everybody fairly, while trying to take care of a sick child who wouldn't even realize if she got up and left the room, as long as there was some kind of distraction.

It's a life of emptiness, waiting to be filled. But it can't, until a light turns on. I must find my own way through life, but I need somebody to turn on that light for me and that lamp bearer is my mother. As David C. Gross said, "God couldn't be everywhere, and therefore he made mothers." She gave me life and when I died, she took me to the hospital and gave me a second life.

The meds are doing their job and the light is slowly coming on; it's growing brighter by the day. In time, I will think of others again.

Chapter 20 – In-and-Out

Monday: November 16th, 1987 – Age 16

Morning bells ring and I wake to the smell of freedom. Then I remember it's not Mom's cooking; it's just an imitation.

I head out into the main room to see if they're serving. Samantha is already out sporting her best outfit and she has a very excited look on her face. It's easy to see why; her bags are next to the chair where she sits talking to Bethany. I walk closer to them, wanting to offer a goodbye of my own, and I see that Bethany is almost in tears.

When Samantha is in my line of sight, I say, "Hey Samantha, I just wanted to say goodbye and good luck with things." I offer as much of a smile as I can muster. I wonder if outside life is better for her.

"Thank you, Rick. Good luck to you." Then Samantha turns back to Bethany and they continue their girl talk. I can either try to talk some more or eat.

I head over to eat and overhear Marta speaking:

"We have a new one coming in today."

I wonder who it will be.

By the time I finish breakfast, Samantha is gone. One of our group members is gone and, with her life, there's no telling if that's good or bad. I can only hope she learns to respect herself and not go on living like a trashcan for men. I have no idea how to solve a problem like that. In my heart, I ask, *Doesn't your dad love you?* I'm finding out that isn't always the case, and it's weird, like I didn't know it before I came here. I've always known about child abuse, just like I've always known that our Heavenly Father weeps for these children.

I suppose, like most people, I just didn't really believe such horrible things could happen to anyone I know.

***

After breakfast, I spend my time thinking of new superheroes to be in my own comic one day, or maybe even save mankind from itself. At least it keeps my brain busy with something harmless.

Time usually flies when I'm in my world and it's no different now. I can see from my seat on the couch that lunch is coming; trays are out. Through the door, I can see the dingy yellowing light of the cafeteria. It comes mostly from overhead lamps, though there are a few places with a hint of natural light.

I wish we had some really big skylights in this place. What are we going to do, jump up there?

That's when the new kid walks in. He's about six feet tall, with a medium build and curly hair edging toward dirty blond.

"Everybody, this is Eric. Please welcome him," says some token nurse I've never seen before. She turns and leaves, but the only people who approach Eric are staff members. Eric is shown to his room and food starts to come out.

I stand and turn to Josh, who has moved next to me. "What do you think?" I ask, knowing he has seen many come and go.

Josh shrugs his shoulders. "Just another one, no big deal," he says.

"Yeah, I guess." *Still, I wonder. What's he about?*

Josh walks away to get some food without another word. I'm left to go on about my business or make friends with Eric.

There's no telling why Eric is here. All I can say for him is there are no bandages on his wrists and his hair is combed. Details can make the difference between being alive or dead, and what people wear says a lot about them, just like a rattle on a snake. Bandages are a red flag that something could be wrong; after all, depression, like crime, has many faces. I need to see a face and know exactly what's in the core of the person. It's not fight-or-flight; it's simply a matter of trust. Friendship without trust is dead.

It's not easy to be a friend. In fact, it's a great responsibility. After all, friendship means, 'I trust and count on you.' But this place is different. It's nice having somebody to talk to and I seek out Eric in the TV area.

I've never been good at small talk. So I cut straight to the heavy stuff. "Ever wonder why people are so afraid of the Unknown?" I ask. My hands fly in motion as I speak.

Eric looks surprised, and rather puzzled, but he goes with it. "What do you mean?" he wonders.

"I mean, people have started to be afraid of me, and I'm not sure what I've done differently. But I've noticed people would rather turn away from me than look at me. It's like an incomplete picture. Have you seen that?" I ask, hoping to find common ground, to feel part of a group or something.

"I guess. I haven't thought about it much, but I think people do fear people who are different, like us." He looks like he's just guessing at an answer.

"Yeah. I see what you mean, but really we're all different. Who's to say that just because we're in the nut house, we're worse off than somebody else?"

Eric looks me in the eyes, smiles and says, "Yeah, you're right, man."

I continue with my ramblings. "I've met some pretty weird people and they are never going to the nut house, but they probably should."

"That's funny, man, and true. I've met some really weird people," Eric replies, still cracking a smile.

"Plus I think somebody is crazy if they themselves think somebody is crazy and tell them right to their face. Seems like a good way to get shot or stabbed or something. I mean, Steve says he stabbed somebody. I don't know if it's true, but there are plenty of people who would kill you out there. You ever watch the news in California?" I ask.

"No."

"I have, and it's filled with 'so-and-so got killed' and I've never even been to places that are supposed to be a lot worse. I mean, I know this is Utah, but I stopped a kid who had a knife from fighting with my brother once," I blurt out, still feeling those love-then-hate feelings for my brother. I reflect that he really hasn't done anything wrong; it's just that his life is a fairy tale compared to mine, and I resent that.

"How did you do that?" Eric asks in disbelief.

"I was at home and I saw my brother being stabbed by somebody at his school. So I ran out and when I got there, he was starting a fight with four guys who went to his school. I told him to go home, because I didn't want anything to happen to him. Not long after, the cops came, but the knife came out just before," I say quickly.

"So do you have ESP or something?" Eric asks with a look on his face that I've never seen before, kind of like somebody who's eaten a hot pepper and doesn't know what to do.

"I guess," I say, not knowing if I should tell him about my church. "I've been in about ten fights since high school, but I was never in one before."

"I guess that's normal. I didn't get in too many before high school either," he says, looking up and to the left.

"Do you have a girlfriend?" I ask, flipping the subject.

"No." Eric looks at the ground for help.

Then I do something I tend to do too often, which is blurt out something I shouldn't.

"Me either. I was after this girl, but she turned out to be a witch," I say without a hint of irony. He probably doesn't think I'm serious, but I am.

"That's funny," he says. Then he points at someone across the room and asks, "What's up with *that* girl?"

I look where he's pointing. "Bethany? She's pretty cool, so be nice to her."

He turns back to me. "What about the others?"

"Josh is cool, but he's really quiet. I don't like Steve very much, he's a punk, and I really don't know Mark well. Marta is the meanest staff person and that huge guy over there's Jaffa, the security guard."

Eric takes a minute to process this information. Then he changes the subject entirely. "Are you a cutter?"

"What's that?" I ask, peering out of my world for a moment.

"People who cut themselves. Kind of like getting a tattoo." Eric says this like it's no big deal.

"No. I don't do that and I don't have any tattoos either," I reply. I'm amazed there's actually a word for hurting yourself like that. "Do you do that?" I wonder. I'm a little worried about what might come back.

"I used to," he says, which to me means he probably still does, and now I want to change the subject myself.

"Where do you live?" I ask.

"In Sandy," he tells me. He looks proud of this fact, and I don't blame him. Sandy is a nice place to live.

"I live in Sandy, too. We should hang when we get out," I say.

"That would be awesome," Eric says excitedly. "Do you know where anybody else lives?"

"No."

"Oh, I thought since you've been here, you might know."

"I guess I didn't think to ask. Jaffa is a nice guy and he would know. On Saturday, Brother Johnson from the ward took me to a ward basketball game and when I got back, Jaffa was supposed to check me for drugs but he didn't; he just looked."

Eric looks confused. "What do you mean?"

"They're supposed to check your butthole. Like I would put drugs up my butt. Man, that's so stupid," I say sharply.

Eric pauses and then says, "Well, somebody must have tried it."

"I guess. I'd sure hate to see those drugs." I laugh, and Eric joins in. The air fills with the sound of joy – rare in such a place.

When the laughter stops, I round out his personal puzzle a little more when he asks, "So are you more of a daredevil or an Icarus?"

"What's Icarus?" I ask.

"Icarus was this guy in Greek mythology who died while trying to flee from danger."

One day I'll learn Eric has his stories mixed up, but for now I say, "Oh, I'm the daredevil. You?"

"Well, some place in between, I guess." Eric looks at the ground.

Okay, so what did he think I was going to say?

"That's okay," I say, not really caring, because it has nothing to do with me.

"I think of myself as more of a thinker," he tells me. "Take chess, for example. It's really just a black king versus a white king, but it's one of the most popular games in the world and has been around for centuries. Plus whenever you play it, it's never quite the same."

"Yeah, my dad taught me to play, but I don't play very much," I say as Bethany takes a seat next to us. I think of chess and link it to reading, saying, "I'd like to read faster. I have dyslexia and some other learning disabilities."

"I've gotten faster the more I've read," Eric replies, giving me some hope that I may improve my own speed over time. "So what do you read?" he continues.

"Comic books."

"Which comic do you like best?"

"The ones with the best artwork," I say. "I like to make up my own superheroes, too."

"How do you do that?"

"The easiest way is just to combine a few different superheroes to make a new one. Or you can write up a list of powers and go from there."

"Eric, you have your counseling session now," Marta cuts in without any thought of politeness.

"Okay," says Eric. And he jumps from his seat and heads off.

I turn to Bethany, who looks up at me and asks, "Do you like tattoos?"

"No," I answer, without stopping to think she's probably asking because she likes them or has one she wants to show me. But snappy replies are standard for me lately.

Bethany turns back to her magazine and I'm left isolated – in part because Eric was pulled away, but also because I somehow messed up an opportunity to talk.

***

Nightfall brings a restlessness I don't want. I'm exhausted, but thinking too much to sleep. For me, self-evaluation is like a kid sticking needles in a Voodoo doll: it hurts, and may be a lesson in bad medicine.

I've gotten sick, which is not my fault, but I've hurt a lot of people emotionally and that's not something I would normally do. I've picked on Thomas a lot and there are, of course, some girls in the ward. I should start trying to be a better person when I get out – try not to lie, accept accountability. If I can figure out everything that's happened to me, that should help me, too.

I wonder if the Adversary has ever gone after anybody else like me. It's said that darkness came over Joseph Smith, so there could have been a lot of pain with that. I need to do my best not to fail myself.

When sleep finally overshadows me, my thoughts turn to the heroes in my comics, the strong ones I hope to be like, if I can just make myself bigger. If heroes are real and can make a difference in the world, then I will do everything I can to become one.

I've started using the other side of the mirror. The side you use when you reflect on the soul and emotions. The side that should say, "And if men come unto me, I will show unto them their weakness. I give unto men weakness that they may be humble; and my grace is sufficient for all men that humble themselves before me; for if they humble themselves before me, and have faith in me, then will I make weak things become strong unto them." (Ether 12:27)

Chapter 21 – Time Removes a Problem

Monday: November 23rd, 1987 – Age 17

My birthday passed and I didn't realize it. It's as if I was a clone and birth had no bearing.

I see Eric walking toward me, and I can tell he has a report.

"Hey Rick, guess what?" he says, with a grin.

"What?" I reply from my doorway. I just finished a conversation with Josh. (Of course, even if you've just started a conversation with Josh, it's already pretty much over.)

"Steven is going home today. In fact, they already took him out to do his paperwork." Eric smiles outright.

"That's good news," I say, hoping never to see Steven again.

"Man, you really don't like him, do you?"

I give a firm, "No."

"Why?"

"He's just cocky. I hate guys that are cocky. It really bugs me." Disgust is written all over my face.

"Why?"

"I guess because most of the time there's nothing to be cocky about, and the rest of it just seems childish. You can either handle things or you can't; it has nothing to do with attitude."

Eric furrows his brow. "By 'handle' you're talking about fighting?" he asks.

"Yeah."

"So like, what should I look out for?"

"Well, it's always in the eyes. For example, if a guy has anger in his eyes and he already has his hands in fists, then he's controlled by his anger."

"That doesn't make sense," he says.

"Okay, let me show you. If I put my hand in a fist at my side like this, I'm actually wasting energy thinking I'll get into a fight.

Well, real life is not the movies. Now let's say you throw a punch at me. Watch my hand."

I move my hand slowly from my side, completely open, and in the course of travel to the target I make a fist, stopping my hand about six inches from Eric's nose, just enough to prove the point. I'm also moving slowly enough that I don't startle him – or the staff, because I don't want to go into lock-down for fighting.

"Okay, I see your point. But could the person be acting out of fear?" Eric counters.

"Yes, somebody could jump the gun out of fear. But like I said, you should be able to see it in the eyes. They say the eyes are the window."

"Hi Josh," Eric says as Josh heads by us on his way to the restroom. All Eric gets back is a wave of the hand.

"That's just the way he is," I try to comfort him.

"Yeah, he does seem quiet."

I think about my recent experiences. "Have you ever felt like you know what the rest of your life is going to be like? But everything is blurred to hide the whole truth from your eyes?"

Eric squints at me. "What do you mean?"

"Like you see things in life and you know something is there for you, but you don't know what."

"I guess you're going over my head, but I think you mean like kinda seeing a vision or something like that."

"Yeah, something like that."

"Time for lunch," a call comes from outside the door by the tables.

"Let's get lunch," says Eric.

"Okay."

We ramble over to eat. I won't have to take a pill since I'm on mornings and evenings. The food smells like chicken, and I'm allergic to poultry, but that doesn't matter, as they will have something different for me. I walk in close enough to see they made me some kind of sandwich, but it's no Subway. Disappointment leaves me feeling trapped in my body. One moment I can't eat, and the next, I can't breathe.

I sit down with my food.

How can anybody mess up grilled cheese? This sucks.

I shudder as I try to swallow the first bite of my sandwich.

I would love to be able to work out right now.

This place is a rat cage. I could get more exercise here by getting into a fight.

I look at Josh, who urgently eats his meal and heads back toward shelter with much of the food still on his plate, just shifted around. Despite arriving at lunch last, he's already finished; it's like the light of the cafeteria shrinks him.

I'm thinking about skylights again when Bethany sits next to me. She glances up at the ceiling as I must be doing, and then looks to me. Of course, just because somebody looks at you, it doesn't mean they want to talk to you, or that you're even somebody to them. People are like houses: sometimes the lights are on and nobody's home, and other times the lights are off, but somebody *is* home. I usually like to be invited in before opening my mouth with somebody I don't know. It keeps you from trespassing or getting the door slammed in your face.

Now Bethany is ready to speak her mind. "I have cramps," she announces. "Do you think you could get me something from the nurse?"

She doesn't look unwell. "What kind of cramps?" I ask.

"The female kind," Bethany says with a snarl.

"Okay, I guess I could go ask." I get up from my seat and walk over to the station nurse. "Hi. I need to get some cramp medicine for Bethany."

"I can't give you medicine for anybody else. I can only give you your medication. Go back to her and tell her that, and let this be a warning to the both of you."

Okay, whatever.

"Okay," I reply. I walk back to Bethany and tell her, "She said no and that she can't give me any cramp medicine for you. You have to get your own."

"You weren't supposed to ask for cramp medicine. You were supposed to ask for Tylenol."

I'm confused. "Oh, sorry. Do you want me to ask again?"

"She's not going to give it to you now," Bethany says in irritation.

"Well, could you get it?"

"I got some earlier, but it's not working."

"Sorry." I feel disappointed.

She was trying to con me.

"Well, maybe if you get some later, let me know," she says.

"Okay." *I guess.*

"You're such a sweetheart. I'll talk to you later."

Why am I a sweetheart? Because you want something from me later.

Bethany gets up and leaves me.

What is up with all these girls?

I grew up surrounded by nurses, and of course Mom, and was left thinking women were perfection. Then I started to learn about them. Turns out they're just like us, only they look much better, and maybe smell better.

***

In the morning, another day is upon me and it seems like I'm not any closer to going home than I was yesterday, even with the therapy sessions.

Josh is on his bed, one of the maybe four places he can be found. The only thing that could be worse is if he never left his bed. He would probably like that.

At 3:16 PM Bethany is put in the padded room, but this time I have no idea why. This time I feel less concerned, since I've now seen somebody go in and come back out again. This time, I'm just glad it's not me and I'm still on track to go home.

I might be the only one in here who really *wants* to go home. I know Samantha seemed happy about it, but maybe she was only temporarily happy to leave here.

The staff finish with Bethany and close the door, shutting her in that silent room. Then she's left alone, and I think maybe she did it on purpose, so she would receive a pill to make her relax.

The night stirs in, not revealing Bethany. I know she will spend the night in the box.

If I could talk to spiders, I could find out how she's doing. She must be asleep by now, but still there's something about the dark and strange places.

The call for "lights out" comes. I'm already in bed and Josh hardly ever leaves his, so our room is good. Staff check will still come in about two minutes, to make sure the boys are in boy rooms and the girls are in girl rooms. My only thought is to get myself out, and so I keep myself in check.

It can be hard to have some of my freedoms held ransom, but it's for a limited time, and in a limited way. Not like before when I lost all freedom only to suffer under the pains of death and despair. Courage must come, courage of the unseen, and that means complete faith in the Lord.

As I fall into a deep sleep, I know I will live to fight another day. My heart still beats, and my lungs carry willpower's breath. I can't lie down to die, only to rest. I can't hope for the best for others, if I don't try to help myself so that later I can help others too.

The darkness that is depression can be beaten back. Life can become beautiful again.

Chapter 22 – Psychotherapy

Tuesday: November 24th, 1987 – Age 17

Psychotherapy is like looking for cancer. It always seems to start with the same questions to ensure the preservation of the patient – in a nutshell, looking for thoughts of suicide or signs that the patient cuts him/herself. It's an intrusion and so I'm hurt by the question; I take it personally.

I currently face this problem as I sit across from a new doctor, Dr Von Sydow, who calls me by my formal name, Richard.

"Richard, are you having any thoughts of suicide or of hurting yourself?" he asks. He wears a silver tie and a green pinstriped suit. I must look like I'm in shock, because he tilts his head slightly to the left and looks me in the eyes.

I must not let my guard down, even if I was *thinking that.*

"No," I reply, wanting to move on to the next question.

"How is your sleeping? Are you able to fall asleep without your mind racing?"

"Yeah." *How does he know about that?*

"And when you're asleep, are you able to *stay* asleep?"

"Yeah." I *have* been sleeping much better.

These types of questions go on for a couple minutes. Then the doctor sits up straight in his chair and takes off his silver-framed glasses, placing them on the desk. He leans forward, and his jet-black hair slips down over his intense face. He pauses like a cougar before the kill, and then asks, "Do you hear voices talking to you?"

"No." I want nothing to do with this question, because the consequences are too much for me to bear.

In time, there's a diagnosis in place for me, though it will take a while to sink in.

Apparently, I have something called Schizoaffective Disorder, with a tendency toward Bipolar Disorder and some OCD – but for now we just say Bipolar. I have no idea what this means, so I have no questions and I want no answers.

The doctor wants to give me these answers anyway. "Let me tell you what *Bipolar* means. It's a brain disorder that causes unusual shifts in mood and, therefore, affects your ability to carry out day-to-day tasks. In your case, based on the notes your mother gave us, you seem to have ups and downs depending on how much sunlight you absorb. Do you have any questions so far?"

"No."

"It's believed that many famous people have suffered from Bipolar Disorder, like Vincent Van Gogh. Do you know who he is?"

"The guy who cut off his ear."

"Well, something like that. But he was also a painter, and has become one of the most revered artists of all time."

But he did cut off his ear.

"Anyway," he says, "the point is: there's no limit to what you can do – and now you, unlike Vincent Van Gogh, have the advantage of modern medicine to aid you in living life to the fullest."

Yeah, like cutting my ear off. Maybe you should get a better example.

"Well, I *have* been sleeping better," is all I can think to say.

"That's wonderful. I bet that feels really good to be able to sleep and then have more energy the next day."

I shrug and say, "I guess."

But he's right. Thanks to these therapy sessions, and the medication I'm taking, I'm surprised to find I'm experiencing what I think is a more normal life…or, at least, as normal as it can be in the hospital. It's not the perfect blend of medication yet, nor is it what I will end up taking for the rest of my life, but it's a start. And it's working.

Monsters are turning back into people, and I'm learning that ordinary humans can be twice as evil as the demons I was seeing. Perhaps if there were a translucent billboard above each person's head giving the board strokes, life would be simpler. You could look up and read, "Serial killer, looking for next kill." Then you could just move to other side of the street.

However, there is no board. I've learned in this hospital that there are daughters being raped in their own homes, which is something I can't even comprehend. Life isn't simple.

I am one person wanting to make a difference, even if it's a small one, in the lives of my incarcerated peers. Yet I'm afraid to understand them too well. Because understanding means knowing: knowing evil, in order to know good from evil. It means knowing why bad things happen to good people.

***

Time goes by, but not as slowly as it seemed to go by in school, and that's cool. Another factor is that I feel more like myself, and at least know for the most part when somebody is trying to influence me.

This life is hard enough without others trying to use you for evil. Evil has many faces; it doesn't need mine.

Albert Einstein said, "The world is a dangerous place to live; not because of the people who are evil, but because of the people who don't do anything about it."

A miracle was done for me...but will it be enough? A story is slowly developing. Will it be of light or darkness?

Chapter 23 – My Reaction Is to Keep Getting Up

Wednesday: November 25th, 1987 – Age 17

It's easy to bluff one session, but to get through one after another is completely different, and I'm feeling there's no way out. I know I'm much better than when I came in, tail tucked and hair chopped up, revealing the horseshoe scar on the back of my head for the first time since I got it.

But hair grows and I have to grow, too. The meds give me time to think, so I sit lingering over humanity, contemplating the options that lie in front of me. But they do nothing but vex me. By this point, it has become second nature for me to get back up when I'm knocked down, both literally and figuratively. Yet even with this confidence, I still wonder if I'm strong enough.

Am I a fragile image, just a glimpse in a shadowed window? Is compassion my guide, or am I torn astray? Am I a friend, or do I cause sorrow?

I still have ups-and-downs, and it will be a lifetime before I take the risk of writing it all down – the kind of writing where every emotion streams from every fiber until it hurts, and then continuing until it doesn't hurt any longer and the pain goes away.

There is light for me stemming from the fact that I recognize the feelings of others, like Josh, even if not consistently. In times when I ignore him, like everybody else does…well, to some degree, that's just being human. But I've never liked being "just human". I've always wanted to be so much more – not famous, but more like a humanitarian who makes a difference – a superhero, like in my comics, only real.

But I look at the people I'm surrounded by and they don't want a superhero. They don't seem to want anything at all, expect maybe more sleep or something harmful.

Bethany, who used to be okay, has proven completely messed up without another girl to lean on for support. Josh is like no one I've ever known, mostly because I've never seen anybody try to hurt themselves in real life. It seems so counterproductive to me, especially in a place like this where staff walk around all the time and there aren't many of us to check on. Josh's Hell strikes me as being made out of shame. But what could someone so withdrawn possibly have done to merit that much shame?

Eric thinks he's really smart, but maybe just about the things he likes. He's a nice guy, but I'm still not sure about him. Right now, he's in counseling with his family; he seems to be suffering from over-parenting. I don't think he belongs here. He *was* caught with some alcohol, but this place isn't rehab.

I've found out almost nothing about Mark, and, for whatever reason, that's fine. I've seen Eric talking to him a few times. Some people just give off a bad vibe and it's easier to do without them.

***

Marta walks over to me. "Rick," she gets my attention.

"Yeah."

"Tomorrow you're going to be released – as long as you don't mess up before then, that is. You better pack up your stuff, just in case." She speaks as if she's losing a prisoner.

I say, "Okay, thanks," the whole time thinking, *Could you act any meaner?*

She turns and walks away from me as if her whole day has been ruined. But for me, this is a good day. Packing will take all of a minute and so I start.

My wait's over; I get to go home. I'll get real meals, and all my stuff will be waiting. I'll get to see Badger and play with him and maybe, in time, my friends will hang out with me.

But home also means going back to the point of origin. For better or worse, I will have to face my family and hope they still feel like family. I will have to face my friends and neighbors. I will have to sleep at home again and can only hope it will be filled with peace and my dreams devoid of pain.

Who am I to say what's the right or wrong way for people to handle me? I haven't done anything wrong, but if somebody is afraid of me, I can't get mad at them for not understanding me. All I can do is be honest and try to help people and know that this won't be easy.

At least I know from being here that I am not alone. Josh and some of the others have it much worse than I do.

For some people, life is strawberries and roses, while for others it's guns and meat. For my little pack here at the hospital, life is pain and regret. I don't want to leave this life with regret. This place has shown me it can be easier to be a man and get back up from an actual fight than it is to face an emotional battle and get back up.

I think I will be okay in time, but I've made some big mistakes. I need to correct these and show everybody I can be a better person. I hope when I get home people will give me a chance.

PART 3:
Going Home

Chapter 24 – My Attack Plan: Heal Myself, Then Others

Thursday: November 26th, 1987 – Age 17

In every engagement there needs to be a plan of attack, and I'm about to establish mine. And with every plan, there's collateral damage. As a teenager, right and wrong choices can be hard to figure out. When the years pass by, these choices will become easier, but at the moment I'm still uncovering answers.

Even as I now talk to Eric, I don't realize he will become part of a choice in life: to leave behind depression and seek the light or continue as I've been.

"Man, I can't believe I get to go home today!" I tell him, excited.

"That's cool, man. What are you going to do when you get out?"

"I don't know, but at least I'll be out."

And I'm not coming back.

"Well, remember when I get out we need to hang out," he says.

"Okay."

I stretch on the couch. Bethany walks over and sits down beside me. I'm not sure why, since the other side of the couch is free, as Eric is sitting on a chair.

Bethany looks over at me. She tilts her head to the side and says, "I heard you're going home today."

"Yeah, I'm going home," I say. Then Eric gets up and leaves.

Before I can wonder why, Bethany asks a question to draw me back to her. "Where do you live?"

"Sandy," I say, still watching Eric's movements.

"I hear it's really nice there," she says.

"I guess." *Does this girl like me or something?*

"I think I'll get to leave soon, too." She flips her hair back.

"Okay, that sounds cool."

I'm not sure I can trust this girl, and maybe she doesn't even like me. Try to keep it together.

"You have curly hair," she says. "I didn't notice because your hair was so short when you came in here."

"Yeah, I don't like it," I say.

"Girls like curly hair."

"Why?" I ask, genuinely curious.

She's surprised. "You're asking me why?"

"Yeah, why?" *What's wrong with asking why?*

"I have to go," she says, getting up and leaving me.

"Okay."

This is kind of a weird last day.

Eric comes back with a piece of paper and a pen. He sits back down in his chair and hands the items to me.

"Here, write down your phone number and address," he says.

"Okay." I do as asked.

I hope this is okay to do. I mean, I'm not sure what I should do, but he does seem like a cool guy. But he could change by the time he gets home, and he might be weird or something.

After finishing, I hand the paper and pen back to Eric, who puts the paper in his pocket. Then Eric gives the pen back to Marta, who glares at him like he just stole counterfeiting plates.

I hope I never see Marta again in my life. What a beast! Why is Eric talking to her? Maybe he's crazier than I thought. Maybe I'll get home in time for the good TV shows tonight. What's on tonight, away? Wait a minute, he got that pen from Marta; I'd better go wash my hands.

On the way to wash my hands, I see Josh on his bed, looking very sad.

I better talk to him.

I go into the bathroom and wash my hands. After I dry them, I head back to see Josh, still on his bed, shaking slightly.

"Hey Josh, what's going on?" I ask in concern.

"Nothing," he answers. But I know the body language, because I've been there myself.

I try to move on from Josh's emotional train wreck. "Well, I guess I'm going home today. My bags are already out there."

"I know," he says quietly.

"I hope you get to go home soon too," I say with sincerity.

"Thanks."

I look up and behold Marta brooding in the doorway. She peers at Josh, and then glares at me. Marta shifts her weight to her right foot and pivots her hips in that same direction.

She's going back to her cave.

"It's time for you to go home," Marta tells me. Then she leaves the room without waiting for my response.

It doesn't matter, though. Those are the best words I've heard in some time. After 22 days in this hospital, they are welcomed in every way.

I turn to Josh, wanting the best for him, and say, "Take care of yourself."

He looks at me and then down at his bed, shifting his body in an odd way, and then just says, "Thanks," in his typical Eeyore way.

I walk out of the room, knowing he will have to face a lot in life. He doesn't seem ready.

Once I'm outside the room, I look around for Eric and can't see him anywhere. He must be talking to a doctor or something. It reminds me of when Hawkeye didn't get to say goodbye to Trapper on *M*A*S*H.*

Marta, being Marta, rushes me through to an outside room, which is okay since I didn't want to talk to anybody else, because goodbyes make me uncomfortable. Something tells me Josh wouldn't like it, either.

Time takes a break as the minutes stretch. When the door finally opens, I see my mom smiling at me. Then she says the most wonderful words I've ever heard:

"Let's go home."

It feels like the nightmare is over and a new dawn is breaking. But will daylight bring me happiness?

The walk to the car brings a feeling of freedom, but no real sign of a smile. The commute home is unceremonious and congested. There must be a freeway sign saying, "Happiness delays the next two exits," because there are a lot of birds in the air. So far, the only positive I have is I can now stretch my legs or hold the TV remote. In other words, I'm not charged up by my freedom. I'm back in shellshock from the pain.

***

Once home, I'm struck by the keyword "shame", like I'm a leper who needs to crawl into a dark cave and die. Nobody knows my problem has a name now.

I put on a brave face, but I feel like I can't put everything behind me until somebody else takes the first step in inviting me back into the group. This is my realization: that after 22 days in the hospital, it's up to others for me to be considered normal.

Not knowing what was said about me when I wasn't around is a blessing. Everybody knows the bad will trash you, the gossips will gossip and the good will stick up for you. I have real problems to deal with.

I want Mom and Dad to be able to trust me, so I need to make a choice. Eric will be out soon and will be my only friend. I could wait for my other friends to come around, but I don't know what they think of me now. What I *should* think is, *Lighten up, you've been through worse* – but I'm not there yet.

It would be cool to have a friend, but I wonder what kind of friend Eric would be. Bishop Cook once said, "You can't soar with the eagles, if you're always hanging out with the turkeys." I learned to think of it as, *You can't teach the turkeys how to become eagles until you have learned to become one yourself.* I'm not doing my best right now and it's not the time for me to be strong for somebody else. First I need to be strong for myself. So I'll need to let Mom know I'm just going to wait it out.

I walk upstairs and find her in the family room watching TV with Mary Ann. Mom never watches TV for very long, and it looks like nothing good is on. I sit down facing them on a bench at the table. After waiting for a minute, I decide I should just tell her.

"Mom, I've decided I'm not going to hang out with Eric," I say, as if I've just unloaded the biggest burden of my life.

"Why not? You told me he was your friend."

"Bishop was saying not to hang out with the turkeys if you want to be an eagle, and I think it would be better for me to wait for my friends to come around. It would be different if I were in a good place, but I don't think I am, right now." I know my actions are self-centered and will hurt Eric, but this time I'm helping myself.

"Okay, that sounds fine." Mom gives me a small grin, maybe because I have the body of an adult but socially I've regressed to some unknown point in childhood.

I decide that's enough talking and walk away without saying another word. I go back downstairs to watch something good. I grab a movie, put it in the player and flop onto the couch, knowing I need a change, but taking comfort from escaping into the film. It's one of my favorite things to do. There's nothing better than a good action movie.

I fade more and more into the TV and my inner voice grows silent – as silent as it can, anyway. Badger comes downstairs to lie next to me. He isn't supposed to be on the couch, but he still ends up there. Badger knows everybody who will get mad at him for being on the couch and everybody who doesn't care. Badger is a smart dog in a funny way. But because I couldn't bear to let his dog-hood be chopped off and thrown into somebody's soup or taken to some lab for medical testing, he runs for the ladies every chance he gets. Not that I blame him. He *is* an actual dog, after all.

Sometimes I wonder if he knows what I'm thinking or feeling, or if he just knows when I'm about to pass out from allergies. Whatever he can do, whatever the plan of attack, it's good to have a somewhat loyal dog at my side.

Chapter 25 – Change for Junior Year

Monday: December 7th, 1987 – Age 17

Today is my first day in a new school: Jacksonville High. It's the first big change in my life since coming home and Mom has decided it will help get my life on track.

I know when I step on that bus I'll be with the handicapped kids, but it doesn't sink in *how* handicapped until I walk outside and see the wheelchair ramp. This seems really weird, because I'm not handicapped; this is just the only bus that comes my way.

Not sure what people are going to think.

I board the bus like a slug moving over salt, firmly set in my belief that I'm not handicapped.

This is really weird. There's that Sarks kid from down the street. I should have known he would be on here.

Sarks looks like a curly haired, slower version of Liam Neeson, who is one of my favorite actors. Sarks misreads everything you do, so to him it looks like you're out to get him no matter what. He may also be the only person who talks less than I do.

The ride to school takes a while because we're traveling from Sandy to Jacksonville and I'm the last stop; some of the kids have had a very long trip. We reach our destination and the bus stops. The overall-and-flannel-shirt-wearing, beer-bellied gas machine of a driver goes to the back of the bus to unload. I'm one of two on foot; the rest leave on four wheels.

I dash off the bus and hold the door for the four-wheelers to enter the building. A couple of them are funny, particularly a girl named Ginger, and I try to make new friends with them, despite feeling out of place. Ginger looks so tiny in her wheelchair, it's like you could pick up the whole thing, and with her sparkling blue eyes and pretty brown hair she would probably love it.

Some really adorable girls pass by while I'm monitoring the door for my new friends, which is all the reward I need. Once my group is in, I make my way to class, up the first flight of stairs on the left, which go up and then bridge off. Then they go up again, reaching the second floor. All the stair wells in the school are built like this. I move south and follow the hallway, steering right at the short end of the school, where my classroom is settled.

It doesn't seem like anybody is watching me. That's good. I hope it continues. I need my space right now. I have so many things to figure out. I just want to get to class and have a normal day.

I have one classroom for the entire school day, every day, for the rest of the year. It's one of those "special classes" but it's in the high school. At least I always know where it is, and the bathroom is directly across from the class.

At least I don't have to worry about moving around during the day.

The idea of school is unnatural right now, but it's still better than trying to translate to Mom and Dad exactly what happened to me.

We have two teachers, Mr Mickelson (the main teacher) and Mrs Rogers. Mrs Rogers is a lanky woman, standing six-foot-three. She always wears a smile, but from the looks of her dress and job, she isn't in the money. Her light brown hair contrasts nicely with her solid brown eyes, and although she isn't really a looker, her face has a friendly glow. Mrs Rogers is also the only female in a class of boys, including Mr Mickelson.

Mr Mickelson has dark hair and a beard. He's the only teacher I've ever had with a beard, although a few have come close. Mr Mickelson is my height with a medium build, and he has on Levi's with a lumberjack-style shirt. It's only the first day, but he seems like a really cool guy with a laid-back style and Mom says both teachers care a great deal for their students.

Mrs Rogers brings me paper and scissors, and then eases them onto my desk. She bends her knees so as not to flash me, a sign that she wants to give and receive respect.

Mrs Rogers says, "Cut me out some shapes, as many as you can with this amount of paper."

Okay, seems easy enough, but Mr Mickelson is at the board doing math. Does that make this my math? I guess I'll find out.

I cut out my shapes while Mr Mickelson works at the board with the other students, who total five, all guys: Bo, Derek, John, Ray, and Tim, who is the quiet one and reminds me of Tiny Tim for whatever reason. One thing that's different about this group from the last group of guys – my poker buddies – is this group are all rockers. I've never been around rockers when they're just being themselves, and these guys seem cool. In fact, I'm cutting out shapes and nobody seems to care. I can tell already John and Ray are friends, as they keep talking in one way or another, despite warnings. They also have on the exact same Def Leppard t-shirt, and try to hide their cigarettes in the same way.

Derek seems the smartest of them all. His eyes say he knows the answers, but his hands won't write them down. Bo, on the other hand, looks as close to a pretty boy as somebody could get, wearing dirt and holes as a fashion statement. Bo carries a pocket knife in the front pocket of pants three sizes too small. Maybe they're his little brother's pants. I have to be on guard against the knife, but the rest is just what makes him Bo.

Once I've finished trimming out the shapes, I bring them up to Mrs Rogers.

"Thank you, Rick, you did a really good job with that," Mrs Rogers says with a smile.

"Okay," I reply.

Still not sure that was really my math.

"You can take your seat now and I'll come over with another assignment in a minute."

"Okay."

I haven't done anything like that since kindergarten.

I take my seat and reflect that Mrs Rogers seems awfully excited I was able to execute the task. I'm not a hundred percent on where they think I should be, but I have a pretty good idea, and nothing is coming out of my mouth to clear it up. After all, it isn't my mistake, and I have other things to think about.

***

Later in the day, I'm at home, sitting down at the table with Melissa.

"I had to cut out shapes," I inform her, with my patent-pending smirk.

Melissa looks a little baffled. "Why did you have to do that?"

I pause and then say, "I don't know, but wouldn't you rather cut out shapes than do math?"

"I guess, but aren't you worried what the guys will think of you?" she asks in her ever-sweet way.

"No," I say with great confidence.

"Do you think they'll find out?"

"Yeah, some time." *But I'm not saying anything.*

"Well, it just seems like a waste of your time," Melissa says. Then, trying not to laugh, she continues, "I mean, cutting shapes is hardly math."

"Yeah, maybe I'm supposed to count sides or something."

"Well, good luck cutting shapes, I guess."

"Thanks."

I get up and slip downstairs for the night, not thinking that it might get back to Mom that I was cutting shapes and she'll make sure I start doing some real math. Or maybe in the back of my mind I want Mom to find out and let them know. You never know what's going on in the back of your mind. It's always planning things for you that it thinks are best.

Melissa is awesome. Man, I have a good family, and it's much better now that it doesn't seem like anyone's trying to kill me. I still need to figure out my powers, though, just in case. If I could figure out how to activate them, I could really make a difference in this world.

It's good to have Badger around again, too. He's such a good dog, though he seems to be rubbing off on me; sometimes we smell the same. I don't think that's normal.

Maybe I'm joining with him in spirit, like the Native Americans who believe they're guided by animal spirits. Maybe I need help with something that's coming up.

If I get sucked into some kind of weird animal spirit world and have to fight my way out, I'm not going to be happy with that dog.

Today has been a good day, a stark contrast with the fortification of the hospital, where they spit you out of an assembly line, stamping your name and diagnosis on your forehead on the way out. At least, that was how it felt, though in fairness, the experience saved my life.

At school I'm a person again, and I hope to keep it that way for a long time to come. It actually feels good to be back in school. I hope it continues to be a good place – or at least a safe place.

I'm seventeen and I don't know much about the world, or even a lot about myself, but I'm learning. The biggest lesson the future will bring is something that I fear now: writing things down on paper. Somehow the wrong person may find out and use it against me.

In time, I will find it my greatest source of strength – writing out the emotional pain so I can let it go. It's not a cure, but it can release my gluttony of emotional scars.

It's one thing to have pain, but to have pain that can't be explained can bring on a sense of insanity all by itself. This is not to speak of the horrific sources of that pain. Really, it's a wonder I still function, let alone didn't think to kill myself. Instead, I made a vow to myself that I would take whatever was thrown at me and fight back.

I will NOT give in.

Chapter 26 – The Real World

Tuesday: December 8th, 1987 – Age 17

Math once again, but this time Mrs Rogers drops a placement test on my desk. Since I'm at least still in the real world, a test isn't so bad.

I guess Mom found out I was cutting out shapes yesterday.

I look at the clock, estimating how long it will take me to complete it, but Mrs Rogers looks like she has her engine purring.

Mrs Rogers smiles and checks her watch. "You have an hour to finish this," she says.

"Okay, thanks, Mrs Rogers."

"Let me know when you're done and we can talk about the results tomorrow."

"Okay," I say, noticing the rockers have seen me taking my test.

I start working, but my thoughts are lost in trivial daydreams.

I need to stay focused.

I try to keep my eye on the ball, but it isn't easy. It would probably help if there weren't so many things going on inside my head.

Eventually, all the time has run out of the hourglass and I have to turn in the test.

Maybe after school, Dad and I can go to the video store and rent something.

I stop at Mrs Rogers' desk and hand her my test.

I have to keep moving forward, I have to stay on track, and I have to beat this thing.

A little later, out of the corner of my eye, I catch Mrs Rogers coming my way. She stops at my desk.

"Rick, you did very well," she tells me. "Is math one of your better subjects?"

Okay.

"I did okay until geometry," I say.

Geometry coincided with me at my worst – not that this school would know that.

"Let's see if we can get you back on track, and next year you can take algebra with the mainstream classes," she suggests. "We would like to get you back in the mainstream as much as possible. Keep in mind that you've missed some credits that we can help you with. You would have to take summer school, otherwise." She sounds optimistic.

"Okay. So by mainstream, you mean…?"

"…you would take regular classes. Do you have any other questions?"

"No. I'm good."

Mrs Rogers returns to base. I've been cleared. Then the bell rings.

Man, I better use the bathroom.

I take care of my business and get a drink, only to look around and think all these kids are normal. It will be some time before I really start humanizing everybody, and even longer before I see clearly the difference between humanizing and demonizing others – before I can see mistakes for mistakes and not intentions to harm me.

When the next class starts, Mr Mickelson motions me to come over and talk to him.

"Rick, you're doing really well," he says. "I don't want to overwhelm you, so we're going to take this a day at a time, okay?"

"Okay."

What are you talking about?

"Alright, I just wanted to make sure you were with me. Mrs Rogers and I would like you to try not to fall asleep during school. We both know you're still trying to get used to your medication. But in order for us to get you to where you need to be, well, you have to be awake. I'm sure you can see that, right?"

"Yeah, I know what you mean."

"Good." He smiles at me. "I believe you can do this. So the first step would be to try to cut down on the number of times you fall asleep. We can make another plan once it looks like you have that under control."

"Okay."

"You don't seem to have too much trouble for first period, but then second period hits and you're out like a light. So just see how long you can make it before falling asleep."

"Okay, I will."

"Alright, you can return to your seat now, thank you."

I get to park it, and Mr Mickelson takes center stage. He doesn't make a lot of radical gestures; he just starts in with whatever he's going to do.

In the middle of his monologue, I fall to my desk like somebody turned off my power.

***

The day pushes forward, with me trying and failing to stay awake, and then I'm out. It's like one of those hidden camera jokes people like to do. Finally, the last bell rings so teachers, students, and fools have a chance to escape the building.

At home I find Mom musing over dinner, Katie laying her books to rest for the night, and Melissa still earnestly working. Thomas does okay in school, but would rather play sports than do homework. Mary Ann has the big room with her own built-in desk so she's usually not found at the table, and Tiffany is hit and miss, being the youngest.

For a stretch, my thoughts are actually focused on the real world.

It looks like dinner is coming along. That's good.

Some kids walk by outside and the sound of loud laughter steals my attention.

I don't really fit in any place, anymore. I'm just different. Who could relate to me?

"Hi, Rick," says Mom, noticing I've started to drift off.

"Hi, Mom."

"What happened at school today?" she questions in an optimistic tone.

"Nothing," I reply as I try to recall what did happen.

"That's good, I guess. Dinner won't be too long. Why don't you take your pill?" she reminds me. I'm on two a day.

"Okay."

I fill a glass of water and then gulp down my medication. One pill down, with many, many more to follow throughout my life. No big deal. I'm only on 50mg, and they seem to be making a difference; I haven't seen or heard anything supernatural lately.

Just like that, my thoughts spiral.

I guess the best thing is just that it works so Satan can't take advantage of me anymore. If he does come back, I want to be ready to defeat him.

But if he doesn't have a body, how will I ever hit him? I'll have to develop my mind. Powers of the mind are much more powerful than just having super strength or speed.

Being able to fly or teleport would be so awesome. I mean, even lifting ten tons would be enough to dominate in this world. But if you could cripple ten thousand with your mind, you could rule on any world.

A force field. If I could get a force field to protect the house, everybody would be safe. That would be really cool if the world went wild.

The last days. How long will they be, anyway? We know the Lord's timeline isn't the same as ours. It could put this event almost at any moment, or in five hundred years.

Contemplation like this can go on for hours, and usually does, since I always seem to have a second processor running. In this case, however, I'm halted. In the real world the table is set; the meal is ready. Dinner has always been important to Mom, because she likes to get the family together at least once a day to have a conversation. Sometimes it even works and real communication happens, while other times hunger wins out.

Dad begins by telling his stories, which inevitably include how Grandpa used to pull his teeth. Everything from string to doorknobs to car bumpers – boy, Grandpa loved those loose teeth. Or Dad loved teasing about it, and waiting to reel in the next loose tooth. I loved all my grandparents, but it's becoming harder and harder to remember them. It makes it more important to listen to the stories about them when they come up.

Later, Badger comes over and lies down on the couch next to me as I flip channels. There's a rap at the front door and off Badger goes like a dog-out-of-Hell. That dog wants his freedom.

Maybe I should have had him fixed.

The sounds from the living room indicate that somebody needs help holding back Badger. I jump off the couch, run upstairs and grab his collar just in time. He isn't easy for me to keep in the house either, but he hasn't gotten away from me yet, once I have a hold on him. He really digs into Mom's hardwood floors, however. It's a sign of Mom's love for me that she lets me keep him.

Moms are always doing things like that and I have a good mom. She does what she can and has to contend with a house full of kids while she tries to keep the peace.

Chapter 27 – Cheerleader

Friday: December 11th, 1987 – Age 17

Days pass by with nothing noteworthy, and then I see her dressed in her cute little size-four, blue and white Jaguars cheerleader uniform. A new figure in my life – a nice little hourglass figure. She has black hair and deep brown eyes with a face that captures Heaven's best light. Her skin has a glow about it. I can't believe my eyes in finding such a rare jewel in Utah, of all places.

I study her every movement, the curves of her body, and even the flow of her hair. Then, without a word from my mouth, she's gone. I'm not in her life. I don't even have a name; she's just the little dark-haired cheerleader. I have to find out her name and something we can talk about.

I return to class with hope. Christmas is getting closer and I just saw something that would make my Christmas golden. The other girls in the school will now be compared to the little dark-haired cheerleader.

When I find my seat, it's business as usual outside my brain, but inside, among the mixed up reflections of demons and puzzles and things that go bump in the night, now the fingerprint of the little dark-haired cheerleader is there.

The mystery of these beautiful creatures is one I've been trying to unravel for a very long time. I still carry a memory from when I was a child and saw the woman across the street, who had the most beautiful German Shepherd I'd ever seen. The woman herself was also something to behold. She had long brown hair with green eyes and probably looked like an ordinary woman, but she was nice to me so I thought she was beautiful. I sat there with her dog and wondered how that lady got so pretty.

Now I'm older and understand the biology behind it all, and I still think, *How did she get that way?*

***

When I return home I'm awakened to how fragile life is. Tiffany broke her nose at school running in the hall – something about a collision with another student. To call it "broken" is actually an understatement since it was moved completely out of joint. Mom is again earning her stripes and the house is full of sympathy for little Tiffany, who has had a hard day with more to come.

My world is pain-free for the moment. The only thing concerning me is the girl. The next step for me is my doctor's appointment the day after Christmas. It's not something I'm concerned about yet, but for Mom, who believes my life is in danger, it's very important.

My days feel long because I'm friendless, and the isolation only serves to remind me how different I am, or at least feel. In reality, there are thousands upon thousands of people who deal with depression, and many who have been hospitalized for it. But I don't know any of them personally and I don't have the desire to talk to someone about it in hopes that we may find a common thread. Instead, I look to improve myself, to be like everybody else.

It surprises me to realize I'm not alone with this goal. People, especially young people, like to be part of some kind of group. I'm lucky to have the support group I have at home, but that's not something I can see right now. All I see are all my differences: my body looks different from how I think it should; I don't have the social life I should have. I see that the world I live in isn't the same as what it used to be. When I look in the mirror, I seem different, although I'm not sure how.

My cute little sister is in pain at the hospital and yet I spend my time thinking about myself.

Everybody in the family knows Mom has had more than her fair share of putting the pieces back together again.

Maybe that's why trying to pick up the pieces of my life is so much harder to deal with: because they can't be seen the way a broken nose can. With a broken nose, a mother can put an arm around her child and then hold that child's hand as the nose is set. But when it comes to something like depression, a mother might talk and talk and never get through to her child.

My mother can't put herself in my shoes, because she doesn't know where I am. She doesn't know how to heal a heart that forgot how to let it out and cry and then move on with life. It's everything and nothing at the same time, and yet with all the pain the world has in it, there's no doubt that depression is a plague on our planet – perhaps one of the worst plagues mankind will ever know. It takes everything a person is and turns that person on a dime until they are, and always will have, the face of depression – unless the spirit within steps up and says, "I am going to win. I want my life back."

The events in my life, painful or not, have been handled so far without complete loss of myself, and for that I'm luckier than I know.

***

I feel most comfortable when I have my comics. So when I'm in my room, I take out the box carefully, as always, and look for an adventure. My comics have served to take me away from my life and into another. Perhaps it would be better for me to paint or golf or something that requires more focus, but comics are an outlet nonetheless.

I think back to the time Mom got me my first comic. It had this heroic iron figure who seemed capable of anything. I carefully looked over each picture, wanting not just to be like him, but also to be able to draw images like the ones on the page. Mom got it for me because we were on our way to the Laundromat, and I would have nothing to do. I don't remember my brother having one, which made it seem more special and also made me wonder why she got it for me.

I said thank you more with my body language than anything else and had no complaints about being at the Laundromat. I didn't realize at the time, but it was probably a hardship for her to buy it for me. Dad worked at Price Brothers Auto Parts, my grandfather's livelihood. It wasn't until much later that Dad made his name in the insurance industry.

Now, I sit amongst my heroes, wanting to be more like them. It must be that child inside me that's the driving force within, clinging to life. Matthew said in 18:3, "Except ye be converted, and become as little children, ye shall not enter into the kingdom of heaven." Going to Heaven hasn't been on my mind for the longest time, even with everything that has happened. There's a place inside that still remembers, though. Perhaps it's the same place that wants me to be a superhero.

Only I'm fixated on the wrong kind of hero – men of steel, instead of men of God.

Chapter 28 – Christmas

Friday: December 25th, 1987 –Age 17

Christmas has come and exhaustion is the headline on Mom and Dad's faces. They are doing everything, including scheduling me a doctor's appointment for the following day.

Christmas morning is sublime. Afterwards, Mom and Dad take a Christmas nap. I attempt to watch a movie in the family room upstairs when Ed comes knocking for some boisterous Christmas fun in the snow. Thomas and I are both friends with Ed, who got pretty big lifting weights with me, and then grew even bigger playing football in Fillmore. He has a hint of red in his brown hair and stands six feet, weighing 220 pounds. But he has the heart of a child.

Thomas goes out to build a snow cave with our freckle-faced friend. There are mounds and mounds of freshly piled snow across the street at the church: a scout's dream come true. Thomas and Ed go across the street, while I start one of my new movies in the upstairs family room.

I'm maybe halfway into the movie when I'm struck with the feeling that my brother needs to come in the house. I get up from my chair and walk to the front door, open it and start yelling.

"THOMAS, YOU NEED TO COME IN!"

"WHY?!" he yells back.

I consider this. "I DON'T KNOW!"

"NOT RIGHT NOW. WE'RE BUILDING THIS COOL FORT, OKAY?"

I shut the door and walk back to my TV. I watch the film again – for a bit, anyway. Then the feeling comes over me once more that my brother needs to come in. I go back to the front door to yell at Thomas.

"THOMAS, WHY DON'T YOU AND ED COME IN AND GET SOMETHING TO DRINK?"

"RICK, YOU CAN HELP US IF YOU WANT!" Thomas shouts back.

"NO, IT'S COLD! COME INSIDE!"

I know something is wrong, but I don't know what.

"NOT RIGHT NOW!"

I shut the door and walk back to my chair. With all the girls either downstairs or at a friend's house, the TV is mine.

Time goes by and I'm diligently watching my show when Thomas also gets the feeling that he and Ed should go in, but dismisses it – or so he tells me later. He's busy tunneling out the cave, forcing the snow to Ed, who then places it on the top or to the side of the fort. Snow caving is a harmless way for two teenage boys to spend the day, but they don't know about the big 4x4 truck heading their way.

The truck's engine bursts out against the cold air as it propels toward the snow cave. The driver is looking to demolish the mound. Thomas's long legs are sticking just out the mouth of the cave.

Ed begins yelling and waving at the truck driver as soon as he realizes what could happen. The driver, apparently thinking Ed is the only one there, continues on course. Hearing Ed's yells, Thomas looks to see the lights of the truck blazing against the cave wall. Ed's attention turns to Thomas.

"GET DOWN!" Ed cries as he jumps out of the way himself.

Thomas dives into the cave, hitting the ground as the truck runs right over him. Luckily for Thomas, the truck goes over his butt where the skeleton has the most support. An inch either way and Thomas probably wouldn't be able to move, but slowly he begins to stir, still in shock from the accident.

Ed rushes to Thomas's side to aid him in getting out of the cave. Thomas then sends Ed to get help. I answer the door and see a very shocked looking Ed.

"Thomas has been run over by a truck," he tells me.

I look over and see Thomas standing up, leaning against the snow cave. "No he hasn't. He's standing right there."

"Rick, get your mom and dad. Thomas has been run over by a truck!" Ed repeats.

I look again and see pain on my brother's face as he waves for help.

"Okay."

I run down the hall and open my parents' bedroom door.

"Thomas has been run over by a truck," I say, fear now in my voice. Hadn't I known something was going to happen?

"What?" they both exclaim in unison.

"Thomas has been run over by a truck."

I'm not sure they believe me, but I feel the need to run to my brother. I dart out of the house in socks and PJs, leaving Ed to fill my parents in.

"I'm not sure I can stand here much longer," says Thomas. He looks like he may pass out.

I put my hands under Thomas' armpits and lift him up for support. Mom is on the way over and Dad is trying to get the car out of the driveway. Ed helps him, as our driveway is pretty steep and there's a lot of snow. Mom looks pale and heartbroken.

"Thomas, are you okay?" she asks.

"Yeah, I guess, but it hurts really bad," he answers, trying to be brave.

We stand waiting as Dad works the car over to us. We're not thinking 911, just "get Thomas to the hospital".

When Dad finally gets over, he says, "Let's get him into the car."

None of us is really thinking clearly, but we manage to get Thomas into the car. I get behind him to try to steady him. Dad drives and Mom sits in the backseat with me, leaving Ed behind to explain things to everyone else.

***

When we get to the hospital, it's not easy to get Thomas out of the car, and as we're taking too long to get out of the emergency zone, some nurses run out.

"What's going on?" asks a nurse.

"My son was run over by a truck," Mom replies, trying but not actually managing to control her emotions.

"He was run over and you put him in the car? Why didn't you call an ambulance?"

"Can we just get him in there!" Mom shoots back.

Thomas is loaded onto a stretcher and Dad offers to take me home, but I want to help.

The next hours go by so slowly, and for Thomas they are some of the most painful hours of his life. He can't stand for x-rays, so they lay him down on a hard metal table to take them. Scattered thoughts race through my mind as I watch this happen: *Will he play baseball anymore? How long will he be in pain? Who was the driver?*

After what seems like an eternity, he finally gets a room and is able to fall asleep, thanks to painkillers. This is just the starting point for Mom.

We head home for the night and even though Mom is totally wiped out from everything, she writes a timeline of anything that could help the doctor with my appointment tomorrow, after now having had another crisis. It's very late when she finishes, but she fears for my life and doesn't dare have me miss my appointment.

I'm glad my brother is still with us, and despite his pain, I know in my heart that he will be okay. But the feeling comes over me that I should have prevented it from happening in the first place, and this brings the guilt of not being strong enough.

Sleep finds me, even with all my worries. What helps in the end is that Thomas was lucky for the placement of the truck, because it could have been much worse.

Mom, on the other hand, will continue to be a mother, and that's a lot.

***

After breakfast, Thomas and I are both in the Alta View Hospital. Dad has just dropped me off about ten minutes early for my appointment at one end of the hospital, while Thomas is at the other. Dad then needs to return home to get Mary Ann, Katie, Melissa, and Tiffany, who each want to see Thomas. Thomas has Mom at his side, as he's stuffed with medication. When it's time for my appointment, Mom runs for my side of the hospital, timeline in hand.

I watch the door, wondering where Mom is. When she arrives completely out of breath, I'm not sure what to think. Mom walks to the counter, where the doctor stands to greet her.

"Here's a timeline of everything I could think of for Richard, who is here to see you. My other son is at the other end of the hospital. He was run over by a truck."

The doctor makes a gut-wrenching noise, obviously a mother herself, and takes the timeline. "We'll be fine," she says, and without another word, my mother turns and dovetails it back to Thomas. As the door closes, the doctor takes a breath, pauses and then says, "Richard, come in now."

I walk into her office like a sloth on steroids. The office is very clean, with lots of books and a really nice oak desk. Dr Savannah Smith is about the same age as my mother, from the looks of it, with light brown hair and blue eyes and leaning toward the heavier side. Her demeanor is sympathetic yet professional, and I notice she has a few toys of an educational nature in one corner of the room.

Dr Smith has me sit down as she does the same, looking over the timeline, which must include my head injury. A normal first session takes an hour and consists of lots of questions. I'm not fond of the questions, but I'm getting used to them.

Dr Smith asks about my stay in the hospital and my feelings about my family and friends. She wants to paint a clear picture for herself of what's going on in my head, either to place me on the right medication or leave me on what I already take.

In the end, Dr Smith says, "Okay, I'm going to place you on Lithium. Lithium is basically a salt that has proven useful in balancing the chemicals in the brain. I think it will be very helpful to you, but it does have some side effects that we'll want to watch. Lithium can result in some memory loss and can make you sleepy while you're getting used to it. But like I said, as a salt it will help balance you out in a more natural way." She gives me a little smile.

"Okay," I say, not even thinking about it.

"Do you have any questions about this medication?"

"No." *Like what?*

"Okay, then I'll need to see you in about a month and we'll need some lab work done for a baseline. You can have that done here at the hospital. I'll give you a prescription for the lab work and one for the Lithium, to give to your mother."

"Okay," I reply, again without thinking.

"Thank you, Richard. It was nice to meet you."

With that salutation, I begin more of the work toward fulfilling my hope of recovery.

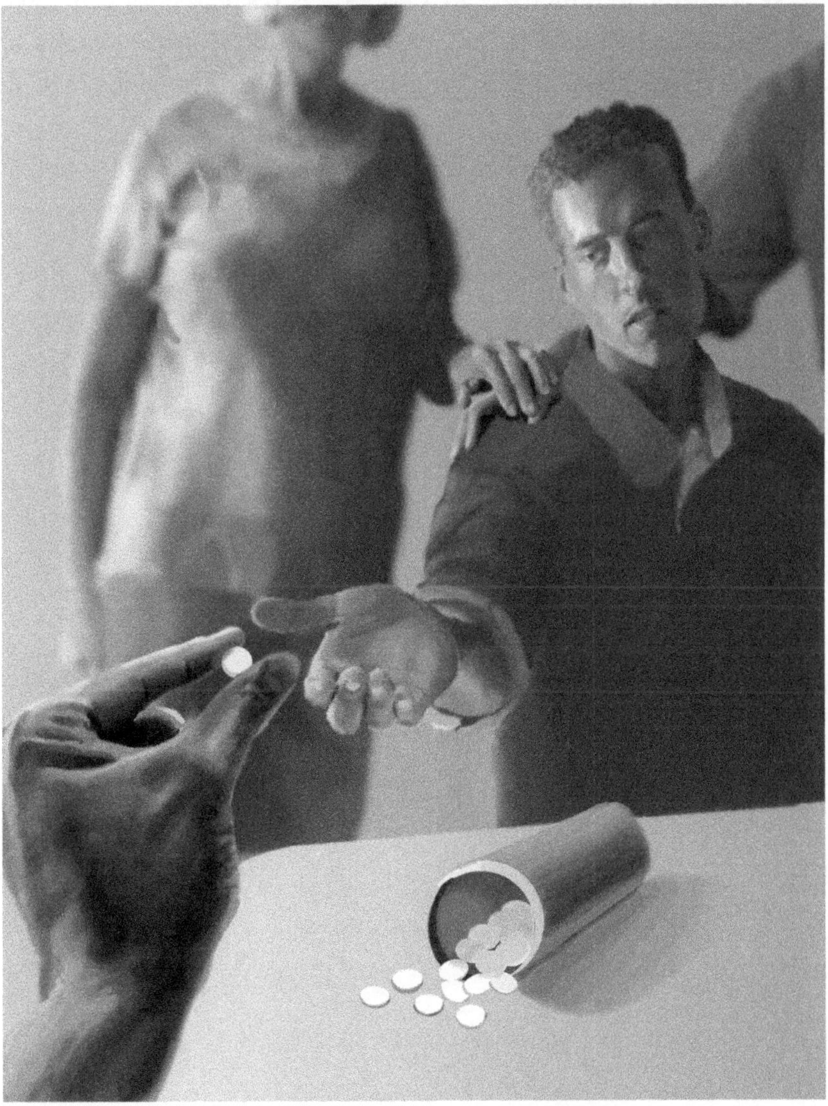

Every time I see a new doctor, it seems like that doctor knows EXACTLY how to help me. But not every doctor can be the best in their field. This doctor may turn out to be who I'm looking for, but there's always a chance that I won't be helped enough or fast enough to make a real difference in my life.

It helps me to remember that nobody is perfect and I can make the difference in my own life by keeping notes on the results of each different medication I take, how they help or hinder me in times of stress.

The fact is that any medication will make a difference, and that difference will be seen in my personality. What remains to be seen is how well I can pick up on the adjustments.

Chapter 29 – The Problem Is Lithium Is Good, Bad, and Ugly

Tuesday: December 29th, 1987 – Age 17

I'm sitting on the living room couch when Mom comes in to check on me. She looks anxious.

"Rick, I know you've been through a lot lately, but at times you push people away in the way you speak to others, and you're getting negative results. I think we should start working on getting positive results. Do you understand what I'm trying to tell you?"

And with that, I'm out like a light.

"Richard. Richard, I'm talking to you. Hello?"

When Mom realizes I'm truly asleep, without any control or warning, she covers me with a blanket as any mother would. Some time later, my head comes up. Mom is sitting in the same spot.

"I understand what you're telling me," I reply to her question of some 45 minutes prior.

"What?"

Puzzled, I reply, "You just asked if I understand you and I said I do."

"Do you realize you were asleep?" she asks.

"What?" I say. I can't believe I could have fallen asleep without knowing it.

"Look down. You have a blanket over you."

I do as she says. "What happened?" I ask.

Mom explains, "I was talking to you and you fell asleep, like somebody flipped a light switch. So I called and talked to your doctor and she said that's a result of the medication. It will happen for a couple weeks or so, while you get used to it."

"How long was I out?"

"I think about 45 minutes. I was just coming back to check on you and you woke up and knew exactly where we were in our conversation. That was kinda cool." She smiles at me.

"Yeah, that's cool."

Wow. That's so weird. I don't remember a thing. If I didn't have this blanket over me, it would be easier to believe she was lying. I hope this doesn't happen when I'm walking around. How will I defend myself if I drop in the school hallway? This thing just never ends. It's like the boogey-man said, "Let's just follow Rick around for the rest of his life."

"Richard. Richard, are you there?" Mom tries to pull me back from my thoughts.

"Yeah," I say, not totally aware of what's going on yet.

"Okay, it's time to eat, let's go."

"Okay."

I follow Mom into the other room. She's concerned about what the other kids might think of me, but doesn't want to ask.

I walk into the kitchen and look into the family room. Everything looks normal.

Mom points out my spot at the table, so I take my seat and wait for the others to join us for our family meal. There we are, with roast beef and Yorkshire pudding and some of the other family favorites. I love Yorkshire pudding. We start with a prayer and then the food is passed around so everybody can enjoy the meal.

The TV is off and that means conversation, something I'm not completely up to yet, but I live in a home where the women do a great deal of talking, talking, talking. I take after my father, who contributes the other 10% of the conversation, so the others won't even notice me not talking.

***

Tuesday: January 5th, 1988 – Age 17

In school, I find myself falling asleep at the drop of a hat – in class or at the dinner table, or while watching TV – becomes the norm for the next few weeks. I'm adjusting to the Lithium, so when I get overloaded my brain shuts down. I have to fight off the sleep, and that means learning to sense when the sleep is coming. The only way this can be done is with help from my mother or a teacher.

I'm currently in math class, so it falls to my teacher today. My brain is already shutting down, eyes closing, and head leaning toward the table.

Mrs Rogers heads my way and places her hand on my shoulder – a big mistake. Startled, I shoot up, my hands going up as Mrs Rogers jumps backward to avoid being hit. My nerves are wound very tight and they jump, as Mrs Rogers just found out.

"I'm sorry, Rick, you were falling asleep. Remember you need to try to stay awake for the whole school day."

"Okay."

"Why don't you go to the bathroom and splash some water on your face?"

"Okay," I reply again. It's a wonder people don't start saying, "Okay," before I do, to save me the trouble. Then I would only have to nod.

I go to the bathroom. I take Mrs Rogers' advice and splash water on my face. Sensing someone has entered, I turn and look. It's the little dark-haired cheerleader. She's looking at me like, "What are you doing in here?" I look about me: urinals – I'm in the right room. I look back at her, but see nothing.

I walk out into the hallway and don't see her.

She could have either gone downstairs or the girls' bathroom; both are close enough. I take my chances with the stairs.

I run down them and jump at the midway landing, heading over enough to look down.

I know I should have caught her.

Give it up. You lost her.

I head back upstairs to the classroom. I've forgotten why I was out of class in the first place. Inside, class carries on as normal, which is a relief, since something is starting to creep into my life again, to ruin it.

I'm doing very well with good grades, in stark contrast with the straight "F"s I was getting before my hospital admission. The classes I now have are geared toward getting a Diploma, not toward higher learning, but I'm still heading down the right path. It's a path with a future – a future with a roadmap to hope.

Hope is an extremely powerful weapon in the battle of life. Hope can bring justice, peace of mind, change in a life gone astray, or even a way to fix something that seems impossible. You don't need money or fame or even beauty to have hope. You just need to believe.

You need to be willing to make the best of yourself if you want to win. The only fight worth fighting is the one fought to be the best you possible, and it's a fight watched by God. Friends are only human and, therefore, imperfect. If they fail you altogether, the only one you can fall back on is that Higher Power.

It's helpful to know Him already.

Chapter 30 – A Friend Brings Hope

Thursday: January 7th, 1988 – Age 17

Winter falls, capping mountain peaks with snow, when there's a rapping on the front door. I answer the door and see an old friend who has some snow caps too. It's Clint, and he stands six-foot-two. Basketball in hand, Clint is dressed to play. His jacket should say, *Heroes go out of their way*. The return of a friend is a sign of hope for a normal life. One person, one step.

Clint looks me in the eyes. "I have the keys to the church. You want to shoot some hoops?" he asks.

I know there's an indoor court we can use there. I turn with excitement. "Mom, can I go play basketball?"

Mom steps into the kitchen and gazes down the hall. "Go," she says.

I'm dressed adequately for basketball, so I throw on my jacket and I'm out. We run outdoors, taking for granted the freedoms we have, sprinting across the lawn toward the church like we're being scouted for the pros. There's some snow on the ground, making basketball impossible outside, but with the church keys, it doesn't matter.

This is awesome.

"How've you been doing?" Clint asks.

"Okay. I go to Jacksonville now," I tell him. I hope the conversation won't turn too deep; I want to enjoy the time out.

"Do you like it there?"

This is a question I'm happy to answer. "Yeah, I like it a lot better."

We make prime time to the church door, where Clint pulls the keys out of his pocket and gets us in. I'm not sure how he got the keys, but he's 18 so I figure it's okay. We stride down the hall and

I jerk open the sticky gym door. I hit the lights just in time to see Clint's ball hit the air, finding nothing but net.

Clint's awesome. I have to play like that.

Something magical happens – at least, it seems magical to me. It's like I never left. Clint takes me back under his wing as a friend and we play ball. I'm just a guy and he's just a guy. I don't stand a chance at beating him at anything we play, but that doesn't matter.

This is one of the best days of my life. Soon things will be back to normal with the rest of the guys. At least, I hope so. I hope Clint thinks I'm okay. I don't want him thinking I'm super nuts or something.

We shoot, play some horse, and even a little one-on-one, which I'm not very good at in comparison to Clint. I don't care as long as I can have some fun, and I always try my best to beat him; he *makes* me try my best. I respect that and need it.

By the end of the night I'm worn out from shooting hoops, which is more entertaining than exercising alone. Plus, my level of hope for what I think is a normal life has gone way up, because of this simple act of kindness.

***

When I get home, I see Mary Ann and Tiffany doing the dishes. Neither of the girls turns around, most likely not expecting me to offer them anything. Tiffany brings the dishes over to the sink and heads back for the last of them, while Mary Ann rinses off the food.

"Hey, do you need any help?" I ask.

"You can use those muscles of yours to scrub these pans," jokes Mary Ann.

"I'm done with the table," Tiffany says as she drops off the last of the dishes from the table and does a little dance to the broom closet.

I follow Tiffany, and then hit a snag.

What was I going to do?

Oh, right, the pans.

I scrub as Mary Ann and Tiffany talk about a girl show on TV, some kind of night soap. I have no choice on that one, but want to show I'm willing to help out, so I make quick work of the pans. I try to get them in the washer. In the meantime, Katie and Melissa are now at the counter.

There's nothing in the world more dizzying than trying to keep pace with a bunch of girls talking 100 miles an hour. Plus they seem to talk at the same time and I'm not sure what they're talking about.

Well, the pans are done now. I think I can go.

Without a word, I walk downstairs to my room for the night, proud of myself for engaging with my family again.

Chapter 31 – Where Puzzles Lie

Sunday: January 17th, 1988 – Age 17

The only thing the Devil has ever done that is truly scary is have so many people not believe in him, but still believe in Hell. Every day I wonder what the scars I carry would look like if they showed up on my body. Every day I wonder how to remove these scars from my mind and soul. Every day I wonder how many lies were told, and how many half-truths.

I look to the sky and see so much that is unknown to me. I look at Badger, as we walk, and even he has secrets I will never know. At times, I want to know how others see me; other times, I don't.

"Badger, what do you think about all this stuff going on around us?" I ask.

He looks, but he doesn't answer.

"I think sometimes you're very lucky to be a dog."

This time he doesn't even look at me.

"I wish sometimes you could talk. But then I guess if you could, you might not be so good to talk to. I wish things were different in my life. So much has happened that I don't understand."

We reach the park and start to walk the path.

At least it's a path that can be seen. It doesn't take brain power to move along it, either.

There aren't many people around, which is probably a good thing, because if there were other dogs, it might make this walk difficult. Pulling Badger around isn't the same as walking.

"Badger, you're doing good. Maybe some day you'll learn to stay by me without the leash." I consider this idea. "Well, that might be too much. But good today."

Badger snorts as if he knows something.

***

After we've done a couple laps, we turn for home. We pass some familiar faces on the way. Being LDS in Utah means going to church with most of the neighborhood. Sticking out as different at church means everybody knows about it. That isn't exactly song birds and pink ribbons. It would be closer to rabbits doing LSD. It's not the kind of thing that can be hidden.

Many people around the world stick out as different, yet we're all still just people. Most of us are trying to have good lives, or at least a life that doesn't affect anybody else's life. To those who are bad, the punishment should be a lot worse. But for the rest of us…we're just people, trying to find our way.

***

Monday: January 18th, 1988 – Age 17

The tyranny of trepidation rules the land, yet the wind blows silent and ever gentle among halls of high learning.

I walk to class half in and half out of the real world. The choice for the new school was a good one. However, after this, the choices are not many.

"Good morning, Rick. How are you today?" Mr Mickelson says with a smile that's almost lost in his beard.

I look into his eyes and check it really is Mr Mickelson. "Morning," I say.

"We're going to start with history today," he tells me.

"Okay."

Mr Mickelson shuffles his paperwork into hand and hits the center of the room. It's a change-up, and it usually draws the attention of more eyes. If I were to think about it, I would have to admit we are a difficult crowd.

"Alright guys, we're going to learn about something I think you're really going to like: the fall of the city of Carthage in 146 B.C. Does anybody have an idea what this battle was?"

Mr Mickelson looks around, but no answers come and no hands are raised. It's obvious he wants to expose us to these things, even if not very deeply. We're always learning about some war or something with action; he must hope it will capture the attention of this small group of teenage boys. But I have no idea what he's talking about. If only I knew how much this means in the real world, and how truly rare it is to find a teacher who cares.

"That's okay, guys, this is a hard one," he says. "We'll be learning about the three Punic Wars between Carthage and Rome that took place over nearly a century. Don't worry. We're just covering it in a broad way, to give you some exposure to history."

While Mr Mickelson talks, Tim gets permission from Mrs Rogers to leave for a few minutes. I don't take much notice of Tim leaving. I'm trying to stay awake and alert so I can listen to the war story. I've always liked war stories. The underdog often ends up winning, and when he doesn't, I like to try to figure out what went wrong.

After a while, we're assigned a writing exercise based on Mr Mickelson's lesson.

Not two minutes into this, I see Tim in my head, and he's in trouble.

I recognize the location, and so I leave the room and bolt down the upstairs hallway. Then I go down the stairwell to run by the lunch room, toward a set of open double doors that provide a hiding place that's still unseen to me.

When I reach it, Tim is about to get beaten up by two kids who have him pinned against the lockers. I push both of them out of the way, using the body of the first one, and then pin the first guy to the lockers.

"This is my friend," I say. "You don't want to mess with him or Rick is going to tear you up."

"Who's Rick?" he asks, newfound fear in his eyes. The other guy doesn't make a move.

"I am!" I growl out in anger that somebody would dare touch one of my friends, and putting on a show at the same time. Something I've learned is that putting on a brave face can prevent a nose-bleed or a black-eye.

The so-called friend of the guy I still have pinned is gone. I release him rather forcefully and resume normal composure. He leaves as quickly as he can, and I turn my back on him, a big no-no.

I put my hand on Tim's back to give him a little encouragement, and start walking toward class.

"Let's go," I say, feeling good that I was able to help.

The two of us walk to the stairwell and the end of our day.

Chapter 32 – Life's Story

Wednesday: February 17th, 1988 Age – 17

Just like in my old school, I'm out wandering the halls when I should be in class.

The story of my life won't end today, nor will it end tomorrow. I'm not very forward thinking when it comes to *my path.*

So much has already happened in such a short period of time that I haven't really taken a look around me. Already the other kids are saying things like, "I want to be in medicine," and are making solid plans for it. I have no solid plans and have no idea what I want to be.

One thing I've learned is that just one little thing makes a difference, changes one path to another, and just like that, your future has changed. Abraham Lincoln said, "The best thing about the future is that it comes one day at a time." The future seems so slow in coming right now, but it *is* coming. For the most part I walk around looking like everybody else, but I haven't felt like everybody else in a long time.

I can only hope things will continue to go well for me. I always wonder what other people's lives must be like. It must be like living in a fairy tale or something, only with school as the backdrop.

I'm going back to class when I see a girl I don't know, but I've seen her many times before. She's different today. Today I see she's pregnant, and her face reads of fear and loneliness.

Oh, man.

She doesn't look at me or anybody else. She's doing a pretty good job of hiding it, but time will end up controlling that.

When she's out of sight, I don't turn or do anything to point her out, something that's not always easy for me.

She looks really scared. I wonder why I've never seen her with a boy. I wonder if her parents freaked out. It won't be easy. At least

I haven't gotten anybody pregnant. That's one good thing about not having a girlfriend.

When I get back to class, I return to the assignment I left behind.

***

Later at lunch, I hear someone ask, "Can I sit with you?"

I look up from my food and see a girl with a tray, across the table.

"Sure," I reply, wondering if she's really talking to me.

She has brown eyes and absolutely stunning hair, not to mention an adorable figure. She's just a little thing, but she makes me nervous, which is weird. In fact, it's something of a first, since I've not been shy for some time.

I look at her, wanting to say something. "You have pretty eyes," I tell her, thinking I've done well.

"But my eyes are brown."

Why does that matter?

"Well, I think they're pretty."

"Oh, thank you. Are you new? I don't remember seeing you," she says.

"This is my first year here," I tell her. "I just transferred in from another school."

"Oh my gosh. This is actually my last day here, because I'm moving. But I'm always looking for a new pen-pal, since we move around so much."

"Yeah, that's a good idea," I say.

Someday I'll look back on this moment and think, *Rick, wake up! Here is this beautiful young girl who wants to be your friend, and you're lost in space!* My shirt should say, *If you're trying to be nice to me, I won't get it for another two decades. Sorry for the inconvenience.*

"You seem like a really nice guy," she carries on.

"I guess so." *So why are people so mean to me?*

"What kind of things do you do for fun?" she asks. She deserves a real answer for asking the question.

"Just working out," I reply, which is true, but the response is so short, it could be taken as rude.

"Oh yeah, I like to swim and do aerobics."

That sounds really good, but I'm not sure what to say, or how to say it. So I take a quick bite of food.

After getting it down, I come up with my best try. "That sounds good."

"You don't say very much, do you?" she notices.

"Not really, why?"

"I can just see you're a man of few words, is all. I like to talk. So I make lots of friends, but no super close friends."

That's not good. I finish my lunch, and then do the stupidest thing ever.

"Okay, well, see you later," I say.

"Bye," is all she says.

When I walk away to discard my tray, I'm walking away from a real girl who showed some interest – all because I can't read the signals. It really is sad that so many times the right thing is within arm's reach, but we can't see it. A friend like this could still call my parents if I went off track, or maybe one day the relationship could grow into marriage. I'll never know, because I leave it behind.

This is only one of my failures in the social world, and as with everybody else, there will be more.

***

The morning's song is fresh as the new fallen snow, but when evening comes, bruises from the day show on the face of time.

One lesson I give to friends and foe alike: our Father didn't say here is your one and only, now go. He said you have free agency, but confirmation on a possibility will come in time. Then He said,

My Sons and Daughters, you need to remember I see no beginning nor end in sight. You will make mistakes, you will learn how to fight. But in Love, the highest call of Natural Law, you will have to climb or fall. So choose wisely, My Sons and Daughters. As we have witnessed the Fall, it's time to go, it's time to gain body to soul. To add a Temple for your days to dwell.

And when you fall with last breath on lips, if you hear the song, then you will know. You will know that you are home.

Chapter 33 – Winning by Living

Tuesday: May 31st, 1988 – Age 17

Days pass and school lingers like it has taken root, leaving me to adjust to class, teachers, and Lithium. What a drag. My intoxication with the little dark-haired cheerleader leaves me blind to the value of *playing the field*. I continue to gain size, all the while keeping in mind my strength, just in case something happens.

I look forward to the end of school and the start of summer, both of which are on the horizon. I feel like I've been through so much and now, in this new school, I can find myself again. I have goals. I want to work out over the summer and try out for some kind of sports team the following year. I want to get a gym membership so I can really lift some weights. All of these are positives in getting me back where I need to be.

Dad is doing awesome at work, which means life at home is getting easier all the time, as well. Thomas is doing great, with his wounds healing normally, and a girl in his group, named Monica, starts hanging around the house all the time. We see guys like Jaxon, Tyson, Taylor and others. At one point, they help Thomas rent a hot tub and stick it in the garage, which barely gives them any headroom, but it's lots of fun. Mary Ann, Katie, Melissa, and Tiffany all seem so different and yet they're also so much the same, because they're all very busy girls and each member of the family is adjusting to life with somebody who has been through a lot and is on medication to level out the depression, but nothing to heal the emotional scars left behind.

The only real concern is over the Lithium. It keeps away the nightmares and helps regulate my body, but it's affecting my short-term memory. By the time summer hits, I find I don't remember details like I used to. It's like I have to reconnect the points. It's very difficult to handle this side effect, because I always got by on memory.

At least the sun is out. The days of summer have always been the best days of my life. It's a time to run and climb things and get into a little trouble.

In my heart, I know that the more I can help others, the more I can help my pain. And with studies showing 80% of suicide deaths are sufferers of major depression, help is needed. Not just because it feels good to help, but also because service is the only medicine that allows the Light of Christ to come in.

I believe. More and more I believe. From that belief in Christ comes the desire not only to help others, but also to fight for them. It's a belief that will be put to the test.

PART 4:
Living in a Dream

Chapter 34 – Senior Year Distractions

Monday: August 29th, 1988 – Age 17

The consequences of summer's last call lie hidden from prying eyes, and senior year whispers in my ear. My path is unsure, my map vague at best. I stand in need of friendship, but the heart still aches under the weight of powers on high, and those below.

Never a girl have these arms held over the months. Yet still I believe the compassion of the right girl will give my life some sense of purpose. I return to a single thought.

Senior year is my chance to express myself to the little dark-haired cheerleader, who will surely see the change in my stature from the summer's workout and fall madly in love with me. I will find a way to have and hold her. I feel like no one on Earth deserves something so beautiful as much as I do, after all the pain I've been through.

These thoughts are probably enough to make a grown man puke. But I'm a hopeless romantic.

On the bus ride to school, I can't help but think, *This bus isn't going to help me get a cheerleader. Somehow, I have to get a car.*

I guess I'm still thinking of my peers, after all.

When we arrive, I jump down from the bus and wade through a sea of empty faces, looking for *her*, knowing Mrs Rogers, Mr Mickelson, and the guys will be in class waiting for me if I wander too far off.

I'm the first student from the classroom to be mainstreamed, and that means I get a class with girls in it. I'm supposed to start in Mr Mickelson's homeroom and move on from there.

I walk into the class and say, "Hi," to Mr Mickelson and Mrs Rogers, who stand by the door to greet everybody on the first day.

"Hi Rick, good to have you back," Mrs Rogers says with a smile.

"Please take a seat, Rick. I'll be over to talk to you once everybody's here," Mr Mickelson says with what could be a grin under his even thicker beard.

"No problem."

I take my seat, facing the door so I can see what's going on outside. Tim and Derek have already zoned out in the classroom when Ray comes in, looking like a tripped-out monkey. Mrs Rogers looks like she might throw a rod, but doesn't leave her seat. Bo and John are no-shows. A couple awkward minutes go by before Bo finally comes in, and Mrs Rogers stands up.

"Welcome to class, Bo," she greets him.

She must be happy he's not stoned, too.

"Hey," is the only thing that comes out of his mouth.

Mr Mickelson walks to the front. "Okay, guys, listen up. John's family has moved away, so he won't be here this year. I'm sorry if you didn't know this, Ray. I know he was your friend," Mr Mickelson says sincerely.

"Thanks," says Ray. He looks like he may not get much else out today.

"I have some good news for you guys," Mr Mickelson continues. "Rick is being mainstreamed this year." No one says a word. "Okay, Mrs Rogers is going to teach first period; she has some warm-up exercises to get you thinking."

Mrs Rogers walks to the front of the room.

Maybe my good news isn't good news to them.

Mr Mickelson walks over to my desk. Being mainstreamed is a huge event in my life, but for me it just seems like what's supposed to happen. Mr Mickelson motions to the hallway.

"Let's go out for a minute so we don't disturb Mrs Rogers' lesson," he suggests.

"Okay," I say, glad it will get me out of class for a minute.

I follow him, seeing a paper in his hand that represents freedom. I try to capture what's on the page, but I can't see it clearly. Once in the hallway, Mr Mickelson faces me and speaks with a very excited look on his face.

"Okay, Rick, this is your schedule. I had it sent to me, because I know you live far away and I want to make sure it makes sense, since you haven't really gone to many places in the school."

He shifts up next to me and lowers the paper so I can view it. "You start with us for first period, and then you go to Mrs Thatcher's for English. Third period will bring you back to us for Math. Then for fourth period you have Mr Tanner for Gym, and following that will be your lunch. After lunch you go to Mrs Christenson's class for Biology, and then sixth period you go to Mr Baylock's class for Art. You'll end your school day with us, and that will be History. I can help you find any of the classes," he says, pointing westward down the hall. "In fact, Mrs Thatcher's class is that corner class right there. Any questions?"

"No, not right now. I'll let you know if I have any."

"Let's get back into class, then," Mr Mickelson says with a warm, although furry smile.

"Okay." *I need to get a beard someday.*

Back in class, I find I'm too excited to listen. The reality of what's happening has finally hit me.

This is awesome. I'll soon have a break from this class and be able to attend more normal classes. I'm sure nobody in those classes will know me. How could they, being off in this corner all day last year? Man, these guys should really get things together so they can do other classes. I mean, how are you even supposed to stretch your legs, stuck to the same desk all day?

I don't know I'm the only person who's going to be mainstreamed. All I know is it's happening, and I have a schedule to prove it. With this schedule, I've become a part of the school. I've been made whole, for better or worse.

* * *

Second period calls for English, served by Mrs Thatcher. She's dressed to the nines, but in a very odd way. Her hair is grey and short, but since she doesn't wear much make-up, that works for her. She has on a red cashmere sweater with a kitten on it, over a white blouse and jet black slacks, rooting into three-inch, vomit-green heels. Yet despite the ugly shoes, Mrs Thatcher has a giant rock on her finger.

The limited seating hasn't drawn a crowd, but at least nobody knows I'm a foreigner. I'm next to a football player who seems like an offensive lineman. My first thought is to bet him five bucks that he can't knock me out with one punch. He's seated, but he looks at least six-foot-three and maybe 240 pounds, though not stacked like a bodybuilder. He has dark hair, bluish eyes, and roll call makes him Mike.

There are some girls in class, pretty ones at that. But my eye has committed to the glory of the little dark-haired cheerleader.

It's not long before I find trouble, not five minutes into class.

"Homework for tomorrow will be to write a paper on what happened to you over the summer, and it needs to be at least 500 words," Mrs Thatcher says.

500 words, are you crazy? I can't write 500 words on anything. This lady is deeply nuts. I hope I can even get half of that. 500 words, man. That really sucks.

Mrs Thatcher looks around before she continues, maybe to make sure nobody has left the room.

"Alright, today we're going to go over a lot of information. How many of you believe studying English is important? By raise of hand, please."

A little over half the class raise their hands.

"Okay, that's a start. Now, let me tell you a few reasons why *I* think it's important. To start, let's get the easy one out of the way: it helps you get a job. It can actually *be* a job for you if you would like to be a writer or report the news in some way. You can also learn to express yourselves by writing poetry, or write the words to a song. In 1839 Edward Bulwer-Lytton coined the phrase, *'The pen is mightier than the sword.'* Let's talk about that for a minute. What do you think that means?"

Mike raises his hand.

Mrs Thatcher points at him and says, "Remind me of your name before you answer, please."

"I'm Mike. I'm on the football team, and the coach always draws out the plays for us before we actually take the field. It helps us be prepared, to have that game plan. I think that's the same thing, right?" Mike asks, looking for approval.

"You're exactly right, Mike," she says. "That's a perfect modern day example. Of course, back in his day, Bulwer-Lytton could have meant something like: penning out a declaration of war puts more lives at risk than one man with a sword. So watching what you write – or say, for that matter – is of great importance throughout your lives. Think of all the magnificent speeches that were first penned, like *The Gettysburg Address* and *I Have a Dream*, to name only a couple. The study of English and the study of history should go hand-in-hand, so I hope you're all continuing with your history classes."

Mrs Thatcher carries on, but I zone out. Maybe she's just not a good speaker, or maybe the adjustment to normal classes is making me tired.

Mrs Thatcher does have her comical moments, but still, the period goes by at the speed of a melting icicle. I get work done, since I don't want to be demoted, and she assigns us a weekly paper. It's so hard to be creative when writing comes so slowly, and soon we have to turn in our papers, typed, which is mission impossible for me, because my head injury affected my finger dexterity.

This is going to be hard.

Chapter 35 – Gym Time

Monday: August 29th, 1988 – Age 17

Mr Tanner is *Chariots of Fire* fizzled out. He looks like he could literally die while going around the track. But by some miracle beyond miracles, he still has all his hair. He wears a white polo shirt, with those gym shorts with the pockets coaches always wear. He seems like a nice man, but the pack of cigarettes in his back pocket doesn't make him the poster boy of examples. And his lesson plan might be a little off.

"Alright, everybody start running laps!" he yells out like a true blue hero.

I'm the only new person, and I don't run; I watch to see what everybody else does. They start walking around the track, so I just wander around, doing whatever to pass the time. Before long, class is over and it's lunchtime.

I'm ready to eat, so I get my two lunches and head for a seat, having forgotten most of what happened in the class just prior. As I walk, I recognize Mike from second period sitting with the "A" crowd. I walk over and sit down next to him.

I open one of my milks, wishing it were bigger, because it's gone in two seconds. I look at Mike and he looks back at me, and then I get a gut feeling that he's Mormon. It's always easier not having to explain the whole Mormon thing, and with that realization I attempt conversation.

"Hi, it's Mike, right?" I start.

"Right. I'm sorry, I missed your name," Mike says, looking down at me, because of his height.

"Rick," I reply, not thinking to ask the names of the rest of the group at the table.

Mike moves his fork through some food. "I haven't seen you before. Are you new?" he asks.

"Yeah, pretty new." I don't want to go into details.

"Cool, maybe I'll see you in some other classes," he says, taking a bite.

"Okay."

I begin to eat, trying not to worry over whether Mike will become a good friend or whether he and his friends will judge me. I don't consider that I might not be the most desirable friend right now. I'm just trying to live what I consider a normal life.

After eating, it doesn't take long to find my next class. I stop in the hallway and lean against the wall for a moment.

At least nothing has happened to me so far in this school. It seems really nice here, even being outside my regular class.

I don't yet know that I've just entered the radar of the "in" crowd. I'm a very small blip on that radar, but I'm still there.

Then the bell rings like a punch in the face. Everybody heads for class.

Chapter 36 – Sunlight Fades

Monday: October 10th, 1988 – Age 17

Fall leaves waft across the sky, marking the change of the seasons, but what marks the change from boy to man? A deeper voice, added muscle, or increased responsibility? All would be good answers, although none really tell what lies in the heart, what makes up the core of a man's soul, good or evil. If you strip away the jokes, the sarcasm and, most importantly, the miscommunication, you can see what a man really is.

Why do so many people misunderstand me?

I've been making new friends, like Mike, though my heart and my head are going north and south on the subject of friends and I'm not always sure how real these friends are…or how real the events in my life are. My head says I don't need friends, knowing how easily they come and go, but my heart wants to make a good impression.

Often I go outside toward the northeast corner of the school grounds, or at least come in that way, since it's where the gym and (more importantly) the girls' dance studio are located. Walking past, my head turns to the left to view the girls dancing. The room itself has wood floors, mirrors, those leg-stretching bars, a door on the north side, and a door on the west side. It's a place where the intangibilities of the heart meet the raw power of the female form.

On this occasion I pass by the north side door, turning left and heading toward class, when an unknown force harpoons into my waist. An overpowering surge of energy courses through my body and the weight of an unseen man forces this weapon into me. I roll backward, shoulders pounding against the floor, the pressure of his hand going for my throat.

I thought I was done with all this! Think.

I force myself to rise and fling my assailant into one of Limbo's doors. It slams behind him, leaving me resting on my knees and head, of all things, unable to move and my attacker at the edge of Hell. I struggle for breath.

I can't be caught in this situation.

My side throbs and body pulsates with a paralyzing force like I've never experienced before. Nothing holds me, but I can't move.

After what seems like forever, I get my hands on the floor and lift myself up.

Thank goodness this hallway is a short one and nobody has come by.

I finally gain a standing position, my left hand against the wall to stabilize me, and I start to walk. When I reach the doorway on the west side of the studio, my hand is firmly on my side with eyes forward, hoping I look somewhat normal.

Breathe. Just keep walking and breathe.

I can't believe it's back. I thought it was gone, because nothing weird happened for so long. I try to stay focused, but it's really hard. The searing pain wasn't that long ago, and I don't want it again. I haven't yet learned how to fight it.

It doesn't matter; I'll find a way to win, even if winning only means surviving...until the Adversary makes a mistake. Then he'll see what I can do.

I have to admit that was well played. He waited long enough that I wouldn't see it coming, and then went for the quick attack. Escalation means he has to get somebody more powerful next time. But someone or something is on my side, protecting me – that door opening up was just what I needed.

I struggle with each step on the way to fifth period. Mahatma Gandhi said, "I believe that a man is the strongest soldier for daring to die unarmed." Every time the Unknown pits me up against one of his thugs, I meet them unarmed. I'm not sure if this makes me the strongest solider, but I do know Mrs Christenson doesn't like people who are tardy. I want to fly under the radar, especially when something is wrong, because I don't want to answer questions.

When at last I reach my seat in Mrs Christenson's classroom, I drop into it with a sigh. Mrs Christenson comes into the room within the next minute, but doesn't say anything to me.

I've got to work out more. It looks like things have started up again and I'm going to have to step it up. If I could only get a car, then I could get a gym membership and drive myself to the gym whenever I want. But how do I convince Dad to get me a car when the bus is free?

I've never asked for something like a car before. In fact, it's been a really long time since I've asked for anything at all.

There's just something about my dad, though – he's inspired, or in tune, if you will, with the needs of his kids all on his own. It isn't even in my mind that my parents actually think about me when I'm not around. I couldn't say why that is. Maybe because my mind is clouded, or maybe I feel like I'm not living up to what I should be doing at this point in my life.

At any rate, I don't realize how hard my Dad is working to make my dreams come true, behind my back.

***

Wednesday: October 19th, 1988 – Age 17

I await the morning bus and for some reason Dad waits with me. When yellow steel lurches to a stop outside the house, I say goodbye to Dad and head outside to the bus – but he follows me.

I'm almost to the bus when I hear him say, "Rick, tell the driver you won't need a ride today!"

"Okay!" I cry, wondering what he's up to. After telling the driver, I run back into the house and a miracle happens.

"I'll take you to school today and then after school, we'll look for a car for you," Dad tells me. Just like that, I get exactly what I want in life, for once, without doing anything.

"Really?" I ask, excitement building into joy inside me.

"Yes. The bus may not be the greatest for your self-confidence and I know you've been trying really hard to get good grades. I'm not saying you need to stop being friends with the kids on the bus," he adds, looking me in the eyes.

"Well, I don't think of myself as handicapped," I say, thinking I'm supposed to give some assurance.

Dad looks less serious and says, "It won't be the nicest of cars, you know."

"That's okay." *It means freedom.*

Dad drops me at school, only today seems to go by quickly. I guess when you know that at the end of the day you're getting a car, life is good. I don't share the news with anybody but Mr Mickelson, who seems genuinely happy for me.

When at last Dad is at the school to pick me up, I can only hope he picks out a car I like, since I know I'm just going to agree with whatever he chooses.

We drive to a used car lot and search for a while, and then he sees it. It's a beaten up old tan Ford Mustang – and not the cool kind. It has rust and dents and the interior is shot, but to me it's the most beautiful thing ever. It's freedom for $877.00 and it's mine.

I have to keep my grades up, work on the car as much as I can, and give rides to siblings. Even with all that, it's the best deal I'll ever be able to make. My new hope is that the car will make it all the way through the school year.

As I put the key in the ignition for the first time and hear the engine sputter the sounds of independence, I know this will be one of the few cars at my high school. No matter how bad the car is, it will greatly improve my standing among the girls.

After driving the car for a few days, I decide on a name: I call it "The Death Car" because you're lucky not to die while driving it. In the morning the windows get fogged up and stay that way for most of the drive to school. I drive crouched over, looking through the clear strip made by the heater. I can't get it un-fogged any other way. No matter. I'm young and invincible and don't want to lose the car for safety reasons. That wouldn't be cool, and driving it brings peace of mind and freedom – both of which weren't in my life before.

It also has a tape player and for some reason I start playing *Dead Man's Party* by Oingo Boingo every day, to and from school, over and over and over. Maybe it's the beat of the music, or maybe the lyrics, or maybe I'm just stuck in a loop. All that really matters is that someplace inside me it makes sense, and for now that will do.

***

Tuesday: October 25th, 1988 – Age 17

The school year moves, as do I. Suddenly I have the compelling urge to try out for the basketball team. I've never done this before, but Mr Mickelson thinks it's a great idea, and with his support I try to get into the world of high school basketball. I don't make the team, but with my great determination on the court Coach gives me an assignment in a supporting role. I'm made assistant to the manager.

The idea is that if somebody gets hurt, I could take his place later on. This means a couple things: I have almost no actual duties, and I get to hang out with the cheerleaders. The little dark-haired cheerleader, that is. Coach brings us all together to announce the team as a whole: players, cheerleaders, supporting cast, and the coach, himself.

But most importantly: I find out my cheerleader's name is Jenny.

I finally know her name. I'm sure glad she's still in school. When I saw her last year and couldn't make contact, I could have lost my chance.

I know for sure she sees me and I'm convinced I could go out with her some day.

Coach is short and stocky with grey, balding hair and green eyes, and a bit cheery for a coach. Coach is also the one who introduces me to Tom. Tom is a junior and the basketball manager and doesn't seem to want any help, but is nonetheless very friendly. Tom is even shorter than Coach and looks like him, only younger with brown hair and green eyes. He sports some really old sneakers, Levi's, and an okay-looking t-shirt. Tom is like one of the neighborhood gang: not somebody who sticks out by himself, but he fits nicely into a group. I decide I should try to make friends with him.

"Tom, it's nice to meet you," I say.

His right shoulder twitches. "Nice to meet you, too."

I watch Tom's body language, trying to determine the meaning. Then I pry for some information. "There are some really cute cheerleaders here," I begin.

He looks around. "Yeah, and most of them are really nice, too," he says.

"Oh yeah? So you know them?" I dig deeper.

"Yeah, I was team manager last year too. If you manage two years, you get a Letterman's jacket."

"Really? That's cool," I say, not really caring.

"I'll have earned mine this year, so I can wear it all next year."

"That's really cool. So you know the cheerleaders pretty well?" I get back to the subject that interests me.

"Yeah, some of them have gone to school with me a long time. But let me tell you what we'll be doing."

"Okay."

"We're in charge of gathering all the equipment for the team, and when there's a game we go along with the team to help, on the road and of course here. Sometimes during the game Coach might need something and he'll get us to help him."

"Okay, that sounds cool."

"Coach said you live in Sandy," he says.

"Yeah."

"Well, I don't need you to travel that far just for practice on Saturday."

"Oh, I didn't even think about that. But I have a car, so I can stay after school whenever I'm needed."

"That would be awesome. Thanks, Rick."

Tom is my introduction to high school basketball. The day continues with my meeting some of the players, at the same time giving them a chance to meet this new kid from Sandy. Knowledge is power and when it comes to me, knowing me on a personal basis, it's much better for me; no depression, no deformities, no bad habits, just me as a person. When it comes to the battles I'm facing, I think at this point I'm winning, not because of how smart or strong I am, but simply because I'm still alive.

Martin Luther King Jr said, "I believe that unarmed truth and unconditional love will have the final word in reality. This is why right, temporarily defeated, is stronger than evil triumphant." This is the story of my life: being beaten down over and over, only to get back up still alive and only temporarily defeated.

After all the battles life has thrown at me, this school feels like a fresh start, and it's always good to have a clean slate. It feels good to be involved with the school's basketball team.

I'm *living* life, instead of just watching it. This second chance brings me new hope, and that's something that has no price tag.

As Tom and I do the few things the coach wants done, a small voice in the back of my mind says, "Freedom."

Chapter 37 – Headache

Wednesday: November 2nd, 1988 – Age 17

I'm late for first period when…**thud!!!** I drop like a beast leveled by a steel hammer.

Ouch, no fair.

By the time I hit the floor, it's lights out. There, a few feet from the corner that blinds the view from the dance studio, I lie as helpless as a half-eaten gingerbread man.

"Hello? Are you okay? Hey, are you okay?" I feel the gentle tap of what must be a girl, which matches the silky smooth voice. "Should I get help?"

Why did I get hit again so soon?

I look up, my head pounding, and see Jenny, the little dark-haired cheerleader.

"I'm okay," I say.

"What happened to you?" she asks, looking very worried.

"I'm not sure. I must have passed out for some reason."

It's not like I can tell you.

Jenny looks me in the eyes and asks, "But why? Do you know? I mean, there has to be a reason."

"I don't know, but I'm sure I'll figure it out," I say, embarrassed that I was found on the floor. "I better get to class. I have a killer headache and maybe I can get something for it. Thank you for your help. Can we talk later?" It's my chance to get to know her, but in a way I hope she says no, because I want her to forget about the whole thing.

"Sure. I'd better go too," she says, looking confused and still worried for me. Jenny heads off with a little bounce in her step, while I slowly make my way back to homeroom for some aspirin.

This sucks. The day has just started and already I've been hit in the head. And it wasn't just an ordinary hit; man, I went out cold.

I wish I had some kind of camera system so I could view what's happening. The doctors made it sound like these attacks wouldn't happen anymore.

But boy, Jenny sure was nice to help wake me up like that. I'd hate to be on the ground when the wrong group of guys happened by. They might start kicking me just for the fun of it.

***

After all the day's musical chairs bring me home, I try to convince Dad he should sign with me on a gym membership, and he agrees. It feels really good to be able to lift real weights and, with the books I've been reading, I'm able to jump in like a pro. I spend anywhere from 2-5 hours each workout session, lifting weights, running, and swimming laps.

For me, this is preparation for battle. After a week without incident, there's already a big difference in my size. My sisters say I should roll up my sleeves to show off my new muscles, but I'm apprehensive as in order to hit my goal I may have to scale down. I've come to realize that you can make changes quickly when you're not very big, but if you're bodybuilder size then you have too much mass to work with for a quick change.

Presently, I'm contemplating my next moves in my room. The East Valley High home game is coming up. My old school. East Valley High holds too many memories that hit me at my core. The guys say they aren't even favored to win, which makes it seem worse. I have to face that place and the team will probably lose while I do it. Maybe when we get there I could pretend to be sick or something. I don't know what to do, and it's not something I can ask about. One thing is for sure: the Adversary is stacking the deck against me, sending in the big hitters.

I've tried to maintain my integrity and some sense of honor, while being pushed by the very definition of evil. I wouldn't say

I'm perfect or even close to it, but I know I have to have gone through all this for a reason.

This world of ours is so very savage at times. I don't think people realize how the Adversary can slowly creep up and take over their hearts. Maybe East Valley High will give me the opportunity I need to show how the Adversary can destroy lives.

I guess if I can't face it, I can always walk home. It's not like I haven't done that before.

I wish I knew what time has in store for me. All I get are these little glimpses of the future that mean almost nothing. These glimpses are so real, yet so out of my control that I'm not sure if it's a curse or a blessing to have them. After all, what does it matter if I see a few seconds of the future here or there, if they have no context?

I need to master the power; then this precognition will enable me to do so much to help myself, and others. It would also be nice to have the gift of regeneration, invisibility, cyberpath, and energy manipulation.

Perhaps it would be easier to find the Philosopher's Stone, but dreams of becoming the hero shine forth. There's no reason to doubt the heart. Aristotle said, "Knowing yourself is the beginning of all wisdom." Some things are even more powerful than superpowers.

Chapter 38 – Will You Marry Me?

Thursday: November 17th, 1988 – Age 17

After a night of East Valley raging in my head, a nice stroll down the hall with a cheerleader named Beckie seems harmless enough. Little do I know that I'm about to have one of my wild, out of nowhere ideas, forgetting Jenny and with no regard for boundaries.

"Hi Beckie," I greet her with enthusiasm.

She flips her hair back and smiles. "Hey Rick, how's it going?" she says.

"I think everything's fine, how about you?" I ask.

"Great. Everything's just great with me," she says without any doubt in her sweet voice.

"Wow. I never noticed how pretty your eyes are," I tell her, sincere in the compliment.

"Thank you, Rick. That really means a lot." She gives me a big smile, showing that I've done my job well.

"Will you marry me?" I then ask. I'm completely serious, but I'm probably not taken that way.

"Sure, Rick, let's get married. Where are you going to school after this? I was planning on BYU myself," she says with a slight smile.

"I was thinking about that myself." Which really means, *I just thought about it and there's no way I can get in there, but I did just think about it.*

In the distance, I see a Tongan friend of mine getting beaten up by five guys. Nobody is going to help him. Plus, as Tongans go, he's not that big, being maybe 160 pounds and an inch or so taller than myself.

"I got to go," I say.

"Wait, Rick, don't!" Beckie calls after me.

It's too late; I'm already running down the hall. The crowd closes off my friend more and more the closer I get.

That's cowardice, to fight somebody five to one. I have to get in there.

When I'm within steps of the wall of people, somebody crouches down to tie a shoe. I leap off his back and into the air, literally stepping off somebody's shoulder and into the circle, where I immediately take action.

For being outnumbered, we fight very well. This is one of the highlights of my life, even though I've really come to hate fighting. For the first time I know what it's like to fight beside somebody for the greater good.

"Nobody move!" yells the Vice Principal. The crowd helps us escape punishment, but the others aren't so lucky. "It was those guys," somebody says, as we get lost in the crowd.

Wow. I did something really good, even if this is my last year here and he'll probably stay away from me the next time I need help. I did something really good and nobody can take that away from me. I stepped in and helped my friend when it would have been easier to walk away; and it's not like I started the fight, so I don't need to feel bad about it.

It's not always easy to see what moments in time will be important. There have been days when I've seen nothing that would lead me to believe I'm worth my own weight in brown rice. Then there are days when I feel so much confidence that nobody on the planet could hold me back.

***

I get to class and take my seat, pretending I was there the whole time. I figure there's no need to talk to the teacher, because I'm either late or haven't been missed. My body, on the other hand, is still pumping adrenaline like crazy and it's hard to keep my muscles from twitching and my hands from shaking. I probably look a little high or something, but it's just one of the ways my body reacts. It feels like I'm being watched so I look around, but I find nothing out of place.

I take three slow, deep breaths and feel much better.

Well, at least I did some good today. But even though I helped him, I still don't think he would do the same for me. I wish I could just change and everybody would think only normal things about me. I wonder how bad some of the rumors are, anyway. Nobody here knows I'm on medication or that I went to the hospital, at least.

I'm trying. I'm trying so hard to figure everything out, so I can be the right person.

* * *

My mind seems to work with different kinds of memory. When it comes to movies I seem right on, and show as much when I walk in the front door later and see my Dad in the kitchen and say, "My brother can make a rocket out of a blender and a vacuum and I can't get my car out of the driveway."

"What's that from?" Dad asks. He himself speaks the same language.

"It's Lane Myers, in *Better off Dead*," I reply, not realizing that to a parent, when I make a joke or quote a movie, it's a sign of hope that their son will return fully to life.

"That sounds like a funny one. I have to see it," Dad says with a bit of a smile.

I smile a little too, and then get distracted and walk downstairs. Once I reach my room and shut the door, I feel like I've reached the place where all battles once started – and at some point, they must come to an end.

Chapter 39 – Teeth

Friday: November 18th, 1988 – Age 17

It's late at night in our little Salt Lake valley nestled in the Rocky Mountains, and nocturnal creatures come out to prey and play. I lie asleep in my bed when creatures of some sort bind me down, and my front upper teeth are filed down. The pain is horrid and the grinding seems to go on forever. *What's going on?* The pain seems never-ending, and then – finally – I'm released.

I make my way to the bathroom and flick on the light.

This isn't going to be good.

In the mirror I see something that resembles a vampire. It's good I don't smile a lot anyway, so people won't notice it much. How would I explain it?

Freak! Teeth don't just grow back. I guess if a dog tries to bite me, I can bite him back and make it sting.

I head back to bed, unsure how to fix my teeth and not knowing what to do to end this once and for all. This is the first attack almost solely directed at my vanity. So the guy who wants to blend in and be normal will once again stick out for some reason that nobody will understand.

I can think of no reason why these things keep happening to me, and I have no way to stop them. It would be nice if life could be reviewed, like watching an instant replay of a sports event on TV.

I head back to the room and close the door, making my way to the bed and sitting down.

When there's nothing left of this world, I'll probably still be here, wondering how to fix myself.

I hear Badger scratching at Thomas's door and I get up to take him out. He's so cute when he wags his tail and sort of hops around. It reminds me of when he was a puppy and I got to pick him out. Those days seem so long ago. Badger is a great blessing for me.

Mom was really inspired when she said we should go pick out a dog. But I think she had a smaller dog in mind.

As I wait for Badger, I think of all the good times with him. *Man, all the times he's pulled me on my skateboard. And babies will crawl all over him and he just lies there looking at us like, "Please help." He's such a funny dog. If I could only get him to stay put when the front door opens, that would really be something.*

There's nothing like a loyal friend to help get you through the hard times. The church teaches us to find that friend in the way of a spouse and to cling to her and none else. Maybe that's why I'm so fixated on finding that one, rather than just trying to date. Or maybe I'm just lonely and don't know that I can date more than one person in life. Just go out on a first date here and there until I find somebody worth more than a first.

I keep getting these little things thrown in, like having my teeth filed down, to mess my head up. By the time I figure it all out, who knows where I'll be.

I take Badger back to my room and try to relax. I hear him breathing at the bottom of my bed and that helps me fall back to sleep. It's now Badger's turn to watch over me. That's one thing he can do very well.

***

Tuesday: November 29th, 1988 – Age 18

For some reason every time I pass Jenny's locker, she's there. I'm not sure how she gets out of class so much.

True, every time I go to the bathroom I wander off, but that's just me.

I walk over and sit down on the ground next to her. I lean back against the lockers, having now completely forgotten about Beckie. I try to think of something to say, but it always seems to start the same:

"Hi."

She looks up at me. "Hi Rick, how are you?"

"Good, how are you?" I return, remembering my training from my mom.

"I'm doing fine. Are you getting excited for the upcoming dance?" she asks, looking me directly in the eyes.

"I don't go to dances," I say as a matter of fact.

Jenny looks as though I've said something foreign. "Why not? Don't you know how to dance?"

"I know how to dance. I've just never seen the point of these things."

"Maybe you've just never had the right girl to go with. Becka would like to go to the Girl's Choice dance with you. You know her, she's on the squad."

"Yeah, that would be fine." *Except I thought you were going to be the right girl.*

"I'll tell her. She'll probably just ask. She's not into all the cutesy stuff."

"That's okay, neither am I."

We sit and talk a little longer when I realize I need to get to class before it begins.

Later, Becka find me in the hall and, just as Jenny said, I can tell she's going to ask me. I'm prepared to accept. Becka is a very thin girl with bright blue eyes and a winning smile.

She looks up at me and says, "Rick, would you like to go to the dance with me?" Before I can answer, she continues, "I'll get out of your car topless and show everybody what a real man you are."

My mouth drops open and I struggle to get out, "That's okay, maybe next time."

Did she really just say that?

Becka's face turns red and she rushes off. I'm not sure what she will do, but I can hardly believe what she just said. I've never even talked to her before, so it's not the best thing to assume I want some cheap toy to go to the dance with. The kind of girl I want would value herself more than I ever could.

I hope she'll be okay. I didn't want to embarrass her, but that was out of control. Now I'm going to have to explain this to Jenny and hope she believes me. Maybe it just slipped out and she didn't mean to say it. I don't know, I guess I'll find out. I mean, how mad could she really be? It's just a dance, and I'm sure she can find somebody else.

***

At lunch, I sit at the table with some guys who have called me over, including Matt. I see what is most likely another student, somebody of flesh and blood and wearing a hooded sweatshirt, headed right for me, his hands in his front pockets. He can't seem to take his eyes off me, giving me the impression that my life is in danger, so I turn to Matt to get him to help me without him knowing he's helping.

"Hey, can I borrow your lunch tray?" I ask as if it's not a weird request.

"Sure." He looks confused, but he lifts his food and slides the tray to me.

I stand. When the guy is close enough, he pulls out a knife and thrusts it at me. I block it with the lunch tray, which sends the knife sliding off my tray, his body hitting my left leg. The table crowd scramble for safety. By this time, I have the tray above my head and I smash it down on the back of his head.

He drops with a thud and I leave with a message that probably goes unheard. "I weigh 125, big man – that means you got beat by someone with the weight of a girl," I spit out, trying to rub in his failure.

I walk, eastbound, destination unknown. When I turn my head left, I see Becka, who goes from a run to a dead stop with her jaw dropping.

I look at her and want to show her that I'm not going to hurt her, but I'm mad so I just say, "You missed me."

Then I walk away, not sure which world I just fought in: the real or the unreal.

Chapter 40 – Predator

Friday: December 2nd, 1988 – Age 18

There's a Predator loose at school and his howitzer is aimed at my skull. He comes from a world where they're close to eight feet tall and stacked with muscle. It's sweltering, and they look something like a cross between a man and a lizard – a really, really mean lizard.

This shows I'm moving up the ranks without even meaning to. One instant I'm waving to Jenny and Beckie, having a perfectly normal school moment. The next, everything changes; my battle begins, and this time I have an audience. I'm struck down by the cloaked enemy, landing not on the school's floor, but in water. I'll soon drown.

I can't breathe. I have to get up.

I look up and see nothing, but I hear the recurring sounds of laughter muffled in the water. The girls think I'm being funny.

Stupid girls. I'm going to die.

I force myself above the water and gasp for air, only to hear Jenny say, "Rick, you're so funny."

Now you talk to me?

It gets worse. My legs are hog-tied up in the air, and back under I go. I know the Predator by sound, but I don't know the exact weight of the huge body that now holds me underwater, its foot on my collarbone.

Out of the corner of my eye, I see Jenny waving her hands at me to get my attention while I struggle for air. I have to get out of the water or die, so I put everything I have into a sit-up that will hopefully throw the beast off balance. I struggle, feeling like my muscles are going to burst. I've lost all awareness of the people surrounding me.

I finally manage to get out of the water, but I'm not free of danger yet.

I have to make a move now.

I make a twist, and then kick a leg free, dropping to the school hallway.

That's it. He's gone. Time to leave.

I get up and make my way in the opposite direction from the girls.

I reach Mrs Christenson's class and grab my seat. After school, we go on the bus to East Valley High School for a game. I plan on waiting at school until we go, to cut my drive time. I was already nervous about going back to East Valley, and now I have a Predator to deal with. What next?

Let's just hope next time it stays on the ground. It's hard to pretend I'm not being hurt, but to fight something flying....

***

The school day slows, but inevitably slips away, and I find myself on the bus going to East Valley with the team, cheerleaders, and coaching staff. The pale grip of death drifts over my body as my heart beats faster and faster.

I'm not sure I can do this. What if I say something or do something really stupid?

We soon reach East Valley and the bus stops in front of the gym. I look out the window and see the place where I experienced my second death – the attack that left me feeling invaded.

Without even realizing it, I say aloud, "I was raped there." Which isn't exactly what happened, but it's what comes out all the same.

I hear laughter from some of the girls, while others ask, "What did he just say?"

The bus clears and I'm still in my seat, trying to remember if I agreed in any way to allow what happened to happen.

I'm not sure how much time passes, but next thing I know, Coach is next to me.

"Rick, your parents are coming to pick you up."

"Okay," I say, knowing my parents will be understanding, and not wanting to go back into the school where I had so much trouble.

"You can wait here. I have to go in now."

Thanks, Coach.

Coach turns and leaves the bus. I sit and wait for my parents to come. I don't realize how much time is passing; I'm lost.

I know I've been beaten and it bothers me. I don't like failing in anything. But I'm starting to learn there are no born winners or losers in life; salvation can only be found through service to others, and in serving others you can forget yourself. If you are forgotten, you can't win and you can't lose; you can only grow. I've been doing better at service and I believe it shows, but no comments yet.

Before I know it, Dad is on the bus. "Let's go home."

"Okay."

I follow him off the bus and get into our car. I don't say a word, and unless I'm asked a direct question, I don't plan on offering any answers. I have no idea what Coach said.

Maybe he just said I freaked out or had a panic attack or something. I'm not sure, but I don't want to talk about it. I don't even want to think about it.

Life can sure kick you in the teeth sometimes.

***

When we finally reach home, I'm so tired that I fall right to sleep – and that doesn't happen very often.

Chapter 41 – Cult Character

Friday: December 9th, 1988 – Age 18

A week passes without another episode and I have to check in with Coach for game night. All I have to do is walk through the school, which is empty because everyone is currently in class.

But before I reach Coach, I'm met by somebody else altogether. Somebody I've never met before. A man who literally came straight out of a horror flick, *Insane Blood*, which I saw, so I know this man's name is Fred.

In the empty hallway, I see the shape of a door crackling with an almost fiery light. Then it slides up, revealing another world, and I see him. I'm looking directly into the eyes of one whom I believe took part in my pain.

I can't believe it. It's him. This freak may be behind what happened to me. I need information.

"What are you doing here, Fred?" I demand, strangely calm. In a way, I've grown used to these visions.

"I've come to advise you," he answers in a deadpan voice.

"Advise me about what?" I ask, knowing this must be some kind of trick.

"You will have to make a choice between having the girl take the pain…or you. Do you understand what I mean?" He cracks an evil grin across his pale lifeless face.

I'm filled with anger, but I try not to show it. "Yes, it hasn't been that long. I remember it as if it just happened."

"Then you will need to decide in your mind. The day is coming soon. In the meantime, *they* have a few more tests for you," he says with a raspy chuckle.

"I'm ready for whatever they throw at me," I retort, now without fear or hesitation.

"Don't count on it."

The doorway zips closed and Fred is gone. I continue on my walk to see Coach.

I find him in his office and he has a question for me: "Rick, are you coming back to help us next year?"

"No, Coach. I'm a senior, remember?"

"Oh, that's right. For some reason I thought I had you another year. We'll miss you, and we better get your name on the list of team members who are seniors this year."

"Why?"

"On the last game you get to run out when your name is called, in recognition of what you've done to help the team."

"That sounds cool." It should thrill me, but I'm too distracted. My thoughts are consumed with Fred's warning.

I have to think this out in a logical way. Why would Fred give me a warning, friendly or not? It's a risky move to show his face to me. I could get my hands on him, or his master could completely destroy him.

"You can go back to class now," the Coach says when he gets no response.

He gets no response from me now, either.

"Rick, are you okay?" he asks.

"Yeah, I'm okay," I make out.

"Alright, then you better get back to class."

"Okay, see you later," I reply.

I turn and do as he says. The way back to class brings time for more reflection.

Will I see Fred again or is it a one-time thing? Nobody would understand a visit like this. Maybe that's why Fred came to me instead of somebody in our world who's gone to the dark side.

It's harder for me if it's somebody on this side working with the other. There are so many people, with so many different kinds of concerns that could lead to being entrapped by the other side.

Where will the light shine when things get complicated? When will I be able to live free from pain?

Maybe that's the wrong question. Maybe I should be asking: how *do I live free of pain? It could be that I just need to increase my abilities even further.*

***

Later That Day

The ball is up in the air and it goes straight through the hoop – two more points for East Valley in the second half of play. I lean over to Tom, as we sit watching from the end of the bench, and whisper, "This really sucks. We're getting killed out there."

"I know – this *does* suck."

"This is my old school and I wanted to beat them." Especially since Dirk is out there and I know he's not a very nice guy. He once told me he liked to throw the ball at cheerleaders, to get them to talk to him. I don't like the idea of him doing this with *my* cheerleaders.

A few minutes of play go by and East Valley makes a bad pass that's headed out of bounds. Dirk races over, leaps up and grabs the ball, throwing off one of our players and running right into sweet Beckie. I jump from my seat, yelling and pointing at Becka. "Hey, she's not the slut! That one is the slut!"

The ref looks over at me and Tom pulls me down to my seat, saying, "What are you talking about?"

"I know that guy. Remember it's my old school. He hit her on purpose."

The cheerleaders look over, wondering what exactly I'm doing. After all, the assistant manager isn't supposed to yell during a game; that's the coach's job. There's some confusion in the crowd, and I haven't picked up that my parents are among them.

Time goes by and Dirk gets a rest. I lean out and so does he. We start by mouthing words back and forth, which quickly turns to saying the words aloud, and before long we're standing up yelling at each other. The coach and the players, along with Tom, are trying to get me down, but this time gentle pulling isn't going to fly with me. Dirk is egging me on, and I don't care that he's a foot taller than me and probably double my weight.

Somebody behind me grabs my nice button-up shirt and pulls, ripping open the buttons to reveal my Sylvester Stallone-like ripped chest. The unimpressed ref kicks me out of the game. I head to the locker room completely pissed off and wanting to fight Dirk.

Once inside the locker room, I sit down on a bench with a clear view of the door and in comes Dirk. I get in his face and we start yelling at each other again. Then the lines of reality start to blur for me as Dirk's raised right hand morphs into claws. Dirk grabs me, lifting me off the ground by the skin of my chest. Just then, I realize Jenny has walked into the locker room and managed to get pretty close.

In fear for her life, I yell, "Run!"

She turns for the door, but Dirk raises his left hand and locks it. Jenny pulls on the door with all her might, when Dirk drops me to rush in for the kill.

I land on my feet. Raising my right hand, I conjure a knife and throw it, piercing Dirk's spine. Reality fades further as Dirk dissipates into thin air. Jenny bursts out the door and I head out the other door of the locker room, knowing it's better for me not to be there.

How am I supposed to prove self-defense when there's no body? And who knows what Jenny will say? Did I kill him?

Maybe it was an incredibly intense astral projection that he sent in. Or maybe it was actually the Adversary made to look like Dirk, to take advantage of the situation.

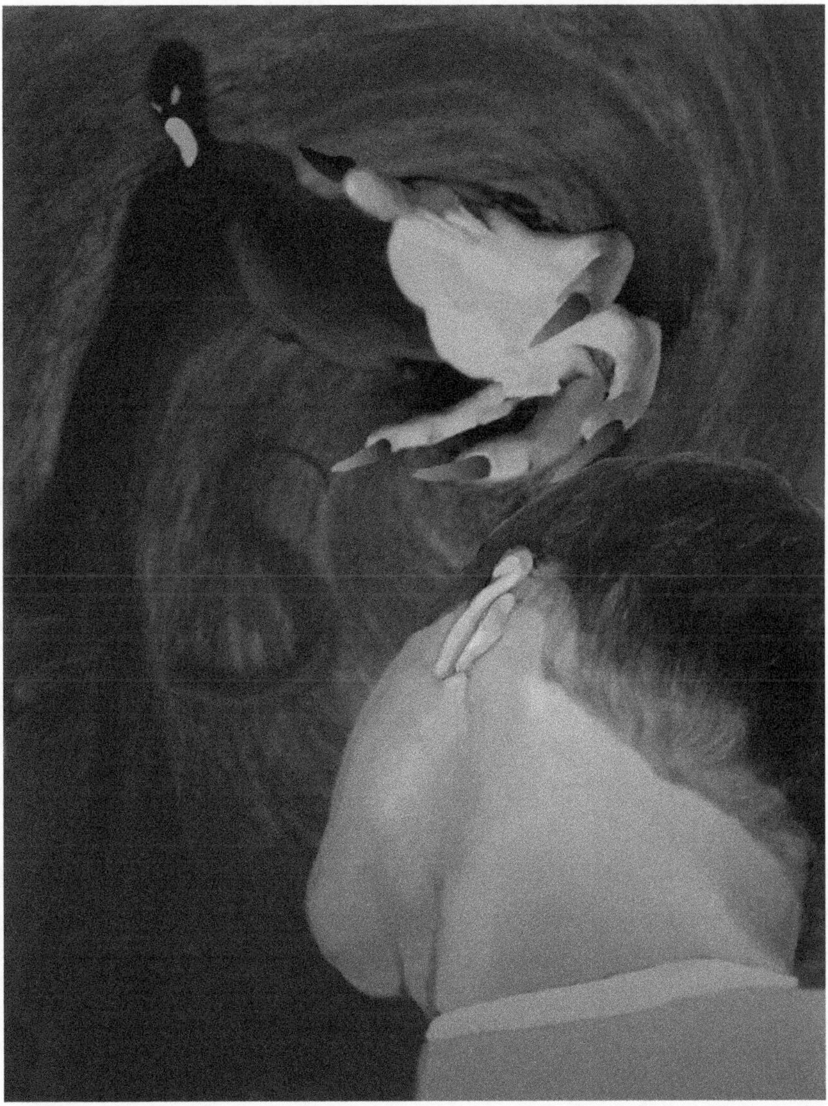

187I feel bad about Jenny, but I have no words to get out of this. I have to get home.

***

Driving home, I wonder if I'll end up in jail. At the same time, I think I didn't kill the real Dirk. The real Dirk must have finished the game, and probably played even more fired up. It's impossible to tell between these demons and real people anymore.

I get closer to home, unsure what's happening in my life and, in some ways, not even caring; I'm just focused on staying alive. Little do I know that after we won the game, my parents talked to the coach.

I lie on my bed as the moon lights the night for all those wanting to know the deeper mysteries of life, and some of the simple ones. The house is quiet and the air seems still as I slip into thought.

There's the power of the stars, the power of the moon, and the power of the sun. I've only been up against those trying to reach the power of the stars. If I have to face somebody who already has the power of the stars, then I could be in big trouble. I've been able to adapt, to take over others' powers, but only for short bursts. I need to find a way to make it permanent.

For me to be a hero, I need to act like a hero, not just have powers. After all, I already know I'm immortal. Church teaches us that much. And if that's true, and we're supposed to become more like the Heavenly Father, then it's just commonsense that eventually we will be able to do more things like him. So why not now? Why not now when it really matters?

If I had just one superpower, I could do so much to help people.

If the goal in life is to find peace, how can I do it? Maybe it's in an embrace that feels like magic. Or maybe it can't be found at all.

Finding this may be asking too much from a kid who's twisted up in an illness that manifests as personality.

If I can find that someone who understands and has compassion for me, will I be happy or is that just the first step? Will I be able to help others, if somebody first helps me? Can I then bond like we're taught, and advance in this life to a place I can't enter alone?

The sun finishes its day with us and go on to give others light, but I don't remember much more than I did the day before. That's the way life has been going for me for a long time. I learn a bit here and there, but for the most part I'm left in the dark, trying to find the light in life and in myself, all the while being beaten down for trying.

Humanity isn't without its irony. Sir Laurens Jan van der Post once said, "In a profound sense, every man has two halves to his being; he's not one person so much as two persons trying to act in unison. I believe that in the heart of each human being there is something which I can only describe as a 'child of darkness' who is equal and complementary to the more obvious 'child of light'."

Without ever knowing me, he summed up my situation perfectly.

Chapter 42 – Death Follows Me

Wednesday: January 4th, 1989 – Age 18

I'm talking to Jenny in the hallway as some of the wheelchair students come in. I guess Jenny notices I keep looking over at them and the door. Then she says, "I'm sorry to tell you this, but it seems like you don't know. Ginger died. It was a couple weeks ago."

I'm stunned by the news. "She died? Are you sure?"

"I wouldn't joke about that."

Of course she wouldn't.

"Thanks for letting me know," I manage to say. "I'd better go. I'll catch you later."

Unable to focus, I forget all about the fact that I've still not been able to cross that magic line with Jenny. I head toward class feeling empty about Ginger's death. Death is very personal and everyone handles it in his or her own way.

She was so young. I mean, we haven't even finished high school yet. I wonder why I didn't hear about this sooner. You'd think they would've made an announcement about it. Maybe they did and I didn't hear it or wasn't here that day.

Maybe I should try to be happy for her, because now she's whole again. She sure was a funny little girl. I always wondered how she had such a good attitude.

I recall a time not long ago when I was running late for class, and I saw three of my cheerleaders trying to help Ginger up the stairs to the second floor in her wheelchair. My first thought was, *I'm late*. But I stayed to help anyway. She looked so cute when I asked if her wheels locked. Then there was the look on the cheerleaders' faces as I picked her up, chair and all. I ran us up the stairs, Ginger laughing and screaming for joy, with the others girls screaming to put her down.

We got up the stairs so fast, I wouldn't be too late, but then Ginger said that was the most fun she'd ever had in her whole life and asked to do it again. I did what she asked. It makes me feel good just to think of it.

What if I hadn't stopped? I wouldn't have been part of her life in such a good way. That's something I can be proud of. I stopped and helped, even though it meant I would probably get in trouble. I've learned a lot this year about life and how it works.

I turn back to look at Jenny one more time before leaving – when the voice of the Unknown comes to me, saying, "Rick, now is the time. Agree to endure the pain…or *she* takes it for you."

What the Unknown doesn't know is that by challenging me, he makes me decide in an instant whether or not to trust again, and I extend that trust in full force.

"Okay, I'll take it. Yes, I'll take it. Just don't hurt her," I reply, knowing that if I don't, Jenny will be tortured to death.

I wish I could tell her the choice I've made for her. Then maybe she would think a little differently about me, and some day she might look at me the way I look at her.

I find my class and sit down, feeling overwhelmed by everything I've heard today. I still have no idea what to do other than to press forward and hope it gets better.

I try to remember a time when I didn't have these kinds of problems, but it's not easy. These inhuman, unearthly, and tremendously painful events plaguing my life are too big to look past. Nothing can be done but think it through and breathe deeply. It's like one of those scenes in the movies where you have to take a deep breath before swimming underwater to safety, and hope the shark with the never-ending appetite doesn't eat you.

***

Wednesday: January 11th, 1989 – Age 18

I have to visit the coach. As I walk down to the first floor, I see that the long cafeteria tables are folded up, probably so the janitors can clean the floors or prepare for some dance I don't know about. The tables might as well be the statues on Easter Island; they stand so tall and there are so many of them that nobody can see through them. But I decide to walk out into the cafeteria among them, thinking it will be faster.

I didn't think tables could fuse together the real and the unreal, but then I see Dirk standing in front of me, and he's angry.

Is he real or am I just seeing things? I thought I finished him off.

"You thought you got me. I'm back to finish this," he says as he moves into position. Our game begins.

I remember him being slow. I throw a punch for his nose, wanting to break it and blind him, but he moves too quickly.

He's so fast now. Something has happened to him.

The next instant, he's behind me and I'm off my feet in a chokehold. His grip is incredible. I know I won't last long before I'm out cold or die.

I press my foot into his leg and kick off, trying for as much speed as possible, while I search for a breath of air. From here, it's all abs and they burn. I pull my legs up into the air and propel myself above him. I flip around, coming back down, grabbing his chin on the way and forcing his head over my shoulder until I hear his neck break.

I release my grasp and feel his body slump against my back as he falls to the ground. I have no desire to see what I've done and no idea how many times this shape will try to kill me, but I'm not going to let it win. I walk away without looking back, feeling once again very lucky to be alive, and wondering when the Adversary is going to stop attacking.

I round the first corner, where I lean into the wall and take a deep breath. Thoughts race in my head, but my body still feels weak from the fight. If there was ever a time when I felt I had nothing to live for, this would be it. But the thought of taking my own life hasn't crossed my mind since I firmly made the decision to fight for life.

Or is it just that place deep inside wanting to live? Is it because of who I *could become*, rather than who I *am*?

Each problem I've faced has had its own unique set of challenges, demanding that I give more than I can.

And nothing can prepare me for what lies next.

Chapter 43 – The Problem Is Pregnancy

Thursday: January 12th, 1989 – Age 18

Three things go through my head on a daily basis. The first is how so much of what's going on in my life is just mind games, like only seeing glimpses of the future; the next would be how much is directly from the Adversary; and finally, how much of my life is real at any given moment. I know the Adversary is punishing me because he doesn't want me to fulfill my mission, but now in my senior year other people are getting hurt, and that bothers me. No more just looking out for myself.

I walk through the school doors knowing that at any moment I could be called on. I look into the dance studio and see something is wrong with Jenny. She lies on the floor of the dance room in her cheerleader uniform. I'm unsure if what I see is real, but what I see is a very pregnant Jenny. Pregnant as in: about to deliver.

Before I can make my way into the room, something catches my eye. There's a scriptural reference above the door that reads, "No man may enter in the flesh."

I rationalize losing my flesh to save Jenny and the pending baby. I feel overpowered by my need to help; I'm the only one who can help in this world that's so intangible and yet so horrifyingly painful if you somehow enter it.

I march in, determined to conquer all who try to oppose me. As I walk through the doorway, it feels like some higher power undid a zipper and then yanked hard, leaving me without skin. I see a mirror in the room and head toward it. I see my skeleton, housed in muscles and standing strong. But without eyelids, I have to use my hand to cause the blinking motion, which gives me my flesh back. I'm now on the inside.

I make way to Jenny. In any delivery, she or the baby could die, and this isn't a hospital; it's an annex of Hell. Vividly recalling a

PBS birthing documentary I once watched, I jump into action and mimic the techniques for delivering as seen on the show.

"Jenny, focus on me and breathe deeply: in, out," I say, trying to comfort her.

"I want it out," she says. Sweat drips down her anguished face.

"Don't worry, I can see the head already, it's very close. You're lucky I have the power to get in here."

"Just get it out!" she huffs.

"I'm trying. Just keep pushing. I'm not a doctor," I reply sternly.

Jenny screams as the baby slips out. I catch it in my arms.

"It's a boy," I announce, stunned.

"Put it back in; let's do it again," she says, completely serious.

"What are you, crazy? We can't do that." I look toward the door I came through and on the other side is a nurse. Without thinking or asking, I give the baby to the nurse.

A tremendous force blows me into the wall and I hear an unknown computer voice say, "Your vitals are down 40%, sir."

Jenny runs out the door across from the girls' locker room.

I struggle to my feet, feeling like every bone in my body should be broken, and start out the door to look for Jenny. But she's long gone, as is any sign of the baby and the delivery. All I see are clouds of darkness swirling, and I hear the sound of breaking glass.

I take a step and fall to my knees. Taking a deep breath, I start again. I begin moving, albeit slowly, like a solider wounded on the battlefield – except no one can see my battlefield. I make my way to class feeling like once again my life has been completely changed in an instant.

My life is so weird; I just don't get it sometimes. I hope I did the right thing. What if that was my son? That time when I blacked out and woke up with Jenny on top of me...she then became demonic and I had to throw her off. That would explain why she was acting so weird just then, and the damage I took being thrown into the wall could have been a warning of some kind. I mean, coming from a demon, I guess I'm lucky to be in one piece. Still, why would she not show? I guess that points to the same explanation – or some kind of rapid growth.

So there could be this half-demon child out there, because of me and what I did twice. What if they DNA-test the kid and people start yelling at me? I don't like people yelling at me. What do I do? What do I do?

There are never any easy answers. Depression is the cruelest form of isolation, because it isolates a person from who they really are, until the only thing left is this empty shell.

Chapter 44 – Told to Get Up

Tuesday: January 24th, 1989 – Age 18

I stand looking at the trophies our school has won in sporting events, wondering if I had one, would my life have been different this year? A verse comes to mind:

"And if men come unto me, I will show unto them their weakness. I give unto men weakness that they may be humble; and my grace is sufficient for all men that humble themselves before me; for if they humble themselves before me, and have faith in me, then will I make weak things become strong unto them." (Ether 12: 27)

I'm blasted with an emotional montage of events from my life, closet skeletons and all. I fall back a step as the bombardment continues for what seems like minutes, but is probably only seconds. This exercise isn't meant to kill; it's meant to cripple or turn psychology. The only fear that sinks in is the fear of self-loathing. Instead of breaking the will to live, I find the need to examine myself emotionally and spiritually, just like I do physically.

I need to create an emotion mirror and examine myself daily, and do better.

Why is it so complicated to know yourself, anyway?

We come down from Heaven and we're supposed to figure our way back there, which sounds impossible. I can't even lock down on something like who I am and who I want to be in *this* life.

I suppose the most important thing is that I've never given up *trying* to figure it out. Despite how many times I've felt like giving in, it hits me now that I was winning the struggle just by living.

I don't know it yet, but this is my turning point. I feel like I've just experienced divine intervention and, with that, a certain amount of clarity. Clarity not just on what's happened in the past, but more importantly: if I want to change my future, I need to look in the mirror and see what's reflecting back mentally, emotionally, and spiritually.

Bruce Lee said, "Some guys may not believe it, but I spent hours perfecting whatever I did." This is a fork in the road of my life and the path I've chosen means I will spend years perfecting myself by visualizing my reflection.

There are some things that can never be started without sacrifice. There will be many obstacles to overcome on a path toward perfection: replacing pity with compassion, anger with controlled aggression if needed. My overall goal would be to replace every sloppy emotion and put a controlled one in its place – and use this control to increase intelligence. Then there's the spiritual path – the Gospel, karma, or anything that works to bring greater enlightenment. There's truth out there and it can be found in many places. But there's something that's easily forgotten: it's one thing to know the path and a different thing altogether to *walk* the path.

Life would be much simpler if a light went off every time you made a right or wrong choice. But in a world of grey, with the only light being the Light of Christ, it's so easy to get lost. I stand at the crossroads of right and wrong, but I can still screw it all up. That's human nature.

It's easy to look down multiple roads and see where they might take me. I race quickly down a different path each time until I meet a roadblock. Every road leads to pain and unhappiness, but divine help is always given when asked for…just not always in the way you ask for it.

In life I may be like *Cool Hand Luke,* knocked down over and over and over, only to get back up and throw another punch. But when will I stop getting knocked down and be able to teach the lessons I've learned? There will be war and peace in this world for years, and I can use my anger to become a part of it – or my passion to stop it.

***

Wednesday: May 31st, 1989 – Age 18

I concentrate on myself and take my medication. I've avoided Jenny since the day she delivered, not knowing what to say, or if it was really the Jenny I see at school or some other-worldly version of her. There are many problems I've felt unable to face, and so I've had to avoid them instead of charging head on in my normal fashion. I've been living the lie. With graduation upon me, I'm about to leave the lie behind me in many ways.

***

"Hey, Rick, are you excited about graduation?" Mr Mickelson asks with a smile.

"Well, I'm excited about not having any more school, but I don't want to go to graduation." *Man, I really don't want to go.*

"Why not?" he wonders with concern on his face, as if this is just as big a deal to him as it should be to me.

But he doesn't know about Jenny.

"It's just a lot of people, and I don't feel comfortable with it," I tell him.

I should have included an apology.

"I'm not sure if you can skip it and still get your diploma," he says, "and we were really excited to see you walk."

Think. I have to get out of this.

"Oh, well, maybe if I asked the principal, could he give me my diploma?" I ask.

"He might do that, but I can't say for sure. I hope you change your mind. You still have a few days."

"Okay, thanks, I'll think about it."

If I go to graduation, I'll have to see Jenny and she might start yelling at me for giving away her baby. It's not like I can just go around telling people that. Plus, what happened to that nurse, anyway? I haven't seen anything on the news or heard anything around school about the baby. It's so hard sometimes, being responsible for all this stuff.

I hope she'll be okay. I'm not sure I can handle the situation if she breaks down. I mean, if she goes, then that means I would be open for a lot of questions. Questions I've never been able to answer, because who would believe me anyway?

Everything has to come to an end with this school year. It just has to end *some time.*

***

The school day finishes a half hour after the final bell with a handshake from the principal. Then he hands me the diploma, signifying the end. Apparently he didn't want to go to his graduation either.

The journey home has none of the normal end-of-high-school reflections. There's no remembering all the proms, as I never went to one. There's no looking back at all the fun dates or crazy things I did with girls, because none of that happened either. And the future holds no "Say Anything" graduation parties for me. I came and went without really being noticed, and that's fine with me.

For me, high school was this horrific time that showed me little kindness and lots of pain. It had moments of joy found in the service of others, like Ginger. But I'm still deeply scarred by moments like when I was racked by hooks and chains and died a death like one I could never have dreamed of.

There's hope and healing found in the comfort of sharing with those who have gone down the same road in life. My road to Hell had no markers, no warning signs, and those who walked it ended up dead or unable to speak. I have no circle of friends and may never get one.

Yet still, I know now that time can heal – if you let it.

PART 5:
Life After School

Chapter 45 – No More School

Thursday: June 15th, 1989 – Age 18

The Church of Jesus Christ of Latter-Day Saints is a church built on a foundation of volunteers. Each Sunday attendance brings members from the ward (or stake) to address the congregation (or audience). When I was young, my dad served as Bishop of our ward. He helped run the affairs of our ward and, at times, had me tell my story in front of the congregation, since a priesthood blessing is very powerful and people like to hear about it. I would say something like:

"The biggest battle I've faced began when I was on a chair at the kitchen sink while Mom was in the other room caring for the new baby. I fell and hit my head. Mom ran into the room and checked me out. I seemed alright...until the next day, that is. I was slowly bleeding, which caused me to have a seizure, so I was rushed to the hospital where my father gave me a priesthood blessing by laying his hands on my head, with my grandfather's, and saying a special prayer.

"Later, Mom still wanted her uncle to give me a blessing. So Mom called him in, along with my father, President Gordon B. Hinckley. He gave me an Apostolic Blessing and 'Rebuked the Destroyer'. I believe it's because of the power of the priesthood and the skills of those doctors that I'm here today. Later, Sister Hinckley asked the President, 'Should we go see the baby?' He responded, 'No, he's fine.' And he was right. I pulled through the operation and everything turned out fine."

I would grow to have my trials, but the fear of public speaking wouldn't be one of them. So when asked by Mom why I wouldn't go to graduation, I couldn't come up with an answer that sounded good, even to me. The truth of the matter was that I gave away a baby and I couldn't for the life of me figure out if it really happened in this world or some other world that I can't begin to explain.

All I know, at the age of 18, is that it's now summertime and I don't seem to have episodes in the summertime. I also strongly believe in my medication and know it's working. It's just that after being through so much, I need to be able to get my head around it.

I've taken what I think is a step in the right direction: on Monday I start a new job at ZCMI as a stock boy. One of the vice presidents for ZCMI, one of America's first department stores, lives in our ward and he helped me land the job. The job is only part of the equation, while I work each day at becoming a better person. I need to be seen as someone stable and good to be around…as opposed to what I really am: barely keeping it together, even with the help of my medication.

I realize I need my medication, even though I appreciate it's not for everybody. A few of my friends have even seen me taking my medication, which isn't something I would have wanted when I was in the hospital. It seemed like admitting defeat instead of just getting the little bit of extra help I needed to put me on the right track.

What has changed between the time I was in the hospital and now? Nothing really important, just time to get used to my new life. I wonder if being like *Indiana Jones* is even possible – running from one deathtrap straight into another. I can't make anything look simple, and everything I do seems to take twice the effort it should. It would be nice to have the gift of speed so I could work twice as fast.

I may never be the Bishop. But I can try to be a good person, to live up to the values of my church.

How do I live up to owing my life to a Prophet? How do I make the right choice every time?

There could be thousands of lives that I'm supposed to touch – or maybe I just need to take care of myself and be a good person.

How do I know? How do I know?

It's not like I wake up every day with instructions.

The church is very demanding that way, which is both good and bad, depending on your state of mind. The only thing that can be more demanding at times is the way people are viewed by other members of the church. This is just part of being human. Even so, it's not fun or easy to be tried in the court of public opinion, and the more popular you become, the worse it gets.

There's one thing I know for sure: it would be nice to have enough money to take care of myself and others, but I never want to be famous. To have to live life with everybody watching is the worst form of punishment I can imagine.

Chapter 46 – Christmas Is Coming

Tuesday: September 19th, 1989 – Age 18

I'm no different from any other guy my age. I want two things: a girlfriend and money. Some of the other stock boys have come and gone already. One asked a really cute girl from the girl's department to marry him and she agreed.

Since girls are a strikeout for me, I decide to spend my time saving money for Christmas. It seems like a fun idea to plan ahead to give back to my family, who have been with me through so much and don't really know what they've been with me for. Each member of the family knows that I became really sick with depression and that I'm trying to recover from it like an alcoholic would, on a day-by-day basis.

What I don't see is the pain each member of the family has undergone *because* I was so sick. Depression has a face, and that face speaks to the outside world just as much as to the sufferer, if it's not controlled.

Silence also brings time for reflection on the good, the bad and, yes, sometimes even the ugly. The weather is starting to change and I haven't had an episode with the Unknown yet, and I have high hopes to make it through the winter without one. I'm living in the moment, and since currently my moments are filled with things of the real world, I'm happy as I can possibly be.

My outside shell, however, doesn't always reflect happiness. In fact, most of the time it reflects more of a blank. It's hard for people to tell whether I'm paying attention to them when they speak to me. I've seen people initially look angry, but upon closer inspection, I've realized that's just their natural face. So a bright shiny smile might not be the only thing to look for.

***

Tuesday: November 21st, 1989 – Age 19

It's now winter and I still haven't had an episode. Even though I'm alone in that knowledge, I still celebrate it, on my 19th birthday. For the first time in a long time, I think maybe I should serve a mission for my church.

At the age of 19 you become eligible to serve, and just the fact that I'm able to think about going on a mission without worrying about being attacked is a first for me. So in that respect, the Lithium is working miracles, and to take it away would be like throwing me back into Hell.

I can't go back to that.

In life outside of me, Dad is having a down period, so the family money is a little tight; but I manage to stay calm about it and even help, with the money I've saved. Dad says things are fine with the house and food and everything like that, but Christmas won't be as big as it usually is. Dad never wants us to worry, and even though I think things are worse than he claims, I say nothing.

I'm so excited for Christmas to come, which shows a great spark of life inside me, and that's always a welcome sign for somebody suffering from depression.

It's not long since the light went out of my eyes and there was no sign of life in me. I'm sure Mom must look into my eyes each time she sees that life and is grateful. I know I would be, if I had a child who was suffering. I wasn't raised in the Bronx and I was never in a gang, but I've felt the cruel temper of the Devil bruise my soul. I know nobody has the excuse that "it's not my fault", when making a choice to do right or wrong. Even an emotionless shell has no excuse in the eyes of God. Justice will be served.

But what of the hand of mercy? What part has mercy played in my life? Because in my times of greatest darkness, I felt overlooked by its gentle touch. Yet the scales can't be balanced if mercy doesn't come into play.

Yes, truly I wandered in the darkness for what seemed like an eternity, but then mercy took my hand in the form of my mother acting for God and taking me to the hospital where I could start to get help. I imagine that for some, mercy comes in the form of God's Angels helping where they're needed, even if they're not seen or felt.

***

Monday: December 25th, 1989 – Age 19

We're all gathered by the tree when Dad says, "Did somebody come by the house and drop off presents? Where did these come from?"

"Well, all the kids helped out, and Rick and I are both working," says Mary Ann, filled with the Christmas spirit.

The expressions on our parents' faces are the best present of all. It's one of the happiest moments of my life, not just because I got two good presents for my brother and each of my four sisters, and then more than that for my parents, but because I feel like I've become part of something bigger than myself. At last, I've joined the family as a complete member, to celebrate the Lord and the gift of giving.

We share family stories, like the time ice cream sandwiches were wrapped and placed under the tree. It's all in good fun, but I listen way more than I share. We eat good food and watch all the movies we got. All in all, it's a wonderful day. It's a day that ends without any trips to the hospital.

Since a truck almost took my brother's life last Christmas, I come to one conclusion I believe can't be debated. In this life, mankind can do pretty much whatever they want to a person, save for one thing: mankind can't take away a person's salvation in the next life, even though we can and often do kill.

Conversely, the Devil himself, who can and will do everything possible to take away a person's salvation in the next life, can't actually kill anyone. I know he brought me lower and beat me up harder than anyone could imagine, but he couldn't kill me.

Sure, he could use his efforts to persuade somebody else to come after me, but he can't do it himself. That means that, just as the scriptures say, if I go on my mission, he can't get me unless I allow it to happen.

John 3:20 said, "For every one that doeth evil hateth the light." That's one way to gain power over evil. Because someone who is evil will have to change or leave you alone or fight. But if I don't fight back, it makes it hard to hold anger against somebody.

I have a lot of power over my life, in that respect, and as a missionary, the Heavenly Father can protect me.

***

Christmas is always a great time of year, but this Christmas day has shown it's important to keep moving forward, and I'm not the only who has been taught this lesson. Not only have we grown as a family, but also we've been blessed by each other; and with all the pain and suffering that goes on in the world, nothing is better than a happy family. I'm still not certain of my place in the world, but I feel at home with my family, and that's a great start. It reminds me of the end of *The Grinch Who Stole Christmas*, when they sing the *Na-Nu* song and everybody is happy. It's a blessing to be able to realize my family loves me and I have support.

When I think back and remember those kids in the hospital who had no support, I realize, sick or not, they will have a harder time adjusting to life. For instance, I have a brother who already has eight friends over to play video games, partly thanks to me. Josh from the hospital, on the other hand, whom I tried to help, may not even be alive. And yet Josh himself looked down before coming to our little home called Earth and said, "Yes, I can do it, send me down."

I may not know how the Earth will end, but I do know we made the choice to live here.

It's also our choice to *stay living.*

Chapter 47 – College Brings Hope

Wednesday: January 3rd, 1990 – Age 19

I continue onward, thinking of one world and living in another; but since I'm only *thinking* of the unknown world, I feel like I'm doing great. It is, after all, January – one of the coldest months – and I haven't had an episode. When my thoughts manage to follow the path of the real world, I think of something I haven't wanted to do in so long: going back to school.

I enroll at the community college. I choose a nutrition class, which, even though it's an elective, is a true sign of hope that I can change my future. I also find a class that sounds extremely fun, but doesn't start until the following quarter, but I want it, so I enroll early. It's called Walleyball, which is volleyball played on a racquetball court. It's played with a ball the size and shape of a volleyball, but made like a racquetball.

I'm looking forward to getting into class, and starting with just one subject seems like a good idea. Plus, all my friends are taking full-time classes, so life isn't the same in the neighborhood. No more spur-of-the-moment playground football or shooting hoops at the church. I begin to see my friends' lives revolve around one word – "me". My dad talked to me about this, because he went through it in his day. It's not a bad change; it's just a change. But for me, at this point in my life, I still need friendship more than anything.

When my nutrition class starts, I'm more than ready to attend and take a front row seat against the far east wall. Then *she* comes in and takes a seat one away from me, in the front row as well. She has long brown hair and looks very fit, and I can tell she's approximately my height.

She must do aerobics.

It gets closer to time to start and students fill the seats.

The teacher walks in, brown leather bag in hand. It's mostly likely the most expensive thing he owns, because the rest of him looks a little shabby. He wears a full beard to go along with the job and is in need of glasses. He sets his bag on the table and faces the class.

"My name is Professor Thatcher," he introduces himself, "and in my class, I do things my way. If you're not here to learn about nutrition, please use the door. This may be a 101 class, but many of your classmates are here to learn and paying to do it."

I look over at my mystery girl and lock eyes with her, despite the blond who now sits between us. We see each other and I hope for the best, but past results tell me I'm going to crash and burn.

But then…that was the past. This is *now.*

Professor Thatcher continues to ramble. "The way I do things is I lecture and you take notes and the tests will be based 100% on my lectures. So you better take good notes or you'll fail, and I'm not one to shy from failing a student."

That statement catches my attention. Out come everyone's notebooks and pens. As promised, the class has me taking notes the entire time, with only the occasional brief glance at this mystery girl.

When class is over, I make my move while she gets her bag together. I say, "See ya."

And she replies, "Have a good one."

Wow. She's so pretty.

The drive home is short and Dad is blending some shakes, just as he always has. It makes me feel good to be home. These little things make me think I have a good life and a lot to live for.

***

In an effort to meet girls and see all my friends at least once a week, I've joined the singles ward. It's a great place and we have an awesome Bishop who admits he has a nose like a parrot, but I think it suits him rather well. And if my theory of how the Lord prefers people with really big noses holds true, then he will do well.

The ward itself is pretty good. In my mind, the function of any ward is to build the community. Since our community is the only singles building, it focuses on the self-esteem of each individual, showing how we can help the community by giving service to others. That service would be in and outside the Church of Jesus Christ of Latter-Day Saints.

I start to show off the new bolder Rick, and meet and greet new people as they visit the ward for the first time. I can say something simple like, "Welcome to our ward," and it means the world to somebody who's new.

I don't consider myself a ladies' man in any sense. If I'm lucky enough to get a first date with a girl, it won't become a second, and most of the time it's just a flat out "no". By this point, I realize my tendency to give the once over is probably the reason for my bad fortune with women, and my efforts to break this habit have fallen short. I have to find the root cause, to pull out of the bad habit. Once I start that interaction, it will take a long time to learn the ins and outs of relationships.

Something I've learned is that to find perfection means to find balance. But balance is something that's barely in my field of vision. After all, I'm only nineteen, and not a normal nineteen year-old at that.

Chapter 48 – A Snowflake in the Flames

Wednesday: January 17th, 1990 – Age 19

I stand outside the school talking to an old friend and see my mystery girl approach. "Catch you later, man," I say to my friend.

I turn and open the door for the girl and this time get out, "Hi, my name's Rick." A good start.

She replies, which is always a good sign. "Hi, I'm Cami," she says with a smile, tilting her head a little to the right. The way she does this reminds me of a young Audrey Hepburn. "Do you like Professor Thatcher?" she asks.

"He's okay, I think, but it's my first class here, so we'll see."

"I'm just getting started myself. How come you decided not to go to the U?" She means the University of Utah, which is in the valley.

"I just wanted to do some basic classes and pay for them as I went, and this is cheaper than the U," I answer.

As we talk, we walk to class and take our seats. Professor Thatcher notices the conversation, which doesn't last much longer as he begins his lecture, ready or not. For a class that could help me with my weight lifting, it sure is boring. That cancels out one career choice the easy way.

I still want to get an "A", however, and since I'm not a full-time student, it shouldn't be too hard, considering we're writing down our testing material. That means even with my snail-like reading speed, I still have a chance at that "A".

When class is finally over, I wonder about Cami and if I should ask her to do something – and what to do. I decide to keep it simple and say, "Have a good night, Cami. I'll see you next time."

"Okay, it was nice to talk to you. See you later." Then she says, "Bye." But it sounds a little different from her normal voice.

That was her flirty bye, I think. I find it hard to believe somebody would want to flirt with me.

I wave, allowing her the last word, and head out the door.

***

What I don't like to acknowledge is that little things are starting to drag me down like a particle of dust entering an engine: it does nothing but wait for more particles to join and eventually cause a breakdown. The drive home goes smoothly for the car, but I'm riddled with questions.

How should I explain to her that I have to take medication? Or maybe I shouldn't tell her right away and let her find out in time....

But is that a lie? Do I show her I'm a nice guy at heart, or that I carry a demon of a disease?

It's all basically the same thing over and over again. The other day, Mom was saying that by the time I'm her age, everybody will be fighting something. But I'm not her age and I don't know of anybody going through anything even close to what I've gone through.

Life is a strange beast that can take you on a journey of ups and downs without you leaving a five-block radius from your first home. Even the most beautiful of creatures can find this place called Despair. It was only yesterday that I had no hope of love, and tomorrow will most likely bring the same.

But after getting knocked down, I will get back up again.

Chapter 49 – What If?

Monday: January 22nd, 1990 – Age 19

Cami and I have an odd sort of relationship, where I try in my own way to get closer to her and she has me sharpen her pencils and things of that nature. As long as she's happy and asks, I don't mind, but certainly something is missing.

We haven't had a single date, due to miscommunication. Then, like a gift from Heaven, Cami says, "Some of us are going out for a late-night coffee. Would you like to come for hot chocolate, or whatever?"

"That sounds good," I reply, thinking actually it will be great.

"Okay, you can follow me."

I get the feeling that if things go well, this will be the start of something, and I've waited so long for something like this.

Alright, you can do this. Just stay calm and watch what you say.

"Sounds good. I'll do that," I say

I make my way to my car and drive over behind her in the parking lot. This isn't necessary at all, since we're driving out of one parking lot into another right across the street, but we do it anyway.

Going into the diner, I hold doors and that sort of thing; I was taught right.

I'm very nervous. I find myself in a group consisting of myself, Cami, another girl who hasn't said a word I can hear yet, and two guys, one who wants to be a minister and obviously has eyes for Cami. It seems to take some time, but we finally get seated. The waitress comes over and I order some hot chocolate.

The whole time I make small talk with the guy seated to my right, I try to focus on Cami, who is directly across from me. I'm not sure if that's good or bad, as well as any of the other signals she's throwing out. It's like trying to read a book full of hard words:

very confusing, but for some reason you just have to find the storyline.

Cami, on the other hand, seems completely at home talking to the others, and to me every now and then.

There are some things you never think about until they happen. For instance, you would never think a man who's going to be a minister would hit on a girl you like until it happens.

Mr Minister says, "Cami, you should really come and hear my sermon."

Holy crap, the way he said that. He's hitting on her right in front of me – and he knows I like her. That dirty little minister. I can't believe it.

"I'd love to do that some time," Cami replies.

Some time. That's not a clear yes, so there's some no in there.

"What church do you give your sermons at?" I ask, not interested in what the answer might be.

Try to show her you're a nice guy.

"First…." I tune him out as he tells me his church and something about it, but I nod like I care. Then he says something weird. "Of course, the church is no place to meet women; it only causes problems."

"Yeah, tell me about it," I reply.

"You sound like you've had woman trouble," Mr Minister says. Cami perks up to hear the answer on this one.

I reply without thinking. "Yeah, you could say that. I had one shoot at me, once."

It's like somebody yelled, "CUT!!" Everything stops and all around the table people are looking at me.

I shouldn't have said that. Now what?

Cami slowly turns and whispers (rather loudly, considering nobody's speaking) in Mr Minister's ear. "What did he just say?"

Mr Minister motions to her like *I'll tell you later*. One by one, the other people in our booth make their excuses and leave. I'm not sure what to do but let everybody go, since I obviously put them on edge. Each one is thinking something along the lines of, *He must have done something pretty bad to get shot at.*

I sit and think about how quickly the table emptied and feel grateful that we each had separate checks. After all, dumb is dumb, but money always counts. Once I've paid my bill, I head out into the cold to drive myself, by myself, home to a loving family who don't always understand what I'm thinking either. So there's no point telling anybody there that I blew it again.

I can only hope the next time I see Cami in class won't be too bad. If I could evaluate myself and the situation better, I would know I had a setback due to some leftover stress and built-up emotional scars. My medication is starting to work at the level that it should, but I'm not a cyborg that can just be reprogrammed; it takes time for my body to adjust.

I should try to remind myself that when somebody says something out of place and even scary, I need to look at the root of the problem and not just the symptoms – even when that somebody who makes the mistake is me.

My day ends with me lying down in bed and trying to sleep. It will be a long time before I drift off. I'm lucky my memory will gloss over the emotional part of it all by the time I wake up. And anyway, my peers haven't liked me for so long that it seems normal, now.

It's just too bad people don't know the right way to study somebody. The biggest mistake people make is judging others by what they would do if they were in the other person's shoes. HUGE mistake.

The other big mistake is caring what others think of you. No matter how foul a thought somebody has about me, it's not going to kill me, so problem solved. No reason to pay attention. Self-worth is knowing who you really are and being happy with it. It all starts with being able to look in the mirror, seeing who you are, and then improving upon the bad until your eyes open.

Real pressure will come someday when there's not enough money to put food on the table for the kids. Then the stress that crumbles men will come, and for that I can hope to be ready. But for now, this is beyond me. For now, I'm a vision of imperfection trying to become better, not knowing many of the tricks of the real world. It's so different from the realm in which I live every day. It's a place filled with a *get to the top of the mountain* mentality.

But what do you do if you get to the top and nothing is there?

Chapter 50 – Thou Shalt Not Bear False Witness

Wednesday: February 7th, 1990 – Age 19

The day of reckoning arrives all too soon. For the first time, Cami beats me to class and now sits right behind Daisy. Daisy has short black hair and is a very mean girl, I think maybe because her parents named her Daisy. She's the one girl in the class I really don't like, as she started calling me "psycho" for everybody in the class to hear and got some girls in the back row to join her occasionally.

It was for the weirdest thing, too. The Professor once mentioned that women used to conceal their ankles in public, because to show them off could have been seen as sensual. I said, "It still could be."

Cami ignored all the gossip...until now.

In all fairness, I can understand why my statement that a girl once shot at me would give rise to the idea that I'm a "psycho". But personally, if I were Cami, I would have asked why. After all, it's hard to play a game if you don't know the rules, and when somebody pitches you a floater like that, you have to take a swing at it.

I'm in this class to learn; my classmates don't matter. I've worried so much about them in the past and it does nothing for me – *they* do nothing for me. Set aside the fact that they're paying for this class (or, at least, their parents are) and wasting their class time making fun of me. It means fewer notes for them, and that makes me happy. I don't lose a beat taking my own notes and when class is over, I leave. It's that simple, and nothing more needs to come of it. If needed, I could go home and get it off my chest by talking to somebody or writing in my journal. It's the best way to get therapy without paying for it.

In the end, I don't do either of these things. Instead, I see if I can pick out a good action movie to help me relax for the rest of the night. I decide to watch *Red Scorpion*, starring Dolph Lundgren, who plays a soldier who blindly follows orders and finds his eyes opened by a little shaman who tends to his emotional wounds. In the end, he takes on the armor of justice by fighting his own people to save innocent lives. All in all, it's a pretty good movie, with the typical small plot and lots of action.

I end the night well, knowing I'm imperfect but have a good heart that has kept me out of big trouble over the years. It isn't always easy to do the right thing, but it's pretty easy to *try* to do the right thing. Even if that means keeping your mouth shut and not unloading on a girl named Daisy who must not have a clue.

It's these kinds of thoughts that keep me up, and I can only try my best to tune them out once again and go to sleep.

***

When sleep comes, I dream about *Red Scorpion*, not class. I'm moving on with my life and sleep is a good way to reset myself. It heals me of the pains of the day. Not so long ago, sleep was something I dreaded, but now it's becoming my friend again.

There really is only one reason why the Adversary would try to play mind games with your sleep patterns, and it's simple to figure out: if you go without sleep long enough, it will bring insanity and eventually death.

You could say the Devil, the Great Serpent, is like an overgrown child pulling strings to try to get his way. Every time a big event comes near, Hell releases a blizzard of fire to torch the soul and cut the face. There's no hiding in dark spaces, and you can't ask for time out. Go to battle with Satan and he will come to fight – only you may not understand the rules.

Remember to have patience until you find your way home. Faith is when you realize the path was there all along. Soon, morning will break.

Chapter 51 – Humble Pie

Monday: February 19th, 1990 – Age 19

I keep lying to myself that peer pressure is nothing, and it's true that I haven't burst into tears or punched anyone. But my peers are altering my actions in small ways.

I use the back door of the school, rather than the front where everybody hangs out. I head straight to my seat, instead of looking for somebody I know. I know that as an adult, if I give in to my anger, there are consequences, like jail.

What I have is routine. I go to class, take notes and leave, over and over. No matter how mean the other students are, this class will end. In time, things start to change, and anger gets easier and easier to manage over time.

Cami moves closer to the front and is back in her old seat by mid-terms. I do great on my mid-terms, meaning I'm on my way to a good grade. Some of the others didn't do as well, which is weird to me, since all the test material is presented in class and there's zero reading outside class. I still have little interaction with my peers, but Cami starts looking at me again.

I'm not sure she realizes I'm the same person. Why does she think I've changed? I have a history that she wouldn't understand, even if I could explain it – and I can't. She's still pretty and I'd like to go out with her, but in a way I don't.

Do girls like guys who are just nice and maybe even a little too humble?

More and more, I want to go on my mission. I'm the right age for it: nineteen. So I wonder if Cami is just a test, to get me off track and thinking about anything but my call to serve.

***

By the time I get to my car, my head is in full-gear trying to figure these creatures out once and for all.

There must be codes. I know there has to be some kind of code. Most of language is non-verbal; everybody knows that. That's why depression breeds liars.

I'm so lost in thought, I don't notice when a cop starts to follow me down the road. I'm pulled over and the officer walks up to my window. She signals to unroll the window, and I do so. She looks at me like maybe I'm drunk and she'd better keep a close eye on me.

"Do you know how fast you were going?" she asks.

"Just give me the ticket."

"What did you just say to me?" she says, astonished and obviously angry.

"I'm sorry, I'm just really tried," I apologize.

"You'll be lucky if I don't take you in. Give me your license and registration."

My mood turns from joking to submissive, and I reach over for the registration. I hand it to the officer, who waits for the license before she steps away to see if I have a previous record. It's a safe bet that she's hoping for a yes on that one, while I sit and wonder why I let my mouth get the best of me.

That certainly wasn't the smartest thing I've ever done. I hope the damage isn't too bad.

There was once a silent film star named Mary Pickford, who was "America's Sweetheart" and, in later years, an alcoholic. She said, "If you have made mistakes, even serious ones, there's always another chance for you. What we call failure is not the falling down but the staying down." Just like Mary, I decide to get back on my feet and take what's coming to me.

The officer walks back up to the window. She doesn't seem as mad as she did before. But you never know.

"Here's your ticket," she says.

The word is like a sharp knife to the heart, even though I was expecting it. I take the clipboard and sign where she has drawn an "X" and is now tapping the tip of her pen over me like I'm a prize buffalo she just killed to mount on her wall. She nailed me for $74 dollars, and all I can say now is, "Thank you."

The officer turns and goes back to her car. I make my way home, steeling myself to tell my story to the only audience I can really capture: my family.

The rest of the drive brings remorse for being so dumb to speed in the first place, and then to mouth off to an officer who could have made me ponder it behind bars.

***

When I arrive home, I decide it would be better to go to my room, which is a good idea since my thoughts are starting to scatter. I go downstairs and see Thomas and all his friends paired up with girlfriends, making out. A feeling of "*why not me?*" consumes me.

Desire for life is within me, as is the desire to love with all my heart. How easy it is for the rich and famous who flaunt themselves on carpets of red, while beautiful cars, and homes too large for the living, await them. Yet even with all these riches, it seems when they find love, they can never make it work.

The art of love takes work – work I may never be ready for in this lifetime. Maybe because love to me is movie love and that's not an easy goal for anyone. Aristotle said, "Love is composed of a single soul inhabiting two bodies." Currently I can't put into words my thoughts on love, because I can't focus on the reality of it.

My dad isn't the most romantic of men, but he's a gentleman and remembers the important times. I remember one anniversary when Mom and Dad took us all along with them to eat dinner at "The Roof", located on the top floor of the Joseph Smith Memorial Building. We were all seated when the host brought over a dozen red roses for my mom, and single roses for each of the four girls.

Wolves develop close relationships. They demonstrate deep affection for their families and may even sacrifice themselves to protect them. The wolf is a noble creature, and even more so are the alpha wolves. This isn't usually the case with their human counterparts, as it would seem the more power or alpha-like a person becomes, the farther off the path they go.

PART 6:
Don’t Lose Hope

Chapter 52 – The Meek and the Afflicted

Thursday: January 25th, 1990 – Age 19

I yield the weapon of hope without control or command, just the aching in my heart and soul. Confusion lies before my eyes and in the depths of my past. Now I know more than ever that the bond between those people who advance the cause of the Adversary do so with clever ideas and a silver tongue to snare their uninformed prey.

It has become my goal to serve a mission in an effort to bring to pass the salvation of mankind, and to better myself while doing so. In order to serve, I have to do a few things, one of which I've accomplished in becoming an Elder in the Melchizedek Priesthood, which is the higher priesthood, the Aaronic Priesthood being the lesser. I viewed becoming an Elder (as most do at my age) as a rite of passage. As far as I know, in reality I'm worthy of that right, and the Bishop felt so as well.

Also before I can receive the call, I must go through the Temple – and before that, I need to receive my Patriarchal Blessing. My Grandfather was a Patriarchal, but he passed away long ago. So I will go to the stake Patriarchal to get my blessing by the laying on of hands, and through the Patriarchal I will receive the blessing the Lord has just for me.

I look forward to it, but it also worries me, and not because He might say, "You won't serve a mission." I know in my heart I will. I'm worried because I have lived in two worlds and even though I tried my best to live by the same code in both, I don't know if I can truly pass the test.

January will be ending soon and I haven't had another attack. Maybe if I wait a couple months and then talk to the Bishop about getting my Patriarchal Blessing, it will work out.

My medication is helping with the episodes, but what about the memory loss? Is it the medication or would it happen anyway? I need to find an answer to that question to regain what I once had. I mean, if I can't remember anything for more than a second, how will I work?

Even scarier than that is if I can't work, will there come a time when I'm segregated because of my condition? After all, racism isn't the only form of hate in the world.

In my prayers, I plead with our Heavenly Father to help me get my memory back, or at least stop it from getting worse.

Mahatma Gandhi said, "What is true of the individual will be tomorrow true of the whole nation if individuals will but refuse to lose heart and hope."

Hope is the key that leads to faith. I need to make the sacrifice and go out to serve my mission. To do so means I have to put everything aside, to serve like my father did. That will be hard. I've never had to do anything like that. I've been focused on myself so much. On the mission, it will be all about others.

Once I go out, there's really no turning back. I'll need to make it work for two years.

That's a really long time.

Chapter 53 – Missionary Training Center

Thursday: November 1st, 1990 – Age 19

My job at ZCMI has come and gone without any episodes, and I've become a missionary just like in the primary songs we used to sing growing up. This means for the first time in my life I'm no longer an "I" but have become a "we".

My mission begins at the MTC (Missionary Training Center), where I currently live with many other hopefuls. I've been assigned a companion for the duration of the MTC, Elder Pinter.

We're all very excited to go out and serve the Lord, but now is the time to learn. One of the Elders announces that he's the cousin of Michael Bierce from *The Terminator.* I have no idea what that has to do with missionary work, but he announces it anyway.

Most of the time, missionaries are directly engaged in teaching the lessons or reading scriptures or perhaps praying. Missionaries aren't allowed to date or do any other things the average nineteen-year-old man might do. But I didn't come here to be average. I came to become the man I've talked about becoming.

Pretty much everybody said it would be okay if I didn't serve, which I took to mean they didn't think I would be able to go out on a mission. Good thing for me I don't listen to things like that.

The MTC will last just three weeks, because we're not learning a language. Everything is scheduled, and we will be kept very busy – so busy that I may fit in without any trouble. At least, that's the underlying hope. I won't have to worry about girls, since there are no girls in my group.

The only thing I have to do is learn the discussions and my scriptures. Really, the only thing any of us has in common is putting "Elder" in front of our last names, so it makes for a rough start. There are two other Elders in the room, which has two bunk beds. When at last we're in our room for the night, I want to find out where Elder Pinter comes from, because I can't place him from the sound of his voice.

"Where are you from, Elder?" I ask, taking care to remember how to address him.

"I'm from Alberta, Canada. How about you?"

"I'm from Sandy," I reply, taking it for granted that he should know where that is, because it's just the next county north of us.

"Where is that?" he asks.

"Oh, that's in Salt Lake County. You drove by it on the way here."

"Okay, I'm with you."

"What do you think President Whittle will be like?" I ask, thinking our Mission President must be a very spiritual man.

"I heard he's a very hard-working man from a returned missionary in my stake, who went to our mission."

"That's good," I comment.

Elder Petterson, whom I met in the Jordan River Temple, is sitting next to his companion and getting to know a few things as well. We're all trying our best to get along. We're just eight guys put together for the same mission. We could hate each other and it wouldn't make a bit of a social difference. It would, however, make time drag, and it would be hard for us to feel the spirit of the Lord.

The room grows as silent as a hamster with an itch. We begin our studies. I want to read every scripture, even the Old Testament. In my experience, usually everybody just goes along with whatever you say about the Old Testament, because they have not and never will read the whole thing. The only problem is I know it will take me forever at the rate I read, so I try to break it down into pieces I can read at one time. Then when I quote Psalms 23:4 saying, "The faithful hand of the living does not desert the hand of the dying," I'll know what it means and where it's from and that somebody isn't actually quoting Walt Whitman like I just did. Knowledge is power and I'm just getting started.

On occasion, a sound comes out from the hallway or in the room that grabs me, like a dog on alert. But mostly I stay sitting up on my bed reading, and wondering who I'll meet out in the mission field.

My journey from boy to man has begun – or maybe it's also to lose the beast – while back at home, the Price family have their first missionary out and are hoping for the best.

Chapter 54 – Elder Green

Sunday: November 4th, 1990 – Age 19

Three days in, Elder Green is grief-stricken and the look on his face spells doom. We're gathered as a group most of the time, so there's nowhere to hide.

"Elder Green, are you okay? You don't look like you're doing very well," Elder Baker notes with concern on his face. He's also nervous, because we've heard stories of Elders going home straight from the MTC.

"I don't know, guys. I think maybe I'm not supposed to be here," Elder Green replies, denoting us as guys and not Elders, a sure sign that he's almost home already.

"Why do you say that, Elder Green?" I ask.

"It just seems like I'm supposed to be working from home and moving on with life. I don't know what to say. This just doesn't feel right," Elder Green says, covering almost the same ground as before.

"We'd all like it if you stayed here, and we'll help you any way we can," Elder Baker says. Elder Baker is from Idaho and was raised in the country, and it's easy to tell right away he's a man of his word. But it doesn't seem to help.

"I feel like I'm breaking," Elder Green says as he tries to hold back the tears.

"Take it easy, Elder Green," Elder Pinter says. I can tell the stress of the group focusing on Elder Green is getting to him. Not one of us has any idea how this has happened in such a short period of time. Elder Green finally walks off by himself in the direction of the President's office.

Elder Green's companion Elder Fisher is dumbfounded by the whole thing. From the look on his face, it's not hard to see he didn't know how deep this pit was dug into Elder Green. I look at Elder Fisher and have no idea what to say to him or where to start.

The sun tells us it's high noon and the lunch bell rings in my stomach. We move toward lunch and hope for the best. It could be much worse; if Elder Green leaves, he will only be going home, not prison or anything like that. He just won't be serving. Still, it's disappointing.

Just before we leave our table, Elder Green walks up, looking like a whole new man. It would seem that he's had some really good news. He takes a seat at the table, along with a leader we haven't seen before and don't pay any attention to now.

"It looks like I'm going to be the first RM of the group," Elder Green says proudly. He means Returned Minister. "I'm going home."

We're all a little shocked by his announcement. Then Elder Pinter replies, "That's really cool, Elder Green." He sounds like he's just giving one of those responses you give when you don't know what to say, but at least it's something.

"Yeah, my mom is really proud of me," Elder Green continues, while each of us thinks, *She must be so worried that she doesn't know what to say, and she doesn't want to let him down by saying the wrong thing.*

Elder Baker looks at Elder Green, then at the leader he's with and back to elder Green, and asks, "When are you leaving?"

"In about an hour, so I have to go pack, but I wanted to say goodbye to you guys before I left. Maybe we'll all see each other again at the reunion."

Glances darting amongst our group show that nobody has ever heard of an MTC reunion. The goodbyes are short, but each Elder wishes Elder Green the best and gives him one of those hugs where you shake with one hand and then pull in with the other hand to give two pats on the back. It's a typical guy thing, no real emotion, with the added fear that he might start crying and then you would be trapped.

We start the walk back to our next class not knowing what Elder Green will find when he gets home, but wishing the best for him. We sit down in the class. We don't know the chain of events that will unfold in front of us, but our eyes have been opened to the fact that free agency means there's much that will happen in life that is out of our control. You might call each of us sheltered in a way, myself included. We all came from good solid homes and didn't know some of the childhood troubles so many children deal with. But we are expected to teach the Gospel of Jesus Christ to all God's children. It's just not possible without divine intervention. That's the moral of the story we have just learned…or at least what I take out of it.

We plow into our studies like a shark cutting a riptide to snag a seal. It's survival of the fittest in a war of words, which has already claimed one of our own. It makes the time sail past and before we know it, we're at the airport heading to the Texas, Fort Worth Mission.

Chapter 55 – Meet the President

Wednesday: November 14th, 1990 – Age 19

President Roy L. Whittle awaits, but first things first. It's time to say goodbye to our families at the gate of the Salt Lake City Airport.

Most of our families are already waiting at the airport, prepared to escort us, except Elder Pinter's family. My dad and brother help me with my bags. Everybody in my family is very excited for me.

We walk to the gate and I answer questions about the MTC, as do all the other Elders, but Elder Pinter. Our plane is due to depart in fifteen to twenty minutes, so nobody really thinks about Elder Pinter too much – not even me, and he's my companion. I'm at least supposed to know his location.

Thomas seems excited for me to go. Maybe it's a way for him to see if it's something he wants to do. Mary Ann, Katie, Melissa, and Tiffany made a send-off sign that says, "We Are Proud Of You, Elder Price." It's a nice sign, and I estimate it took at least a half hour to make.

It feels really good to receive attention for something positive, after previously getting a ton of attention only for my mistakes. I haven't had an episode the whole time I've been at the MTC, which makes me feel like I can do this.

"Now boarding Delta flight 316 to Dallas, Texas!"

There's nothing left to do but give hugs and say goodbyes that will have to last two years. We all begin, except Elder Pinter. It's nice to say goodbye because everybody in the family is healthy and happy and that's enough. Some of the other Elders look back one final time at their families before boarding the plane. This time, Elder Pinter is not alone; I get on the plane without looking back. Nobody told me I was supposed to look back.

Like cattle, we're driven to our seats, as the captain prepares to steer us toward the great open sky. It feels like forever and the in-flight instruction seems to have been poorly written, or maybe the delivery is just off. But the lift-off is good, so the overall score leaving Salt Lake isn't bad.

It doesn't take long to travel directly from Utah to Texas, and the landing is as smooth as an A&W root beer. Getting off the plane is another matter altogether. The humidity makes the air hot enough to boil an egg. But each one of us knows Texas, the greatest place on Earth (at least for the next two years of my life), even Elder Pinter.

President Whittle is at the gate, beside his wife, waiting to meet his newest Elders and tell us where we will go. President Whittle has expensive taste, with cuff-links and a suit made by some designer that I wouldn't know. He has grey hair trimmed up high in the back, so high it looks really weird. He has the look of high business and a resumé to match. President Whittle introduces himself and begins shaking hands with each new Elder. We wear name tags to make things easier.

President Whittle shakes my hand firmly and says, "Your uncle called and said you were on the way and I better look out for you." He's referring to President Gordon B. Hinckley, now President of the church.

My mouth falls open and I'm not sure what to say. I purposely didn't tell anyone about my uncle when I was in the MTC.

"Okay," I reply.

I thought I was going to be a normal missionary like the other guys. We just got off the plane and I'm already being treated differently. Well, I'll just have to prove myself as a hard worker.

Luckily, I'm not last in line, so he keeps going while I get a hug from Sister Whittle, who has very becoming shoulder-length dark hair even at her age. She wears a long dress (no pant suits) and a warm smile.

When the introductions are over, President Whittle has something to say: "Elders – welcome to Texas. Now, there are a few things you need to know. If somebody says, 'Do what?' it means, 'What?' If somebody says, 'A little bit,' it could mean something that's actually really big in size, because everything is big in Texas. Texas is hot, humid, and will really beat you Elders up while tracking, but the people are very proud of their state so while you're here, you *are* a Texan."

I'm only half-listening.

Why is he wearing those cufflinks? He seems so business-like, and I was expecting Christ-like.

But then, what is Christ-like supposed to look like?

I continue to think as we collect our bags and get into the mission van to be brought to our first home in the mission field. For most, this means an apartment, as there aren't many missionaries staying with members anymore. I don't have far to go, but it's still around 10PM when I meet Elder Richards.

He's tall with dark hair and probably weighs about 220 pounds. He says he loves to play basketball more than anything back home. Currently he's the District Leader, meaning he supervises about a half dozen Senior Missionaries, each with a Junior Missionary. I'm Elder Richard's Junior.

I soon find my bed, which is only a spot on the floor, because we're supposed to move. I try to sleep and begin what will be 709 nights of gastroesphogal reflux disease to one degree or another. Many of those nights will be horrible. But I'm a missionary. I'm away from home, experiencing life on my own for the first time.

Well, somewhat on my own. We're glued in a companionship and I have a doctor already set up, so I didn't exactly do the work on that one. But when all is said and done its good, and I'm ready for the work that no movie can prepare me for.

I turn to scriptures for help:

"For behold the field is white already to harvest; and lo, he that thrusteth in his sickle with his might, the same layeth up in store that he perisheth not, but bringeth salvation to his soul; and faith, hope, charity and love, with an eye single to the glory of God, qualify him for the work. Remember faith, virtue, knowledge, temperance, patience, brotherly kindness, godliness, charity, humility, diligence. Ask, and ye shall receive; knock, and it shall be opened unto you. Amen." - Doctrines and Covenants 4: 4-7.

When at last I fall asleep, I do so without so much as a bad dream. Although it may not be the soundest sleep I've ever had, it's sleep and it's with a roof overhead. There's something to eat in the morning and something to do the next day. Because without something to do, we're all just sitting around waiting to die.

And I'm not playing that game anymore.

Chapter 56 – On Bended Knee

Thursday: November 15th, 1990 – Age 19

The awkwardness of the first night is abandoned and missionary life begins. It's a good life, all in all. I can't say it's perfect, but what *is* perfect in a world of imperfection?

I get different companions and teach new people all the time. When I teach, I hit the zone and things just happen for me. Also, not having to learn a new language (as my mission is not overseas) means 100% scripture study. My reading speed picks up and I learn the many life-changing principles found in the scriptures. My favorite book is *3rd Nephi*, where Jesus comes down and visits the Americas.

One of the hardest steps for a young missionary is to ask somebody to pray about the Book of Mormon to find out for themselves if it's true or not. When you've gone, they'll start to ask questions from their friends, who convince them to turn away from anything you've taught, even if it still follows the Bible's teachings. You could say that asking them to believe is like getting down on bended-knee to ask for your love's hand in marriage.

Brother Packer honks his horn outside our apartment door; we arranged for him to pick us up after we ate a quick dinner. We walk outside and see him in a brand new car, a gold Cadillac that looks like it could seat twenty. Brother Packer himself is dressed to the nines, and with what's left of his grey hair, he looks the part of authority.

Seeing how Elder Richards is so tall, I head for the back seat before anyone can yell, "Shotgun!"

We start the drive over to the Robinsons'. While I notice just how flat the landscape is, Elder Richards and Brother Packer talk about the Robinsons. It's the second discussion, but the fourth visit to their home. The lessons are broken up into six discussions, as we call them, since they cover a certain amount of material, but they can be tailored so the individual doesn't have to be as well-read in the material as the teacher. It's a 101 class of sorts, with the end goal being completely up to the student and not the teacher.

This does more than just help those who want to learn about the church; it follows the layout for the Plan of Salvation itself:

Before the world was, there were two plans laid before the Father, one saying *I will go down and force them to do the right things to return unto you Father*, while the other plan allowed for free agency. Free agency is essentially free will and, here on Earth, something worth dying for. Any form of forcing one's will over others is dangerous and it can truly be found as a wolf in sheep's clothing.

When we arrive at the Robinsons', I have no reason to believe anything is wrong in the way they are receiving the discussions. They have a nice house, although it's not exactly surrounded by a white picket fence. We knock on the door and Mr Robinson answers the door. He wears business casual, he's not much taller than I am and he's balding on top.

"Please come in," Mr Robinson says warmly.

We each take a few swipes at the mat outside, before entering the house. I'm last to enter and the only one in the group who hasn't been in the home before. It looks like an average home, but then I see Mrs Robinson, who isn't average herself. I've never in real life seen a woman as heavyset as Mrs Robinson.

She says, "Hello, Elder Richards. Where's Elder Evans?"

"This is Elder Price, my new companion," Elder Richards replies without missing a beat. And why should he? He's been out in the field for a long time and has had many companions.

"Welcome to our home, Elder Price," Mrs Robinson greets me with a smile.

"Thank you," I reply.

My people skills aren't great, but I feel like I do a pretty good job at not making a face or anything. Mrs Robinson is very kind and seems very well kept, but her size reminds me of the hospital in some way and it makes me uncomfortable.

Brother Packer heads for what I assume is his normal chair. It's funny how those things happen. Elder Richards and I have the couch across from the Robinsons' love seat. As this is my first discussion in the field, Elder Richards offered beforehand to teach first and that didn't sound so bad to me. However, now that we're actually in the home, it doesn't seem that different from the MTC.

Elder Richards begins the discussion by asking Brother Packer if he will offer a word of prayer, and he gladly gives a humble yet powerful prayer. Elder Richards opens up his scriptures with the discussion booklet already open on the table in front of him and begins:

"This is 1 Thessalonians 1:2. 'We give thanks to God always for you all, making mention of you in our prayers.' What this scripture says to me is that it's important to give thanks to our Heavenly Father in our prayers. I know I've always tried my best to do this in my life. Sister Robinson, do you feel it's important to give thanks in prayer?"

"Yes, Elder Richards. We believe in giving thanks for what we have received." Sister Robinson takes a breath as she prepares to turn on a light bulb for us. "We just don't feel ordinary people like us have what it takes to receive answers to prayers. I mean, we aren't like these people you're telling us about, or the people in the Bible."

Brother Packer looks at Sister Robinson, and then he closes his eyes and smiles just a bit. When he reopens his eyes, he says, "When I was a boy, we knew nothing about this church. It wasn't until I was fifteen that the missionaries came and gave us the discussions. The whole idea of a boy prophet didn't seem like it could ever happen, and then these golden plates on top of it. But the missionaries didn't say, *Believe us*. They said, *Pray and find out for yourselves*. In time, we were all baptized. But I had to pray for myself. It was hard at first, but I remember feeling warm inside, like I had just returned home, but to a home I hadn't known before."

I listen and ponder as Elder Richards speaks to show how much he would like the Robinsons to receive answers to their prayers – any kind of prayer, really. This goes on for what seems like five minutes, but is most likely only one. Then it hits me that I have to share my testimony, and that is something I'm not yet used to doing.

When Elder Richards pauses for thought, I begin, "Brother and Sister Robinson, I was like you were, not long ago. I got very sick and I fell away from the things I grew up knowing, even to the point that I felt like God no longer answered my prayers. One day at school, I was jumped by about five or six guys who were beating me up pretty bad. They forced me to the ground and they were going to do things to me. I prayed in that moment. All I could think to say was, *Oh God*. But He listened to me and gave me the strength to free myself, so I could get away from them."

I can't control my emotions very well, so I look at the ground for a moment and then look back at the Robinsons. "I would like to get down on my knees with you right now and pray until you receive an answer to your prayers, to know whether the Book of Mormon is true or not."

Brother Packer and Elder Richards agree to join the prayer, although the look on their faces is one of shock. Brother Robinson agrees to get on his knees, but Sister Robinson is unable to do this because of her size. We take turns praying and finally allow Brother and Sister Robinson to pray on their own, while we kneel in silence praying for them. We must be on our knees for twenty minutes.

The silence is broken with tears streaming down the face of Sister Robinson. Brother Robinson, filled with light himself, gets up to hold his wife. And before long, my first real missionary discussion ends.

Chapter 57 – A Few Days Later

Sunday: November 18th, 1990 – Age 19

Elder Richards and I are almost done eating breakfast when the phone rings. Elder Richards answers, saying, "Hello Brother Robinson, how are you this morning?"

I see a look of panic come over Elder Richards' face and a very one-sided conversation ensues; Elder Richards can hardly get a word in. There's nothing for me to do but watch as the whole thing plays out. I don't have to ask what's going on; it's painfully clear.

It seems like time has almost stalled when Elder Richards finally hangs up the phone and turns to me.

"Elder Price, the Robinsons don't want anything to do with us ever again. They said we were trying to brainwash them and they're going back to their old church. I can't believe what just happened."

"Did they say why they think that?" I ask, already knowing the answer.

"They said they were up really late last night talking to some friends who helped them see more clearly."

"Yeah, right. We didn't lead them to any conclusion. We just asked them to pray and find out."

"Well, it isn't the first time that's happened to me and it won't be the last, I'd bet," he shares. "That's the way it is down here in the Bible belt. But after hearing your testimony and praying together, I was certain they felt we were teaching truth."

"I'm not sure what to say. This just doesn't make sense to me."

"The worst part," he says, "is they won't even let us come over, and he started to sound so bitter that I'm sure if we showed up, they wouldn't open the door. In fact, we'd be lucky if they didn't call the cops or something. It was like talking to a completely different person."

"I'm sorry, Elder. I know you've been teaching them for a long time."

"Yeah, but that's nothing compared to the loss I feel right now. It's like losing a family member."

"I'm sorry, Elder," I repeat.

The room grows silent. Neither of us knows what to say or how to say it to remove the burden of loss. But then, grieving isn't supposed to happen all at once.

I try to think of a reason why this has been the result of my first big missionary discussion. It's like the ground has been yanked out from under me and there's no place to hide, only room to fall. Silence can be a friend or an enemy and today it feels like the latter.

My Grandfather and his companion walked across Australia, sleeping on the ground with the snakes and scorpions. All Elder Richards and I have to do is go back out and track for the day after receiving disappointing news.

It won't be easy, but it will be worth it.

Chapter 58 – A Depressed People

Monday: March 11th, 1991 – Age 20

I have known many tricks of the Adversary. But in keeping with my faith, I've decided to extend the same amount of trust to everybody, until they prove unworthy. Basically, it's the *do unto others as you would have them do unto you* approach. And now we're not just representing ourselves; we are representing our savior.

This day is the same as many others, out knocking on doors, when we knock into a nice Caucasian man with light brown hair, blue eyes, a fairly plain looking polo shirt, and Levi's. He has a pleasant smile and looks us in the eyes when shaking our hands. He tells us his name is John.

"You guys hungry? Come in and get something to eat."

"Sounds good to me," Elder Richards says. He and I follow John into his house and then into the kitchen. I'm so hungry that anything sounds good, and this is an opportunity to teach somebody and not add to my missed meals count.

John motions to the small dining room table. "Please have a seat," he says.

"Thank you," says Elder Richards. He reviews his seat for structural soundness before committing to sit on it. I didn't think of that myself.

"You guys like ham and cheese?" John asks.

"Yeah, sounds great," we both reply at the same time, a true sign that we have now been together too long.

"All right, we're doing good, then. I got some chips and lemonade to go with the sandwiches. Tell me a little more about what you guys are doing," John invites.

"We're out representing our church, the Church of Jesus Christ of Latter-Day Saints. You might have heard of the Mormons," Elder Richards says.

"Oh, right, the Mormons. I've heard of you guys," he confirms. "You have the Book of Mormon. I have something for you guys; I'm sure you'll like it."

"Sounds good," I say, not knowing what he has in store.

In a couple minutes the sandwiches are served and John has left the room. When John comes back, he has two books and he hands each of us one of them. They are both entitled the Koran. We look at the book, not sure what to think of it, but our faces beam back gratitude.

"Thank you. I remember my Grandfather having an older copy of this," I say, still reviewing the book. John seems relieved and sits down to eat.

"This is nice of you," Elder Richards adds.

We continue to eat and talk and enjoy the air conditioning. It's one of those times when you know you're talking to a nice person, but not somebody who wants to take the lessons you have to offer. When the meal finishes, there's a moment of silence.

"Hey, I want to show you guys something," John says. "Come with me."

Elder Richards and I follow John out the back door of his rambler. Without another word, John starts climbing a ladder to get on the roof.

"Okay," I say as I start to climb the ladder.

"Let me know when you're good, Elder Price, and I'll come up," Elder Richards calls up.

"Okay, you're good to go now," I reply from the top.

When Elder Richards finally steps onto the roof, John says, "Come over here, guys. Look at this view."

We do as instructed.

"Isn't it beautiful?" John continues.

"You're right, John. That's a great view!" Elder Richards exclaims.

We look out across the vast Texas terrain, and even with the houses you have to feel like a cowboy. I can imagine the days of the open range when cowboys rode, roped, and carved out a living with the snakes and bugs. A time when the word "grit" still had meaning.

We stand enjoying this awe-inspiring view, two Mormons and a Muslim each respecting the other. At this point, I have no idea that the violence that comes out of the dark ages for most cultures is still alive in more radical Islam. Perhaps Elder Richards knows, but he hasn't said anything yet. It's possible we wouldn't be on the roof, if he did. But John isn't like that. We even take turns getting a picture with him on the roof.

***

Before long, we're on our way to more houses, and since at least one of us carries a backpack each day, the extra books aren't a problem. We come to a large field that has some apartments on the other side. Elder Richards spotted them while on the roof. We knock on a few doors and when a nice-looking African-American woman answers the door, I look at Elder Richards and he looks at me and then I look at the lady and she looks back at us. Then I start laughing and Elder Richards starts laughing and the nice lady starts laughing, and then she invites us in and we're all still laughing when we sit down. It's a unique entrance.

Our discussion starts and ends on a friendly note. What more can you ask of laughter?

After such a great lesson, we go on our way, and I can't help but think: it's not an easy thing to be a missionary with this depression. Sometimes I think I'm getting ahead and other times I feel like I'm getting nowhere. What good does all this do if we never have any baptisms? Does that mean it's all for nothing?

NO.

But it's hard giving lessons and then losing people around the third lesson.

I know better than to think this way, really. It's just hard.

One might ask: why don't you just talk them into it? Since by the fourth month out, most of the Elders, including myself, are good enough to do it.

I once heard a very wise man say, "The definition of meek is *enduring injury with patience and without resentment*." As missionaries, both Elders and Sisters, we embody that definition.

Joseph, my brother. Joseph, my friend, what must it have been like for you? You were beaten and tarred and then feathered to make you look like a fool. Oh, how I wish I could have been there for you. Returning each time to your wife, and mother too. I imagine you cried, but not because of what they did to you. I imagine you wept, because when you went home you didn't look like you.

What will I look like, when I've completed my own mission? Who will I be?

I am not like Joseph, John the Beloved, or the Three Nephites. I'm just somebody trying to serve, and make a difference by doing it. It's hard at times, not eating much food, getting limited sleep, and endlessly traveling. But I'm making a difference.

Chapter 59 – Missionary Life

Tuesday: December 17th, 1991 – Age 21

I have a new companion: Elder Thomas. It's about the halfway-home point when Kim answers the door to our call. She is glamour shadowed by the clouds of an unjust life that could only be saved by the love of God and spouse. I feel like Kim is one of those people I was sent out to find and she's looking for somebody or something.

Her home is gloomy, with lots of dark colors and not much natural light. We begin to talk and it's not long before Kim tells us how happy she was as a child, wanting to have children of her own someday. She goes on for a bit, and then things take a turn for the worse. Her son comes into the story, and it looks like there may be a reason behind the grim decor.

"My son died in a car accident when he was fourteen years old," Kim reveals.

"Oh my gosh!" Elder Thomas and I say in unison.

"I can't believe I let him go that day," Kim continues while looking at the floor. "It was just supposed to be fun. He was out with some older boys and they were being good, but they were hit by a drunk driver."

Nobody really knows what to say when these things happen, and Elder Thomas and I are no different.

"I'm sorry, Kim. It's really hard to lose somebody," Elder Thomas tries to empathize.

"How have you been doing with losing him?" I ask. I want to know how deep the pain runs, to get an idea of how much help she'll need from us.

"It's been awful. I started to go to the cemetery all the time. I even made friends with some other people who also went to the cemetery a lot. I've had a lot more trouble with the whole thing than my husband has. I don't think he understands what I'm going through."

"Honestly, neither of us can fully understand what you're going through, either," I reply, "because we come out on our missions before getting married and having families of our own."

"But through our Heavenly Father's plan, we can be together forever someday, and we would like to teach you how this is possible," Elder Thomas says with an inviting smile on his face. He's always good with the smiles.

I step in. "It all started in this dispensation when a young boy by the name of Joseph Smith was unsure which church to join. He read a scripture, *James* chapter one, verse five: *If any of you lack wisdom, let him ask of God, that giveth to all men liberally, and upbraideth not; and it shall be given him.* In reading these words, Joseph Smith did just that. He went out into a grove of trees and prayed with all his might."

I continue with the lesson and Kim receives it well. When we finish, she says she wants us to come back.

Elder Thomas consults our schedule and says, "We could come back tomorrow sometime after noon, or on Thursday pretty much any time."

"Could we do it on Friday? My husband doesn't work on Fridays. Then he could be here for the lesson."

"That sounds great," Elder Thomas replies with one of his smiles, and with that, we shake hands and say our goodbyes.

Elder Thomas and I walk out the door and I can't help but wonder how much we've helped her and if she will be strong enough to make it through all the discussions.

Dr Burton Grebin, whose leadership guided St Mary's with the first certified Pediatric Traumatic Brain Injury and Coma Recovery Unit in New York City, the first Pediatric AIDS Home Care Program in New York State, the first long-term Pediatric Home Care provider in New York State, the first Pediatric Palliative Care and End-of-Life Program in the United States, and the first and only Interdisciplinary Pediatric Feeding Disorders Program in New York State, said, "The death of a child is the single most traumatic event in medicine. To lose a child is to lose a piece of yourself."

Elder Thomas and I walk out of Kim's house knowing we'll be fighting a battle on a different front with Kim. We need to be open enough spiritually even after the death of her son, which has clouded her willingness to receive an answer to her prayers. We can't force her to believe or talk her into it.

It's personal inspiration from divinity and that feeling can't be faked. No spell, no mystery, and nobody can do it for you. You are stuck in a world of despair, much like the theoretical communist view of the proletarian who can free himself only by abolishing private property. But since the walls of depression can't be seen, they aren't easy to tear down. First, the sufferer must see a light to destroy the mould-infested barrier of what feels like a soulless prison.

***

Thursday: December 19th, 1991 – Age 21

Tonight, we're visiting the Turners for dinner. The Turners are members of the ward in our area. When the time comes, my companion and I start cycling for their home.

I go with a plan in mind: I want to ask the Turners to fellowship [befriend] Kim and her husband. Kim doesn't seem to have the right kind of friends. Her life was changed instantly, the day her son died. From what she told us, she sank into a dark depression that spun her downwards until she went out of control. Kim's excessive time at the cemetery was most likely her way of trying to reach out to her son, and soon she ran into other women of a similar nature.

In a town this small, the reputation she's gained for that kind of behavior has probably been awful. I felt great pain when we spoke with her, and I know she needed what we were teaching. I hope tonight we can get the Turners' support.

I hope we have pasta, too. That would be really awesome. Or maybe some brisket.

In Texas, you have one guarantee for most of the year: that it will be hot. The humidity doesn't help, so when we get to the Turners', it's nice that they understand we stink doing the Lord's work.

After locking up our bikes, we head up to the house, remembering not to walk on the grass. It's Texas, after all. I knock on the door three times, which is followed by ten seconds of staring at a door that doesn't move. It's finally opened by Brother Turner, who looks happy to see us, with a big smile on a face that's in its forties.

Brother Turner extends his right hand, while holding the doorknob with the other. "Hey guys," he says. "Come on in."

We make our way into a house full with five kids, plus Mom and Dad. There are three girls and two boys; the eldest child is a high school girl named Mary Beth. Brother and Sister Turner have a very nice home and we're invited right in for dinner.

Brother Turner offers the prayer over the food and then Sister Turner and Mary Beth serve the food. It looks good. Plus, you know what? It's brisket with a pasta side dish, and some other stuff a vegetarian might mention. As always, we are (or at least I am) starving, but have to eat like everything is fine. Talk about acting! Those Hollywood types have nothing on me.

After eating for a minute or two, I think it would be good to mention Kim.

"Do you guys know the Snoopers over on Plum Place?" I let out, hoping they know them at least a little bit.

"Yes, Elder, we know about them. Why do you ask?" Brother Turner says with a questioning look on his face, not one I expected to see.

"Well, we were wondering if you would fellowship them for us."

"We can't do that," Mary Beth says, rather startled that the question was asked.

"Why not?" I ask, while my companion decides to stay clear of the whole thing and keeps eating his food.

"Because she's a witch," Mary Beth replies.

I instantly look to Brother and Sister Turner for back-up, because this can't be right.

"That's what we've heard, Elder," says Sister Turner. "She goes to the cemetery with other witches and howls at the moon and all kinds of weird things."

I can't believe what I've just heard, and I know from experience that things are not always as they seem. Yes, Kim is mixed up, but not the way the Turners seem to think, and so I explain:

"Kim got mixed up in some things that were way over her head when her son died and she fell into a very bad depression. She didn't grow up learning or even knowing about the Plan of Salvation, but she did grow up wanting children.

"We talked to her for some time and, yes, it was clear she was doing some strange things – so I can see why you've heard these things. But…but we were led to her by the Spirit and I know she needs these lessons in her life.

"I can't say how the Lord would judge what she's done, but we're not supposed to make such judgment ourselves. We're only supposed to try our very best to teach the Gospel. Please remember: faith takes a beating when depression sinks in, and when it comes to clinical depression, you can compare it to being an alcoholic."

"Okay, Elder," Brother Turner says, stepping up to the plate for his family and for us. "I'll tell you what. You can have them come over here and we'll try, as you say, to welcome them as we would anybody else."

"Thank you. Thank you very much," I say with a rare smile on my face.

Before long, it's time to go, so we read them a scripture and bless their home with a prayer. Being a missionary has its advantages. Being able to serve as a representative of the Lord Jesus Christ means having His spirit as long as you stay the course, and wow, what a feeling! As we leave the Turners, their home is so full of the Spirit, you could cut the feeling with a knife.

It's so awesome that things are going to work out. We got a family to help and everything should be much smoother for Kim from here on out. If we can just get her to church to show her there are people in the world who will help her, befriend her, eventually she can build others up the way I'd like to see her get built up.

I'm finally seeing true power at work. Priesthood power, the power of God Himself here at work on Earth. To think, if I'd known exactly how much power I had against the Adversary in high school, things would have been so different for me.

There's no denying that I need to understand what happened, but the whole time I was fighting, I was doing it wrong. The power of the fist – what a joke. The power of the Priesthood – now that *is something real. The Priesthood can be worked with full power, even at ninety. Nothing else will ever come close, and nothing else can or ever will crush me like I was crushed then, as long as I stay true to it.*

This has been a great day – and to top it off, it looks like my teeth are back. I didn't even notice when it happened; I've been so busy.

Chapter 60 – Bad News

Monday: December 23rd, 1991 – Age 21

The day arrives for our next discussion with Kim. I'm on a split, which means a trade of companions for training purposes and things of that nature with Elder Grover. Elder Grover comes from Iowa and has only been out for two months, making him pretty green. He has brown hair, blue eyes, and is built like a shooting guard, which I learn is what he played.

We head out for the day and I'm very excited about our next appointment with Kim. Most of the day is spent in a very unassuming way, tracking. Finally we arrive at Kim's door. I gladly knock and wait for an answer. Kim's husband answers the door and he begins in a calm yet broken voice:

"You must be the guys Kim said would be coming over today. I'm grateful for what you did for her. I hadn't seen her so happy in a long time. She said you guys were teaching her about Joseph Smith. But…I'm sorry to have to tell you Kim has passed on. She...she hit a downward spiral and never came out of it and lost her battle against depression."

My heart breaks and I reply very sincerely, "I'm so sorry. Is there anything we can do for you or your family?"

"No, but thank you for the offer. I'm sorry to cut this short, but as you can see…I have family over. I just wanted to be able to thank you."

"Thank you for letting us know," I reply with a wave of the hand to indicate that we will let him tend to family matters.

We turn to walk away, and the door shuts behind us.

I won't see Kim again in this life. But I will always remember you, Kim. I wish I could have been there or had been stronger for you. I only hope you find peace and the missionaries beyond the veil find you soon.

Seconds later, Elder Grover says, "Well, that's one that may not make it on the other side."

"Elder, you don't know what you're talking about," I respond. "He just told us Kim killed herself, and the reason she did that was because she could never deal with the death of her son. I don't know what's going to happen to her, but I do know our Father above will know what she's been through, and what to do for her."

He looks surprised. "I'm sorry, Elder Price, I didn't know."

I take a breath. "I know you didn't and I'm sorry if I'm coming down on you too hard, but I could have helped her. I *know* I could have helped her. We teach a lot of people and most of them I don't want to lean on me at all. I want them to build their own testimony and grow in the church without me. That's the way it should be. Each person needs to be able to stand on their own two feet, so to speak.

"But with Kim, she was hurting so much that I was willing to let her lean on me until she didn't need to anymore. I know most of the Elders like to feel like they're part of the reason for baptism – but we're only supposed to teach the lessons, and teach these people how to pray. The rest is between them and God. I just felt like Kim was so unhappy, she needed a boost to get to the place where she could pray and feel good about it."

"I didn't realize you felt so strongly about it," Elder Grover says as we start to walk our bikes.

"Well, when I was little, I fell and hit my head, and it caused a very small bleeder that went unnoticed because it was so small – until I had a seizure. When I hit puberty, things got really bad.

"The point is: she could have seen happiness. I know that if you said a killer smile is worth a million dollars, mine would only be worth a dollar-twenty-five. But I *am* happy, and sometimes I think I'm actually the happiest person in the room, because I'm learning who I am and what I can do and that's enough to find happiness."

"I guess there's just a lot more to that kind of stuff than I realized," he says. "I never dealt with any of that growing up, and I never met Kim. Now, I'm wishing I could have met her. You've given me a lot to think about, Elder Price." He studies me a moment, and then says, "You're different from what I've heard."

"Well, yeah, when I was first out I was on fire, and then I found some of the things that were going on hard to deal with. We kept going through the paces, just not with the same drive. When I came to terms with the fact that all the other missionaries and even our Mission President are really just people in the end, it became much easier to get back into it."

"Oh, yeah, I know what you mean," he agrees. "The President isn't always the easiest person to see eye-to-eye with. That's something each of us has had to deal with."

"And then there was my reading speed," I continue to share. "I guess I thought it would just start getting so much faster once I got out here, but that didn't happen at first either. It *is* getting faster now, though, because I've read everything and now I'm just rereading and that's faster."

"Yeah, I know what you mean. It's easier to read something the second or third time."

"It's getting late," I notice. "We'd better start riding. That hill takes a lot of time to get up when you're tired." Something about this strikes me as metaphoric for our whole situation.

***

The ride home doesn't come easy. That Texas mountain seems to take longer than seven years in Tibet. To make things worse, when we return, we see extra cars in the parking lot. I recognize one from the ward, and all the lights in the house are on. Someone must have given a key to the ward mission leader.

We live on the second floor of a small two-storey apartment building. We carry our bikes up the stairs and lean them against the wall outside the apartment. I pull the key, thinking I need it, but the door is unlocked.

"Surprise!!!" shouts ring out.

With my temporary companion at my heels, I step inside to meet the shining faces of our ward's young women and leaders, all gathered for a Christmas party. My hair is longer than I would like and wind-blown, but I try to put on my best face. I receive a tie with leaves on it, from the young women. It's a moment I will remember for the rest of my life.

Only, they don't know we lost a life.

Chapter 61 – Sorry, Elder

Tuesday: December 24th, 1991 – Age 21

The following morning brings Elder Thomas back from splits, and I have to tell him the news – news I'm not handling all too well myself yet, since I'm taking Kim's death personally. I'm not sure how Elder Thomas will take it, so I wait until the other Elders are gone, to give him space.

"We went to Kim's house yesterday to see if we could catch her and her husband," I begin.

"How'd it go?" he enquires.

"Not good. Her husband answered the door and informed us that Kim had passed away."

Elder Thomas looks shocked. "Do what? What *happened?*"

"She didn't survive her depression."

He stares open-mouthed, and then shakes his head in sympathy. "I'm sorry, Elder Price. I know you felt like you could help her."

"Yeah, I was really upset about it. The most upsetting part is I won't know how she does in receiving the Gospel for so long."

"Well, I guess you could pray about it," he suggests.

"Yeah, I guess I can. I'm sorry to have to let you know, but you had to find out at some point."

"Yeah, it's never good to hear that somebody has passed on…but sometimes, it can be for the better. At least in Kim's case, she can see her son now."

"I didn't think of that," I say. "That's a good point."

"Well, thanks for letting me know. We can say a word of prayer for the family before we go out today. We better get moving."

"Yeah."

Kim is only one in nearly thirty thousand deaths by suicide every year in the United States; every minute, somebody considers suicide. I'm heartbroken and not sure how to express it. I was really trying hard to make a lasting connection with Kim and show her a new way of life. It's not right that Kim was suffocated by misery, by howling, and by gnashing of teeth going off in her head. Kim was a happy child, who grew to lose her own child, something that would kill most of us. But so many were confused by the mask and missed the chance to help bring out the joy that was once Kim.

I may never know what happened when she awoke on the other side of the veil, but I can hope her son was there to welcome her with open arms. I can hope she will be cared for and find happiness over time, not just because she has her son back, but because she will find a light inside. Then she can find peace, though she will also know that she selfishly left her husband behind.

I know as much as anybody that Kim was sick, and help for depression is hard to come by.

It's hard for me to think as we ride our bikes and do the things we need to do each day. However, life moves on; time never stops for us. I've been changed from having known Kim. Kim was wrongly viewed in such a small town, when in truth she was just a lady who became sick, suffering from the loss of her son. Ralph Waldo Emerson said, "Sorrow makes us all children again – destroys all differences of intellect. The wisest know nothing." I wish I could have helped Kim find her inner child; to remember times when she was happy, to remember how to cry and ask for help.

I wish I could have helped Kim remember that her son loved her back, and his wishes for her would have been to live a long fulfilled life. I wish I could be there for each person out there going through these trials of life that just aren't fair.

Life is filled with these lessons. I'm not sure how many of them I've missed while my head was down, but I received this one loud and clear. Just knowing Kim has caused me not only to mourn her, but to work harder in my mission.

***

It isn't until breakfast the following morning that I wake up to the fact that we need to include Kim's family in our prayers. After the prayer, we head out the door to track for the day.

At this point, I'm missing a ton of lunches because we're engaged in the work. I'm also the only Elder who can't go home at night and eat a full meal without getting reflux. It's taking its toll on me. My weight has dropped and I no longer look like I have any muscles. I knew I would lose weight, but not exactly how or how quickly.

I promised the Lord to work hard and He promised the bones in my chest would not come uncovered, and they haven't. But I'm about as skinny as can be, and now my health has started to drop.

Chapter 62 – The Letter or the Spirit of the Law

Monday: April 6th, 1992 – Age 21

In my next area I'm with Elder Thomas, and we love the Bradshaws and they love us. The Bradshaws are an elderly couple living in our ward who have signed up to have us over for dinner several times. Each time, we've enjoyed great food and a great spirit in their home. This evening, we're signed up for dinner with them again and we are both very excited.

Elder Thomas is District Leader, so he really wants to set the standard for teaching and show up the Zone Leaders. We always seem to do great with our efforts.

After the day's tracking and teaching, we ride our bikes to meet our dinner hosts. Only we're met by Brother Bradshaw at an overpass on the way to their house. He rolls down the window as we get closer.

"Hi Elders. I'm sorry but something's come up and we can't eat with you tonight. Here's some money for McDonald's." He hands Elder Thomas the money, but I feel like something's not quite right.

"Is everything okay, Brother Bradshaw?" I ask.

"Yes. Yes, everything's fine, I'm just in a hurry. You guys enjoy and we'll see you next time."

That's all we get out of him before the car drives away. Elder Thomas and I are left looking at each other, trying to figure out what just happened. It's not like the Bradshaws at all, to push us out.

"Elder Thomas, I have a feeling something's wrong."

"He was acting kinda weird."

"Not just that. I feel it in my gut: something's wrong."

Later that evening, we return home and find a message from the ward mission leader, Brother Gray, to call him no matter how late.

Elder Thomas calls Brother Gray, who informs us that Sister Bradshaw is in the hospital following a stroke, and we need to go see her. Only one problem: the hospital isn't in our area and it's against the rules to leave your area.

Elder Thomas calls to ask for permission and gets the answer: no, you may not go and see her; we have to stick to the rules. Now we have a choice. It's not my choice alone, but still a very important choice: follow our leaders, or visit the sick as we imagine Christ would have done.

Am I thinking with a clear enough head to be able to make this choice? I haven't had any problems for a very long time now.

Elder Thomas and I decide to go see Sister Bradshaw and take whatever punishment comes from it. So we start out the next morning, visit as many houses as we can, and then peddle the long distance to the hospital.

When we arrive, we're directed to her room and head there as quickly as we can, because it took us so long to get there. We enter the room to find Brother Bradshaw sitting at his wife's side. He sees us and stands, walking toward us with tears in his eyes. His wife is lying in bed, not speaking or even moving. Brother Bradshaw welcomes us and gives us each a hug.

"How's she doing?" Elder Thomas asks.

"Not too good right now, Elders, but things will be fine."

"I'm sorry this happened. Is there anything we can do?" I reply.

"No. I'm just so grateful you came."

We each take one of Sister Bradshaw's hands and wish her the best. She can't speak, but she does try. It comes out all mumbled. However, Sister Bradshaw is still in there; you can see it in her eyes.

What a wonderful lady.

We call it a short visit, because of the distance we have to travel to get home. As we cycle back, we both feel good that we did the right thing. We made our choice. But each choice carries a consequence.

When we arrive at the apartment, there's nobody there. Elder Thomas gets a phone call and it seems it's not going very smoothly.

"Elder Price, I have some bad news," Elder Thomas says with a grim look on his face.

This looks bad.

"Yeah, what's going on?" I ask, knowing that it concerns me.

"We're being transferred tomorrow."

"What?" *This can't be right.*

"Yeah, I'm going out west and you're meeting your new companion when you drop me off at the airport." He looks at me. "Do you still think we did the right thing in going to see the Bradshaws in the hospital?"

"We did the right thing," I say. "I know it."

"Yeah, I feel the same," Elder Thomas replies, this time with a smile.

"What do we need to do tonight?"

"We need to pack and get a ride."

"Okay."

This doesn't seem right that we did the right thing and are being punished. But it was against the rules, so I don't know. I just hope the Mission President weighed it all out and prayed before making his decision.

Elder Thomas calls Brother Gray, who says he can pick us up and would like to talk to us anyway. We pack in silence, and then pray for the Bradshaws.

***

Wednesday: April 8th, 1992 – Age 21

Brother Gray drives up; our time in this area is over. We pile our bags into Brother Gray's light blue Volkswagen van and head off. Brother Gray is a very laid-back guy. This morning he wears casual clothes with his movie-style brown hair and blue eyes. He seems uneasy about something, but takes a little time to speak. When he starts to let us know what's on his mind, we're more than ready to hear his news.

"Thank you for going to visit the Bradshaws in the hospital," he says. "I wish I'd known when you were going to be there, because I could have taken you home. I just missed you, and it was so important for you to be there."

"Why?" we ask in unison.

"Didn't you know?"

"What are you talking about?" I reply. *What are we supposed to know?*

"The other day, you were supposed to eat at the Bradshaws'."

"Yeah, Brother Bradshaw gave us money for McDonald's," Elder Thomas says.

"Sister Bradshaw was very excited you were coming and she was hurrying to take something out of the oven when she fell. That's how she got the stroke."

Brother Gray waits for a response, but gets nothing but silence. "What's going on, Elders?" he asks after what seems like a long time.

"I called to get permission for Elder Price and me to visit and they said no, but we went anyway. Elder Price felt like something was wrong and so did I, so we just went. But he didn't tell us that."

"Is that why you're being transferred?"

"Yes. President Whittle said, 'We can't pick and choose when it comes to the rules.'"

Brother Gray considers this. “Well, that’s true, Elders; I can see his point. Then he might have Elders breaking the rules for every little thing. But this really wasn’t a little thing.”

Elder Thomas and I sit in shock for the rest of the ride. Life seems somehow different, like we did something that really mattered. So many times when you’ve done the right thing, you just *feel* like it was right. You never actually know for sure. Oscar Wilde said, “There are moments when one has to choose between living one’s own life, fully, entirely, completely—or dragging out some false, shallow, degrading existence that the world in its hypocrisy demands. You have that moment now. Choose!”

Here Elder Thomas and I drive along the highway in a vehicle that could be older than we are, not just because we chose to go on a mission, but because of what other things we chose *not* to do. We’re at an age when most guys are hitting spring break, chasing girls and getting really drunk. Yet here we sit wearing a white shirt and tie, having learned a valuable life lesson.

Sister Bradshaw was a good lady. I didn’t realize how good she was until now. It’s sad to think that death or near-death experiences are what it takes to wake us up to life.

***

When we get to the Zone Leaders, they don’t look happy to see us, that’s for sure. But I look at Elder Thomas at the same time he looks at me, and just like that, we both agree without saying a thing that we made the right choice. We say our goodbyes and are taken in different directions.

I’m certain the number of bumps I’ve had in my life would far outweigh those Elder Thomas has experienced, but a true friend is worth his weight in comics or gold, whichever you like better. I will miss him.

Chapter 63 – I Can't Swallow

Wednesday: June 10th, 1992 – Age 21

Time passes and I'm in another area with another companion, Elder Groves, who has red hair and a frame for running, something he loves to do. I hear he's quite good at it, but I didn't hear it from him, as he won't easily admit to such things.

It's dinnertime and we're with members – the Johnsons, an empty-nest couple with matching grey hair – when I start having trouble swallowing my food. I try my best to do two things: eat and not upset the Johnsons, as Sister Johnson has made a wonderful meal and we've just started. It's only the four of us at the table and it's becoming painful to swallow each bite.

When I take my first bite of pork, it begins to go down, but then comes up again. I try to force it down. I'm scared to death. I put the napkin to my mouth before the food can spill out – and notice all eyes are on me.

"Elder Price, I never!" Sister Johnson lets out rather loudly and in some shock, her blue eyes opening wide through her silver rimmed glasses.

"I can't swallow." *What's happening to me?*

"What?" she replies.

"Elder Price, are you okay?" asks Elder Groves with a look of compassion on his face, which is nice because we've only just been placed together.

"I don't know." *I'm going to die if I can't eat.*

"Loosen your tie and shirt button and try drinking some water. Maybe that will help you," says Brother Johnson. His tie is already off his white shirt; he's a bigwig with the Boy Scouts.

I pick up the glass of water in front of me and take a drink. It goes down my throat and I force it hard as I can force something with that part of my body.

"It's bulging your neck out. Spit it out into your cup," Brother Johnson instructs. I do just that, along with small pieces of food that were in my mouth, making my cup look gross.

On the bright side, now that Sister Johnson knows something is wrong with me and I wasn't being rude, she jumps into mother mode.

"Has this ever happened to you before?" she asks.

"No."

"We better call your mother."

That could get me in trouble.

"We're not supposed to call home."

"Elder Price, this is an emergency. I'll call her for you. Then I'll call your Mission President."

"Okay."

I tell her my phone number and, in return, she gives me a Popsicle to suck on and a cup for spitting into. She then leads me into the other room so I don't have to watch them eat on an empty stomach. I have no idea what's going on, but I do know I won't last long if I can't even drink water.

It seems like forever when she finally comes back into the other room. She walks over to where I sit on the piano bench, leaning slightly on the instrument. She takes a seat in the adjacent chair and looks at me with empathy in her eyes. I'm guessing she knows what it's like to go without food, but she doesn't know exactly how much this food means to me at this time.

"I called your mom," she says. "She thinks it must have something to do with the scar tissue in your throat. Your mom also said to say they love you and you'll be in their prayers. Then I called your Mission President, who said to make an appointment for you ASAP. So I called Saint Joseph's Hospital and made you an appointment for tomorrow."

"Thank you," I say.

"Brother Scott will pick you up in the morning and take you to the hospital. You'll need to be there by seven."

After a pause I say, "Okay, that sounds good."

"I also called the Bishop to let him know."

"Thank you, Sister Johnson. That was really nice of you to do all that for me."

"Well, you got us all a little freaked out," she says.

Yeah, well, I thought I was going to die for a second there.

After another pause, I admit, "Yeah, it freaked me out."

"Your Mission President asked us to take you home so you can rest. We can have somebody bring your bikes over to you in just a little bit."

"How long will I be in the hospital?"

I can't be in there long. I need to work.

"I don't know, Elder Price. It depends on what they have to do."

I haven't been worried about my health for a long time, so this little choking trick has caught me unawares. It really is hard for me to think of myself as mortal. I can't stand the thought that something could actually hurt me. Because of my head injury and all it has put me through, I don't feel pain the way others do.

I have the heart of a cowboy, in many ways, and dying from a simple lack of food and water isn't exactly going down in a blaze of glory. Neither is old age, and maybe that's another reason this mission is so hard on me, because I'm unable to take care of myself. I miss my old life, and that is the real point driving this whole event. The Man of Misery is saying, "Give up and go home or I'll hit you again."

I haven't given my response yet, as I'm still a little too freaked out to think it over. There's always tomorrow, and I will go forward. I will keep getting back up over and over again.

To ruin the end game, my Adversary will have to do better.

***

When we arrive at the hospital, I find that most of the nursing staff are nuns. I'm not really sure what to think about it. Nuns are very nice and all, but I can't help thinking they should be in a church or something. But after a while, they really start to grow on you.

Before I know it, I'm no longer an observer. I'm out on the table while they try to determine my diagnosis. The room is probably pretty full, I would imagine, by the number of doctors that come in to see something they've only heard of before. By the time I see the light of day again, they have fixed the problem and made sure it doesn't happen again.

Hours later, I'm visited by a Doctor Filmore, who is tall with slight covering brown hair and round glasses.

"Let's see, it says your name is Richard. Is it okay to call you that?" he asks me.

"Yes."

"It looks like you have all that scar tissue in the back of your throat and you're in one of the worst places for allergies in Texas. Your allergies must be pretty bad because between the two, your throat was completely closed off. But next time, you'll know what's going on."

"So that's all it was?"

"Yep, that's it. So you'll need to drink plenty of water while eating your food and you should be able to resume your normal activities."

"That's good news," I say. "Thank you."

"Can I answer any more questions for you?"

I consider this. "No, I think I'm okay for now."

"Okay, Richard, get some rest. You should be able to go home once we know everything is working right."

"Okay."

With that, Doctor Filmore gets up from his seat and heads out the door, leaving me with my thoughts.

For whatever reason, my body seems to generate a lot of scar tissue. In a number of hours, I'll see this is a turning point. It's the first time in my life I've gone through something like this without my parents.

Chapter 64 – An Hour with Mr Keaton

Monday: September 21st, 1992 – Age 21

There's an older gentleman who lives in an apartment downstairs from us, probably in his eighties. We've noticed he has a new car every week. Each one seems to be nicer than the one before. It's like he's a test driver for *Luxury Cars for Reckless Geriatrics.* Or maybe he's a former spy.

Something happens when you pray to meet people. Doors open up so you can meet them. In this case, the door actually closes, just as we're carrying our bikes downstairs for the day.

We set our bikes against the wall and walk up to the door in unison. I knock on the door, and a few minutes later the door opens. The man has some white hair, but he's not too heavy around the middle and he stands about five-foot-three. He looks like an older Anthony Hopkins. He glances at each of us and extends his hand.

Then he says, "I'm Sterling Keaton. How can I help you today?"

"My name is Elder Price, and we're from the Church of Jesus Christ of Latter-Day Saints."

"Oh, I know who you boys are. Some of the others that have come through here have stopped by. Please come in."

"Thank you," Elder Smith says. Then he introduces himself too.

Mr Keaton leads us inside to sit with him, coughing into a handkerchief along the way. "Don't mind me. I'm okay," he says before either of us can comment.

"You have a nice home here, Mr Keaton," I reply, taking care not to stray too far from safe conversation.

"Thank you. I have lots of old books and stuff, as you can see."

"Thanks for having us in for a little bit," says Elder Smith, who can be overly polite. Maybe that's why people like him so much.

But he may just have met his match with Mr Keaton, who grew up 'old school'.

"Don't even worry about that," he says. "How can I help you boys today?"

"Well," I say, "like I said, we're from the Church of Jesus Christ of Latter-Day Saints. We're just out talking to people today, like we do every day."

"Do you know Elder VaClaw?" Mr Keaton asks. "He was a nice young man."

"I've met Elder VaClaw. He's very nice." Elder Smith looks Mr Keaton right in the eyes and waits for him to turn toward him, which he does. "What did you do for a living, Mr Keaton?" Elder Smith then asks, which is a great question to find common ground.

"I was in the banking world for most of my life, and I enjoyed it so much, it was just heartbreaking when we went to paper money. You know, I have some Silver Certificates around here someplace. Let me get you boys one."

We both assure him he doesn't have to do that, but he either doesn't hear us or doesn't care and goes anyway. It takes him some time, and we sit listening to cabinet doors opening and shutting. Then he comes back and hands us each an envelope with a Silver Certificate in it. He's so proud to be able to do it, we can't say no. Then he returns to his chair.

"Thank you so much, Mr Keaton; this is awesome," I say, beating Elder Smith to the punch.

"Yes, thank you so much," Elder Smith agrees.

Mr Keaton begins to talk about banking and the history of the Silver Certificates he gave us. We know we should just listen, and we do so intently, making sure he knows we care for what he's giving us – and that his Father in Heaven loves him. That's why He has sent him missionaries to comfort him in his elder years. It's truly an hour to remember.

As we leave, we know we will never see him again in this life. I want to part with a hug, rather than a simple handshake.

Chapter 65 – Winding Down and Breaking Down

Friday: October 30th, 1992 – Age 21

If asked, I would have to admit that in a way, I'm glad my mission is almost over. I've had much success and met many great people. But you wouldn't believe how easily I'm falling apart,

I sprained my ankle. Then it swelled up to a size I've never seen the likes of before. I sit, trying to study, with my ankle resting on a pillow at the other end of the couch. I'm not sure what's worse, an ankle that's two sizes too big or the lack of food I have for the last week, because I gave all my extra money to a homeless guy who needed to eat. Then we got him into a motel with the help of the ward and we caught the maid coming out of his apartment, mostly undressed. The guy promised he would turn the corner and look for work. But no. With my luck, he just spent our money and had fun with the maid on the Lord's bill.

That guy was a real piece of something.

The ward mission leader tried to cheer me up about it, since I was trying to do the right thing. He said members from the ward learned from my example. I just had the misfortune of learning that the gift was not well received.

I find myself reverting to old thoughts.

I look forward to working out again. Then maybe I can get some dates. I think I've changed enough that girls won't think I'm so weird, now.

I hope things will continue to go well for my family and friends. Since Malcolm has gone back to his mission to teach English to Japanese students, I won't see him.

Thomas has waited for me to return from my mission before he goes on his own, but I'm not sure why. I've never been much of a big brother. At least Dad's career has taken off while I've been out.

He could become a professional artist with his oil painting. It would be cool if we could do something together someday.

All the girls seem to be doing great and Mom seems happy that I'm coming home. I may even still have a dog. This last year has gone by very quickly. I hope the next one goes by as quickly and sees me continuing in the right direction. It's a great feeling, like everything is in control, even when I know too well that I have very little control in this life.

The hardest thing I'll have to do is get a job that I want to do for the rest of my life. I have no real idea what that would be, while most of the guys out here know what they want.

I look around the apartment and see all the things I need to pack. Packing's never fun; some of this stuff may not even fit. Plus, I might have to leave my bike here and that would be a waste. We both have our bike boxes, so that is something if I can get the right price, or free.

There's no time to write home for money and phones are off-limits; I don't need to break any rules and make it worse. Although maybe I should think about that each time I start arguing with the Mission Presidents, both new and old. I have no respect for authority when it's wrong.

***

"Elder Price, it's getting close to time to go," Elder Smith tells me. "I have some extra pancakes. Would you like them?" he asks with a smile.

"Yeah, that would be awesome," I reply. Despite my ankle, I start to get up.

He motions for me to sit back down. "I'll bring them over to you."

"Thank you," I say.

A peaceful feeling comes over me, like a warm blanket. Elder Smith wants to be Christ-like and he's doing just that. He hands me the plate and I pour the syrup over the pancakes. It's a joy to have food. I would rather fight a polar bear than go without food. When I finish, Elder Smith takes my plate and I get on my knees. When he comes back, we pray.

Then we have lessons to teach. We are baptizing a ten-year-old boy the day before we have to go to the airport. He's a great kid who's full of life and energy. We want it to be a great baptism, as it will be the last one for Elder Smith and me before we finish our mission and go home.

Thankfully, we have a car, so I don't need to worry about cycling with my swollen ankle. But we're only permitted so many miles per month, so we turn off the car when going down steep hills. It makes it hard if the steering wheel locks up. But we're still young and stupid in many ways, so we shrug this off. That's the real beauty of the whole mission: that young men will volunteer to serve the Lord, asking nothing in return.

"We need gas," Elder Smith announces. "I'm going to pull over."

"Okay."

"Alright, let's see…there's a place. We'll go there."

We pull in and then step out of the car. We walk up to pay when I notice a really pretty blond lady struggling to get oil into her engine.

"Do you need help with that?" I ask.

"Yes, that would be wonderful," she says. "I never really know what I'm doing around cars."

"It's not a problem. I'll take care of it for you," I say as Elder Smith pays for our gas, just behind me.

"Thank you."

"Are you a model or something?" I can't help asking.

"Yes, I am," she says with surprise. "What are you guys?" She glances around me at Elder Smith.

"We're missionaries for our church," I tell her. "Do you have a picture I can have?"

She lifts her eyebrows at me. "You want my picture?"

"Yeah, I want to show my dad I met a model, when I go home this week," I say, smiling at her.

She smiles back. "Okay, I'll get you one." She goes to her purse and pulls out a wallet-sized headshot and gives it to me.

"Thank you," I say, closing the hood to her sports car. "Have a nice day."

"You too," she says.

Elder Smith and I walk back to our car to pump the gas. Elder Smith seems to be thinking hard about something. He doesn't look like he's going to say anything, but then changes his mind.

"I can't believe you did that," he says.

"What do you mean?" I ask.

"You asked for her picture."

"Yeah?"

"And she gave it to you."

"Yeah."

Elder Smith finishes pumping the gas and puts the nozzle away. The whole time, he wears a bewildered look on his face.

"Can I see it?" Elder Smiths finally asks, as if to clear up something in his mind.

"Sure," I say. I take the picture out of my shirt pocket and hand it to him.

"Well, she *is* cute," he admits, "but you're kinda crazy, Elder Price."

"I get that a lot," I reply with my best good-humored smile.

***

When the only thing left is to go home, I've read all the scriptures and lost count of how many times I've read the Book of Mormon. I've helped bring to pass twenty-four baptisms and, more importantly, I've helped my fellow missionaries when needed. I entered the mission field riddled with allergies, but now I'm only allergic to poultry. I used my last week's McDonald's money to feed somebody and shelter someone in need, only to have him turn his back on me, my companion and our gospel with his free agency. For good and bad, these are the best years in the lives of many young men, as this is the time to prove they have the right to be called men.

For me, it was about more than becoming a man. It was about proving to myself that I'm more than just the Adversary's whipping boy. I needed to prove to myself for a surety that helping others is the difference between the joy of man and Christ-like happiness: one is done out of selfishness and the other selflessness.

Chapter 66 – Homecoming

Saturday: November 7th, 1992 – Age 21

My missionary days are over, and I'm honored by my fellow Elders who carry my bags. I even shed a tear, but I hide my face so it doesn't show. On arrival, I'm welcomed at the airport by my family, as are some of the other missionaries. The look of shock on the faces of my family tells me I did well. I left for my mission at the pinnacle of health and returned home decimated by time, hunger and, above all else, full service to the Lord.

Going home is all about having time to think about getting a job and how I might have a life, one step at a time. Everybody knows I'm looking for work, so I actually networked – a little bit, anyway. I hope somebody can help me.

My brother and father carry my bags as I begin to tell the stories of my mission. There's just one thing missing: Badger, my great dog. Surly Mom gave him away the minute I left.

I will miss him.

The drive back goes by quickly. When we arrive home, Mom has something for me.

"I have a surprise for you," she says, clearly hoping for a really big reaction.

"What?" I say.

Mom signals Tiffany to open the back door, and out comes Badger, running and knocking me down, only to start prancing around and licking me. Without question, he has never been happier to see me. I'm thrilled to see him, but he won't let me up. When I finally get to my feet, I try to figure out what to say.

"I thought you would've given him away," is what makes it out of my mouth.

Mom balks at this. "How could I have given him away? You were so adamant about us not throwing away your comics, I thought we better keep him."

"Well, those comics are worth a lot of money," I point out. At least, I like to *think* they're worth lots of money. Later I'll learn that even if you have a first edition or the first comic in a series, it's printed so many times that it becomes worthless, like the Fed printing too much money.

"It was worth it," Mom says, "to see him greet you."

It's a wonderful homecoming. To have a good dog is to have a true friend. I've never known a dog to misjudge me. I've never known a dog to gossip about me. I've never known a dog to hate me based on my mannerisms, whereas humans do this all the time. Frankly, I'm guilty of all the same things. If only people were like a good dog, then maybe we would all get along, even those of us with fleas.

***

Now that I'm home, my troubles aren't over. They just take a different form. I want to get back into college and find a job. I contacted the military before going on a mission and know I can't go in that direction, even into something with computers, since I can't pass basic training without my medication. Or at least, it wouldn't be a good idea.

The next question is: what kind of collar should I wear, blue or white? The biggest thing to consider is what will lend well to what I can do, and how much I can cope with. Keeping my journey from a normal employer wouldn't be a lie. But if I went into law enforcement or public service, I would need to be honest and admit I have clinical depression. I don't think I need to go into vast detail, as I don't believe we should be judged in this life for every sin ever committed. But a clear picture of each person in office is necessary.

***

November 1992

I return to the singles' ward, which has a plethora of unknown faces. The big announcement of the day comes from a guy named Adam: there's going to be a game of Ghost in the Graveyard on Tuesday, which is really just hide-and-seek, but the scale is as massive as you want it to be. Everybody attending is going to wear black clothes and it sounds like fun, plus there are people I don't know.

When Tuesday evening hits, I head over to meet the others. Adam is there. He looks like a buffed up comic book soldier but is very down-to-earth. He's a big guy, perhaps six-foot-two and maybe two hundred pounds. Basically, the kind of guy I've always wanted to be just like. Adam isn't concerned with how people view him and he's nice to everybody. I, on the other hand, have become outgoing by my standards, but cover most everything with jokes that usually don't make sense to others.

When the game starts, I hide just like everybody else. Some of the couples are never seen again (not sure why they came in the first place), but most of us just run around and climb up on people's houses. Stuff like that.

It's the second round when a guy named Trent finds me. He's a carpenter who looks like he stole Van Halen's clothes.

We start looking for more people when he says, "It was a lot more fun when we used to play in the actual graveyard."

"Why'd you stop, then?"

"The guy who watched the graveyard filled shotgun shells with rock salt and started shooting at us."

"Oh, yeah, I guess I could see how that would kill the game," I reply. I look at what's left of Trent's blond hair blowing in the wind. Then I see something else in the back of a 4x4. "Look," I say, motioning to it. "Let's go check it out."

"Okay, remember you have to tag them once you find them, so be quiet."

"I'll go this way, you go that way." I point right and left.

We get up closer and find that it's Adam. We're lucky to have caught him off guard, because he's really fast. Adam laughs when he's caught, but it's kind of like he's laughing at himself, because he must be very competitive or something like that. Now that we have Adam, we have the edge.

***

The best part of the whole evening is walking home by myself. No more looking back to see if I lost my companion, which happened a lot with Elder Kaine, a guy who rode his bike like a two-year-old; or feeling forced to have a conversation while on foot for hours at a time, but having nothing. The good parts of the mission can't be shared; they were felt.

PART 7:
Returned Missionary

Chapter 67 – After the Silence

Thursday: January 21st, 1993 – Age 22

Lithium has brought life and understanding back into a body that shared two worlds. The emotional scars still burden an otherwise carefree person. The second fracture comes in the form of memory lapses that crash down upon me like the waves of the mighty ocean. It's a continued battle to regain my footing and relearn old skills, before the next wave crashes.

It is a game I can't win without help, but I've tried to learn the rules. I leave key items in the same place every day when I'm done with them, like my wallet and keys, which come out of the same pocket every day. It's like something out of a bad movie.

Hope walks through the door as Melissa comes home with the name of new doctor for me, Dr Earp, whom she came across while doing a school project. Mom schedules an appointment to see him. She has seen me through so much and hopes he's the right doctor for me. Then she lets me know about it, and I'm thrilled, but unaware exactly how much this doctor will mean to me with life's trials to come.

***

Dr Earp is tall with light brown hair and brown eyes, and young enough to be my doctor for a long time. He shakes my hand firmly as we enter the office. When he smiles, it's easy to see he's sincere. The best part about Dr Earp, though, is that he's LDS, so I don't have to explain that part of my life.

I find that Dr Earp is a stickler for the questions.

"Have you been able to maintain friendships?" he asks, to establish my ability to keep common ground with others and maintain a give-and-take relationship.

"I haven't had any trouble keeping friends since I've been on my meds," I reply, hoping it will get better, and that when it comes to my turn he will really listen to me.

"Do you have thoughts of hurting yourself or others?"

"No, I don't."

"Does your mind race or do you have trouble getting to sleep at night?"

"No, but I'm having really bad problems with my memory."

"What do you mean?"

"Well, I've been on Lithium for a while now and my memory has gotten worse and worse. It's to the point now that I'll write a note to myself on my hand, but then I forget to look at my hand. I'm basically leaving notes for myself every place, just trying to get by. But I used to have a memory that was almost photographic. My memory was how I got by."

"Well, I can't just take you off Lithium and put you on something else," he tells me. "You have to wait two weeks until it's out of your system. Also, you should know that depression itself will cause memory problems. After the two weeks, though, we can start you on something else. I'll need to ask you some more questions so we get you on the right medication," Dr Earp says with compassion.

"That sounds fine," Mom replies, and I actually smile.

With that, the long process of repairing my memory begins.

The visit is fairly standard, but I'm in La La Land the whole time.

This is so cool. Maybe I'll be able to finish college at some point. This is the best thing to happen. I can't believe it. Maybe one day I'll be able to get my life back.

There's one other piece of information I pick up after sort of explaining my episodes to Dr Earp.

He says, "It sounds like a schizo-affective disorder. It would be hard for me to determine for certain, since I wasn't the doctor who saw you at that time. You're doing so well now, but from what you've said, that's what it sounds like to me."

I leave the office feeling so good about being able to get my memory back that the new diagnosis doesn't sink in. In fact, it is, ironically, forgotten pretty much on the spot and won't be realized in full until I come to write this book.

I'm once again on the right track and encouraged to continue my self-evaluation, which has come to mean a lot more than just trying to determine whether the meds are working right. The evaluation has become a way of becoming a better person.

I remember being a person who wasn't liked and was losing friends one after another. In typical fashion for me, I don't just want to make up for my mistakes. I have to try to become the best I can be.

Chapter 68 – Adam

Sunday: August 14th, 1994 – Age 23

Adam and I sit next to each other, waiting for sacrament meeting, the first church meeting. The sound of the Elders putting together the sacrament itself rings out. The stage fills with the normal line-up, when Adam turns and looks at me like something's on his mind and says, "I have an opportunity I think you'd like."

"What is it?" I ask, hoping it's some kind of work, because I need something.

"I'm starting up a little business that I was doing before my mission and I'd like some help. You interested?" A warm smile highlights his chiseled features.

"Yes, I am," I say, excited at the chance to earn my way in this venture of free enterprise.

"Great! I already have our first job lined up working at the dairy where my dad works. Then there are lots of possibilities for other jobs," he gushes. "We'll be painting. Have you ever helped paint your house or something like that?"

"Yes."

"Well, it'll be like that, only we have power tools to make it go so much faster. We'll be using a high-power sprayer to take off the old paint and then a regular sprayer to paint it on," he explains.

The hymn music starts to play, signifying that it's time to start.

"Cool," I reply, slightly awe-inspired.

I can't believe Adam wants *me* to help him with this. There are several guys in the ward he could get. He must know my history. Everybody else seems to, and it's not like I've tried to keep it secret.

I hope I don't let him down.

I start thinking about the "what ifs" already.

If this goes well, I could be a partner in a good business. I mean, I don't know what Adam is planning for the future, but I know he's a really smart guy. I hope I can show I'm worthy of being a good partner. It would be awesome if it could keep going for a long time.

It will be nice to learn from somebody who's so smart. And it will be good to have a job, since the holidays are getting closer.

When at last church is over for the day, I rush home to tell Mom and Dad about my new job. There's something extra special about getting a job. It gives a feeling of independence and freedom from the bonds of poverty. It says so much, especially for someone who may have been out of work for a number of years, or will always have a hard time getting work. It's more than a sense of self-worth; it is the *embodiment* of self-worth. That is why the Great Depression was just that: depression.

But not anymore. Not for me.

***

Monday: August 29th, 1994 – Age 23

I sit on the passenger side as Adam drives us to our first day on the job. With the progress I've made on my meds, I could do just about anything I want. This is a great day for my reputation, even with the two-year mission. To me, it shows trust, and that's something more important than money, in this world. I hope this will put the sick teenager phase of my life behind me, once and for all.

We head onto the freeway. It's a bit of a drive to West Valley.

Adam breaks the silence by saying, "I took Rylee out last night for a movie and some dinner."

"Oh, how did that go?"

"It was nice. Rylee is such a sweetheart."

The name sounds familiar, so I ask, "Where did you meet her?"

"At a church dance," Adam says with a little grin.

"I think I've met her. Does she have blond hair and she's about this tall?" I hold my hand around the level of my shoulder.

"That sounds like her. Have you seen her at one of the dances?"

"Well, if it's the same girl – and I think with the name Rylee and in our area, it would be. She was actually nice enough to dance with me. She was very cute, as well as nice. You're a lucky guy," I say, a little embarrassed by the fact that it's still so hard to get girls to pay any attention to me, despite being told over the years that I'm so cute, by older women.

"Thanks, Rick," Adam says as I drift into space.

I wish I were more like Adam. He's so close to perfect it's not even funny: tall, muscles, and a great education. Then look at me. I lost all my muscle on my mission, I'm average height, and have practically no education, and the kicker is that it won't be an easy thing for me to get it because I have to keep relearning everything as I go, however many times.

I'm still out of it when Adam says, "We're almost there; just a few minutes."

Just like Adam said, in a few minutes we arrive; in about fifteen more, we start working. The work is easy. All we have to do is take turns lifting one another up in a cage attached to the forks on a forklift. Then, with high-power sprayers in hand, we spray off all the old paint from the overhang above the dock. It means spraying right overhead, which gives the shoulders a workout. While Adam is spraying, a dry breeze sweeps across my face from the cemetery that looms next to us.

I'm compelled to keep up with Adam, even though he's three times my size. After a few rounds of this, it's lunchtime and we get free chocolate milk.

I love this job.

And when I actually open the container and taste the thick, rich chocolate milk, well, the gods of chocolate milk are shining upon me. The blessings of lunch have come to a place called Winder, Utah.

Adam and I head back to work with few words spoken, due to the fact that we just ate like Vikings. Work becomes routine and time-consuming; we cover a large area and this is just day one. Time is the master of all things great and small; it makes mountains and then crushes them. It makes the young old and the dumbfounded dumber. I have to keep at the work, if only to remind myself that I'm not alone – even when it feels like it.

***

Tuesday: August 30th, 1994 – Age 23

Rylee is the kind of girl who makes love songs live, a true better half, a compass of compassion, and somebody for eternal marriage. Adam doesn't seem to be reflecting on his blessings in life this morning, but his mind is someplace. As we drive to work, love is not in the air; God is.

We haven't being driving long before Adam says, "You know how I was saying I'm going on a trip to Texas and we would start working when I got back?"

"Yeah, I remember."

"Well, I have tons of CDs that I listened to all the way down, but coming back as I was driving, all I did was pray."

"Why were you praying that much? Is something wrong?" I ask, marveling at the way people have always felt comfortable talking so personally with me.

"I feel like I might not be here much longer."

"You mean you feel like you might die?" I ask, looking at somebody who is the picture of health.

"Yeah, I can't explain it. I just feel it."

In the seconds before Adam continues, thoughts race through my head.

I don't see how that could happen. This guy is so healthy; he would have to get hit by a truck or something. And I know I'm not going to pass away until I've accomplished whatever it is the Lord wants me to do, so we're not going to crash. It's just not possible.

As if reading my thoughts, Adam says, "I know I'm healthy, but this is something I just feel."

"Well, if it's on the Lord's time, it could be a long time from now," I say. "I mean, for all we know, ten years could be the blink of an eye to the Lord. That would give you lots of time here."

He frowns at this idea. "Yeah. I don't know about that. But I do know I'm at peace with it."

The car fills with a warm sensation and silence becomes us. I've heard of people knowing their time is near, and that's something I won't face for years to come. I feel the exact opposite; my time is far away. And maybe because I somehow know I'll be here until I'm done, part of me wants Adam to be around just as long as I will and forget all this talk about going home to our Father in Heaven. I want him to stay here where we need him – where *I* need him.

Adam has become like the big brother I never had. The big brother I wish I could be. The kind of *person* I wish I could be. To end something like that isn't fair. It's not right and if his intuition proves correct, I don't think I'll ever understand something like that happening.

Maybe Adam telling me all this stuff sets off the guard dog in me, or maybe it's just me being selfish – or maybe it's something I'm not even aware of – but it won't leave my head. I may never know what causes a bond of brotherhood to grow until you have become brothers in spirit – but I know when it *does* happen, it's as real as being flesh and blood brothers.

When the morning drive is over, we break into our normal routine of blasting off old paint and getting soaking wet in the process. It's fun spraying the old paint off the metal cover, because the force of the water throws the paint everywhere. It falls down onto the big metal dock, making it look like it's covered in snow. Then, with the next wave of water, it's gone. The steel cage of the lift adds to the feeling that this is the kind of manly work I could see myself doing for a long time. It's a first.

As the water is continually forced through the long black, rubber hose, I wonder if someday I could help bring in some business and contribute to the bottom line. It's a good feeling to think about building something in the real world. It's a step in the right direction and as I ponder, my thoughts turn to real life problems.

If I can find a way to meet my expenses with so many dollars per hour, then go beyond that and make money on my own, like with a comic book or something, I could become rich over time. First I have to keep out of debt and then pay for a house with cash. I can do it. I am, after all, very creative. Maybe I could invent something.

The days of the future often move so quickly that when a moment comes that will change your life, it may not be noticed until later. I feel like in many ways life is changing for the better, but perhaps life is just slapping me in the face again, or getting ready to. I don't hear the sound of footsteps running down the hall in the morning, hoping to wake their father. I don't feel the breath of my young bride as we honeymoon in a faraway place. And I certainly don't see love at first sight. All of these things are merely dreams to me, but for Adam they seem not too far off. I envy him that, with the best intentions.

In the world outside my world, life is just life and work is just work. I do what I must, to hold up my end, because my name and the pride I have in myself are on the line. It doesn't matter that Adam is bigger and stronger than I am. I won't let myself down, or Adam – in that order. After all, God above said, "Prove yourself." He didn't say, "Prove yourself to Adam." This is who I am.

In times of old, when men were men and you didn't eat until the beast was dead, what did they do to stem the tide?

I could ask the riddles of my mind, but this I know and this I say: I won't be outdone because I am not the same.

Forget your fears and troubles of men,
Forget the fire, and live to the end.
It is not the fight that makes the man;
It is staying in the battle until the end.
There is not breath inside and yet I fight;
It is the spirit, not my might.

Chapter 69 – Beautiful Depression

Wednesday: August 31st, 1994 – Age 23

Depression is hard to transform into something beautiful; you can't do it alone. You can look in that enchanted mirror and turn your life around, but if nobody gives you a second chance, then it feels like it was for nothing. Adam is giving me this chance and my aim is not to blow it.

The reality is that while going through depression and the episodes that surrounded it was the hardest part of my life, for better or worse the experience made me who I am today. I may always be depressed, but if I can find that perfect muse, then I will have Beautiful all the time – Beautiful to remind me to smile, because her smile lights up the room – Beautiful to show me that what I have inside is beautiful too; it just gets surrounded by clouds sometimes. Then maybe one day I will be beautiful too.

When I look out my window into the great big world, what I see is that every single person out there will be depressed at some point in their lives. Taking one day at a time is the key to finding a way to beat anything. What's today? Today is another day in my life, because I choose to live my life no matter how bad others try to make it – no matter how hard the Adversary tries to make me slip up.

Today is another chance to help somebody. Today is life and in my life I have a job, and friendship that means a lot. Today is another day spraying off paint in the steel cage, which means more money in my pocket and more time to prove my worth in what could be a growing business. There's no easy way to show Adam I can work hard, and I'm not looking for one. I know I can work hard and that's something I would like to think helped get me through my troubles.

However, Adam has done more in his life than just hard physical labor. He went to BYU, a college open to all religions and widely known for academics, and graduated with honors. Do you know what I mean?

I mean, I've never felt ahead of the class in anything when it comes to academics, and maybe I never will. So here stands this giant and a scholar next to me, little and not advanced according to anybody in the academic world (*so far*, that is). The only thing I can do is work, and so I do just that. My greatest hope in working with Adam is that I will learn to become more like him. So every time we break or sit down to lunch, I talk with him.

I'm just not that good at chitchat and perhaps I never will be. I'm becoming very aware of who I am, and of what I can and can't do – without divine aid, that is. I want to express myself in ways people will understand so they won't only know what I mean to say, but respect my ideas. If I actually said what I'm thinking at times when I'm in such deep thought, I'm not sure language would be enough.

***

When break time comes and we sit down, I ask Adam, "So, have you been playing Ghost in the Graveyard or what? I haven't seen you much after work."

"No. I've been too busy with family and with Rylee."

"That sounds fun," I reply, wanting the best for him.

Adam looks at the sky and says, "Yeah, it's been a good week so far."

"I haven't been doing too much myself, other than hanging out around the house," I say.

"I'm getting closer on that next job for us, when this one ends, so at least you won't have to worry about that much longer," he tells me.

"That's awesome, man. I haven't been worrying; I knew you could do it."

And I still live at home anyway, so no problem.

"Cool. You thirsty?"

"Yeah."

"Let's go get a drink."

We start to walk and I guess I feel like a little brother must feel, because I want to do and be better. Adam doesn't pressure me about girls or only want to be my friend if I meet a certain standard. He's just my friend, and that's good enough.

We walk toward our watering hole and I see a spider falling from its hidden little home under the overhang. It is a common thing to see, but the way the web reflects the light reminds me of small miracles. So I begin to say something to Adam and get out something entirely different, like my head skipped a beat:

"You know what I think Hell really is?"

He looks at me. "Tell me."

"I think Hell for somebody like Hitler is having to relive the deaths of all those innocent lives he took, over and over and over for eternity, without ever getting the release. I think for the child molester, Hell is to live in his childhood body knowing full well what he did and having to face it over and over, with no hope of saving grace. Hell is having the rapist stripped of clothes and left alone as the voices of his victims cry at him and razors sear into his flesh one at a time, only to heal a second later while he's torn open someplace else."

Adam continues to study me. "Wow, have you given this a lot of thought?"

I shrug. "I guess. I mean, it's just something I was thinking."

"That may have been the most I've ever heard you say in one breath, outside Elder's Quorum lessons at church," he remarks.

"If I really try, I could probably think of worse," I push on, disregarding his last comment. "It's just that people think of Hell mostly as the torment of the body, and that's not right."

"You say that as if you're pretty sure of yourself," he notes.

"I am."

"Strong words."

"What do you mean?"

"People will follow you with words like those."

I'm startled by this. "Oh," I say. "Thanks, man."

Sometimes great bursts of clarity come out of thin air and there's no turning back. It would be easier to break a tidal wave or split a mountain in two. Life isn't just what dreams are made of; it's the breath of God, giving the light of every soul who enters this world. And yet so many quickly tune out the light to dwell in darkness and keep the secrets of men. There's no eternal hope for these people, but as Children of God we're not supposed to call judgment upon anybody, and that's something that surrounding myself with good friends like Adam will help me with.

Chapter 70 – The Problem Is a Plug

Friday: September 2nd, 1994 – Age 23

Friday is finally here and we're finishing our week of stripping off all the old paint, hoping to clear the loading dock with our power sprayer. We continue forklifting each other up in the cage. Earlier, I found an outlet that was different from what we were using, but because we didn't have a long enough extension cable to clear the dock, we grabbed Maintenance. Jim, a young guy dressed in overalls and a button-up cowboy shirt, came over to help. Even though the plug was a different type, he felt like an adapter could be made, a simple thing.

We continue our work until Jim shows up with the adapter. I think we can quickly try it out, so I run into the building and down the stairs, grabbing the end of the extension cord to plug it into the new location. If the adapter works, we can finish without buying more extension cords.

I plug it in and run back to the guys. The maintenance worker flips the switch and we have power.

Cool, it's working.

Jim says, "We have to see if the motor is turning the right way. Could one of you hold the nozzle so it doesn't flip around?"

This morning, like every morning, the forklift is pulled up to the three-foot-high cement loading dock, which is covered by a great big metal sheet for the platform. The dock is butted up against the building so the metal conveyor belts can load and unload crates. Pieces of the belt lie against the wall at our end. The metal nozzle of our sprayer is connected to a rubber hose, and there's rubber on the sprayer's handle.

Adam and I both say, "I got it."

Adam is closer, standing near the end of the dock. He jumps up and grabs the nozzle, putting him right in front of me. When the switch is flipped, Adam and I look into each other's eyes.

He's thrown back into the wall and I jump to his aid.

"No!" Jim shouts.

I'm determined to help my brother. I grab the hose and the rubber handle to yank it out of his hands, but I can't. His hands have clamped onto it because of the raw power. Adam's body has become a board.

I'm going to lose him if I can't get this free.

My tunnel vision expands as the power is cut, and I see the spray of water dissipate. I rip the nozzle from Adam's hands and throw it to the ground. He needs help now.

Adam is against the wall like a piece of lumber and he outweighs me by at least sixty pounds. I bring him down to a resting position as carefully as I can, struggling with his weight. The metal assembly line rollers loom overhead, so I shove them off the dock and away from Adam. I hold his head. I brush the hair out of his face. I look into his eyes.

He's in real trouble.

"Adam. Adam, can you hear me?" I ask, my voice betraying panic.

I get no reply.

"Adam, please, can you hear me?" I say, starting to fear the worst.

Adam's pupils don't look good and his pulse is fading. His body is failing and he starts convulsing.

Need to clear his airway.

I remember CPR from when I was a Boy Scout. Within 10-15 seconds, I give him his first breath with my mouth. 20-30 seconds in, I start compressions and don't stop. In about a minute, I go from happy to fully engaged in saving Adam's life, to what sounds like cracking bones.

People gather around. Some ask, "Is this really necessary?" while others offer help. I have one man rip open Adam's shirt and garments.

I have to know what I'm doing.

"Can I still help?" asks the man.

"You breathe for him," I respond, because the man looks like he has good lungs and Adam is big.

"Will I get sick?" he asks.

"Maybe a cold," I say, knowing what a good person Adam is.

"What do I do?"

"Watch. Hold his head back like this and plug his nose." Then I breathe and finish my instructions. "On five, it's you."

"Okay."

A stranger to Adam, this man must be scared, his mind racing over that first breath.

I count off my breaths until it's his turn, and he fills Adam's chest with air. I have no idea how much time passes before the ambulance arrives, but his father arrives before it.

"Rick, did you give Adam a blessing?" asks his father, also named Rick, with a grief only a parent can understand.

"No, I didn't have time."

"Okay."

Rick watches me perform CPR on his son and gives Adam a blessing, but my heart is pounding; my thought process is singular; I don't even realize he's there. Our work to save Adam continues.

Then the EMTs take over, but not quickly enough for me.

When they load him into the ambulance, I fall apart. I'm in shock. I've never witnessed anything like this before. The uniformed policeman doesn't care about my feelings as he begins to probe me for details; I'm a suspect. Adam isn't just anyone; he embodies everything I want to be, and he's my friend. But I'm a suspect.

The officer finally concludes it was an accident and turns me loose. I'm free to go home, but I'm still in complete shock and in no condition to drive. I can't leave without knowing what happens to Adam, so I wait.

Five or so minutes pass and the answers don't come, so I start looking. There's no one to ask but that officer, so I go to him.

"How's my friend?" I ask.

He tells me rather coldly, "He's dead. He didn't make it."

I'm speechless.

I walk to my car and drive away. Tears stream down my face, and the cars around me aren't completely there. It's a miracle I don't crash, because I'm barely functioning.

Somehow I make it home without crashing. I stumble out of the car and go in the house.

I walk down the hallway toward my parents' room. I hear Mom in the bathroom, the sink running, and I head that way. I stand in the bedroom just outside the bathroom. I can tell she's been cleaning, because the door is open and the smell hits me even in my still-soaked clothes.

"Mom," I let out, trying to stay strong.

"What are you doing home so early?" she asks.

"Adam's dead."

"*What?* What did you say?" Mom replies. She walks out where she can see me.

"Adam's dead."

"Richard, what happened!?" Mom asks. She puts her arm around me from the side and we sit on the end of her bed.

"We were working and he got electrocuted."

She looks stunned. "I don't understand. How could he have been electrocuted?'

"I found this plug and we asked a maintenance guy if we could use it and he said he would make an adapter."

"Wait…you what?"

"We didn't have a long enough extension cord, so we asked a maintenance guy for help and I was the one who found the plug," I explain.

"Okay…then what happened?"

"He came back with an adapter, so we tried it out and it wasn't grounded right."

"Oh, dear…." Now Mom is crying.

"Adam was blown back against the wall and I jumped up there to try to save him."

Mom looks horrified. "Richard, what were you *thinking*?" she exclaims. "You could have been killed!"

"I *wasn't* thinking; I just did it." Mom holds me tighter and cries even harder, and I continue. "Then I grabbed onto the rubber parts and tried to rip it from his hands, but I couldn't get it out. I wasn't strong enough." I pause. "I got it out of his hands when the power was cut. Then I laid him on the ground, which was really hard, and had to do CPR."

"You remembered how to do CPR?" She looks impressed.

"Yeah."

"Then what happened?"

"Then Adam's father was there and I was swearing."

"I'm sure it's alright that you were swearing," she assures me.

"Then when the ambulance came, they took over, and this mean cop started asking me all kinds of questions like I tried to kill him. And when Adam was gone I didn't know who to ask, so I asked the cop and he just told me he's dead."

"Oh, Rick." She wraps her arm around me and hugs me to her. "I'm so sorry," she says, and she means it.

***

SHOCK has struck – a point clearly illustrated when Bishop Bowman comes over and says, "We wanted to visit with the other victim in this tragedy," and I ask, "Who's that?"

The visit isn't a long one, and I'm not really there anyway. When the Bishop and his lovely wife leave, I watch TV, trying to focus on something else. But it's not easy to pass the time with the image of Adam's final moments replaying in my head, even in front of the TV.

Dad arrives home and says the doctor told the family they had never received anybody in such good condition; if it weren't for the amount of brain damage, Adam would have made it. It doesn't help, but over time it will.

In the days to follow, I remember the accident even when I try to think of Adam alive.

He was and will always be my friend.

Chapter 71 – Getting Up

Saturday: September 17th, 1994 – Age 23

For a couple weeks I've been in state of shock. The fact that Adam's gone hasn't truly sunk in yet. I'm not sure what's worse: to be the one who made it or the one who passed on. The pain seems unbreakable.

How am I going to get past this?

I can't wrap my head around it. It happened so fast and then he was gone. I keep thinking I'll see him the next time I go to church.

I wasn't able to stop it. Why couldn't I stop it?

Despite my best efforts, I wasn't strong enough to hold back the hand of death, nor fast enough to beat the current that hit him harder than anything my eyes have ever seen.

What I see when I look in the mirror is a failure. What I have is guilt. I haven't had an episode, and thank God for that, because it seems like I should have. In dealing with the guilt of being alive, the guilt of not being good enough, and the guilt of knowing that of the two of us, he was so much better…I'm at least handling the loss normally.

The biggest problem I currently face is that after all my dreams to be a superhero like in my comics, *now* of all times people keep telling me I *am* such a hero – now, when I feel so low and "hero" sounds like a joke.

Don't they get that he died?

A thought floods through me: *"Greater love hath no man than this, that a man lay down his life for his friends."* (New Testament | John 15:13)

Did Adam lay down his life for me? Did he know what he was doing in that instant before? Adam knew his time was close, because of his relationship with our Heavenly Father. He could have known that very morning it was coming. He probably thought it would be a car accident.

Maybe his last thought as he grabbed that nozzle was, "My time is here." Or, "Rick, you're safe." Or, "Send my love."

His last moments haunt me.

Life also has a way of haunting me. I was too young and wide-eyed to see life wouldn't magically be perfect now, just because I finished high school. I haven't yet learned how to accept when things go wrong.

Adam isn't the only person I've lost. I know of death; my grandparents passed away. But I was younger, then, and I wasn't the one to find them. For me, it was the regular steps: viewing, funeral, and so on. Not the face-to-face experience that comes from seeing somebody actually die.

Death can also bring to light the Plan of Salvation. However, I haven't been in the most spiritual of places, so even though I understand Adam is in a better place, normal depression pushes this fact to the back of my mind and I'm left without hope.

I have an appointment with Dr Earp and Mom comes with me. We both know I'm taking the whole thing really hard, but I think Mom, more than I, is wondering how it's affecting me after having already been through so much. I feel like things will be better one day. I'm just not in a rush, and I feel like it's okay to take time to deal with Adam's death, as long as I carry on with my life. I know Adam wouldn't want his family, loved ones, or me to stop moving forward.

Moving forward doesn't mean I have to storm the globe taking out bad guys like Thor or some other hero, which has always been in my mind as something I would do if I could. Rather, it means spending time with family, letting them know I'm still here. Allowing myself to get out with friends and be happy while doing it. All the positive things life can offer. Plus, I still have my appointment, and that means working with one of the best doctors in the world, and it's not taken for granted.

There are so many things I couldn't do if I didn't have the medical treatment that I have. In fact, I'd be dead without it. I would have died once shortly after birth, and then again from my head injury.

Only the third time, with Adam, is the one the medical world wasn't there for.

My battle scars run deep. The question of whether I still believe in myself and can move forward is no longer there. The only question is: how long will it take?

What if I slowly slide down into the underworld again? Or what if I can't think well enough to hold down a job? What if I can't think clearly enough to love somebody? What if? What if?

Then again…what if on my next mission I change the world? What if life brings me children? What if I make a difference in one person's life? What if I fall in love just like in the movies? Then it won't matter if the scars show through, making me look like a nightmare, because I will be at peace with myself. It's only a matter of hope – and my mission is to extend hope.

Chapter 72 – Attack the Grief

Tuesday: September 20th, 1994 – Age 23

I sit with Dr Earp and my mother, recounting what happened to Adam. Mom waits to hear how the doctor thinks I've been affected. Interestingly, Dr Earp tells us something we weren't expecting:

"It sounds like Rick has developed post-traumatic stress disorder."

I look at him in confusion.

"I thought that was only for people who went to war," Mom says.

The doctor shakes his head. "No. Actually, any event of this magnitude can trigger the disorder, and since we already have Rick on medication, we can either up the dose or just watch and let time do some of the healing. In other words, as time goes by, things will get easier to deal with."

"Why, then, did Rick get this now and not with his past experiences?" Mom asks, looking concerned.

"It's probably harder for Rick to have something happen to somebody else and witness it than to have it happen directly to him. Plus, we need to consider that past events may have already set this off, and now with Adam's death, it's just being triggered again." He gives us a smile that says everything will be alright.

"So, do I need to do anything?" I ask.

"Nothing you're not already doing. We'll keep up the medication, and I'd like to see you next month instead of three months out like we normally do. Is that okay with you?"

"Okay," I reply.

Mom, still looking worried, says, "So this is something he'll most likely always have, then? I mean, from here on out?"

"Yes. It will get so it doesn't bother him on a daily basis. At least, that's what I'm expecting from Rick. But it will always be there."

"The dairy offered him a job, but he didn't want to work there," Mom tells the doctor.

"That's typical of the disorder, to avoid the place where the event happened or maybe even certain people, depending on what happened," Dr Earp says in a stately way.

I'd like to take a quarter off from work anyway, so I ask the doctor, "What if I take a full load in school this quarter, to get back in the swing of things?"

"That's a good idea," he says.

"Does that sound okay to you, Mom?" I ask out of respect.

She smiles at me. "That's fine," she says.

***

Before long, we're out the door and I have a new diagnosis to add to my list of problems. It will not be the last. Over time, I also struggle with Obsessive-Compulsive Disorder to sometimes lesser and sometimes greater degrees.

I end up doing CPR again and take care of a lady having a seizure. I remain cool under fire, but feel some anxiety around those who could be in need of medical help. I become almost normal in most cases, aside from my nervous quirks.

On the other hand, my left arm sometimes twitches out of control and I develop two kinds of stutters: one where my brain can't seem to send the words to my mouth, and the other that's just a regular stutter, but mostly just when I get a fever. Yes, I am truly one for the books.

One day, I will marry and have two children, whom we love and adore very much. I will learn to recognize when my body is crashing under the stress of too many hours at work, poor nutrition, being around the wrong crowd, not enough church, belittling bosses, peer pressure, lack of sleep, going through a divorce, trying to keep the kids fed and hitting bottom without knowing it, and then the loss of a job, because of what would best be described as a mental breakdown brought on from working myself too hard, as if I'm a machine.

Sometimes it's hard to see that not everybody is out to hurt me. If I could see the future, I would see the numerous times people step in to help me. One day, I will want to say thank you and ask our Heavenly Father to send blessings to those who came to my aid.

When I was a teenager, it was hard to see that life has *ups* as well as downs, when all I had ever known were the downs. But now I know things *do* get better, as long as you're willing to work for a better life. In time, I will do just that, going on to receive many certifications, then my Bachelor's Degree, and finally my Master's degree – all the while learning to beat my own limitations…and there have been plenty of those.

Thomas S. Monson said, "Some are young people who don't know who they are, what they can be or even want to be. They are afraid, but they don't know of what. They are angry, but they don't know at whom. They are rejected and they don't know why. All they want is to be somebody."

My current thoughts are more like: *Just don't think about the problems in that way. I have to keep moving, because no one can help me with my problems but God and me.*

I have hope in the unknown future, again with the knowledge that I control the outlook of my life, even when the events of my life are out of my control, simply by maintaining a positive attitude. Being negative kills hope, and without hope there can't be faith.

I continue to live life as an imperfect man, striving to have perfect faith, because with hope leading to the right medication and faith leading to Christ, I've changed my life for the better.

There's no way to tell how a person's life will end. The important thing is to keep pushing forward, and learning. Because

I'm still here, I can tell you to make your Depression into something Beautiful.

The End

Appendices

Useful Resources

***** Rick Price's Official Website *****
http://richarddavidprice.com/

Schizoaffective Disorder Information and Support Groups

National Alliance on Mental Illness
http://www.nami.org/Content/NavigationMenu/Inform_Yourself/About_Mental_Illness/By_Illness/Schizoaffective_Disorder.htm

Mayo Clinic
http://www.mayoclinic.org/diseases-conditions/schizoaffective-disorder/basics/definition/con-20029221

Mind (Charity)
http://www.mind.org.uk/information-support/types-of-mental-health-problems/schizoaffective-disorder

Mental Health America
http://www.mentalhealthamerica.net/conditions/schizoaffective-disorder

Schizoaffective.org
http://www.schizoaffective.org/

Depression and Bipolar Information and Support Groups

Depression Alliance
http://www.depressionalliance.org

National Alliance on Mental Illness
http://www.nami.org/Content/NavigationMenu/Mental_Illnesses/Depression/Depression_Resources.htm

Depression.org.nz
http://www.depression.org.nz/waythrough/resources

Psych Central Support Groups
http://psychcentral.com/resources/Depression/Support_Groups/

Depression and Bipolar Support Alliance
http://www.dbsalliance.org

NHS Depression Support Groups
http://www.nhs.uk/Conditions/stress-anxiety-depression/Pages/depression-help-groups.aspx

Depression Tribe (a social network for sufferers of depression)
www.depressiontribe.com

About Conditional Publications

The name 'Conditional' means a few things. First, it is the aim of the imprint to provide a specialist home for publications written by people living with neurological conditions such as Tourette Syndrome, Obsessive-Compulsive Disorder, AD/HD, Autism, Epilepsy, Bipolar Disorder or other related conditions. These writings can be about, but are not restricted to, these conditions.

Second, the imprint also aims to publish informative non-fiction about these conditions, written by those who live with them.

Finally, we mean 'conditional' in the theoretical sense. In the case of this imprint, it means the 'human condition' or, the many aspects of what it means to be 'human'. The ultimate goal is to help people realise that just as a valuable diamond needs its multitudinous facets in order to sparkle so brightly, so we must embrace the many faces that make up society in order to be a beautiful whole.

Links and Social Media

Conditional Publications Website and Blog

www.conditionalpublications.com

'Like' Conditional Publications on Facebook

www.facebook.com/conditional

Follow us on Twitter:

@NeuroBooks

Also from Conditional Publications: *Check Mates*

The first EVER collection of fiction, poetry and artwork about OCD – by people with OCD

#3 best-selling short story anthology on Amazon.com

#2 best-selling 'compulsive disorders' book on Amazon.co.uk

#3 best-selling 'anxiety disorders' book on Amazon.ca

Check Mates is an original collection of fiction and poetry written about Obsessive-Compulsive Disorder by the people who know best – Obsessive-Compulsives. Split between 'realism' and stories of the 'beyond', there is a diverse range of styles and genres, and a mix of rage, frustration, tears, violence, pain, heartache, subversion, love, strength, metaphysics, philosophy, friendship, hope, and even a bit of humour. And maybe – just maybe – it will knock away a few stereotypes.

This exciting new book takes the fresh approach of fiction in order to express to the average reader what the world really looks like in the mind of an obsessive-compulsive.

It is a project conceived and developed by genuine sufferers and survivors of the condition, who met via a social networking website dedicated to OCD.

Praise for *Check Mates*

***'A fascinating and enlightening read**, so **brave and honest**. OCD: I never really knew. And now I'm so glad that I do. Thank you for this.'*

~ Nia Peeples
Actress, Singer & Writer – Los Angeles, CA

*'This **powerful collection** offers readers a **rare and intimate glimpse into the mind of those who struggle with OCD.** We hope this book contributes to a **sense of community** for those in their journey with OCD, as well as **help to educate** those who want to better understand what it is like to live with OCD.'*

~ Ryan & Kristin FitzGerald
Founders, OCDTribe.com

*'For far too long, OCD has remained largely misunderstood and misrepresented around the world. Stitched together in this collection of fiction and poetry is **a literary patchwork of OCD insights, each offering the unique wisdom and intimacy of personal experience.** What a wonderful opportunity this book presents readers looking to understand such a complex and multifaceted disorder!'*

~ Jeff Bell, author of
***When in Doubt, Make Belief: An OCD-Inspired Approach to Living with Uncertainty* and**
Rewind, Replay, Repeat: A Memoir of OCD

Check Mates is available in paperback and at all good e-book shops

Also from Conditional Publications:
The Ladder

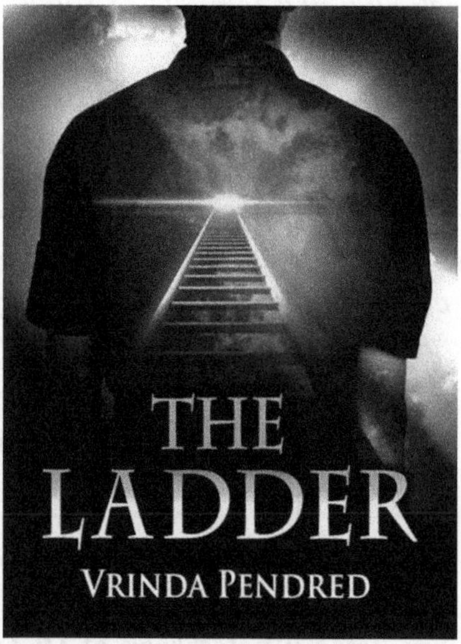

Ansel has no idea what might lie at the top of that ladder, but he knows he has to get on it.'

Ansel Hilliard doesn't need anyone. He doesn't need friends. He doesn't need family. At least, that's what he's always told himself.

But when the troubled boy moves in next-door, Ansel finds himself drawn into a lifelong friendship he never thought possible. As they grow together and dare to allow others into their hearts, they find that the turbulence of life doesn't always have to destroy you.

Inspired by the author Vrinda Pendred's background of living with bipolar disorder, *The Ladder* is a story of self-discovery, and learning to face – and embrace – the darkness we are all afraid to admit lies inside of us.

The Ladder is available at all good e-book shops

CPSIA information can be obtained
at www.ICGtesting.com
Printed in the USA
BVHW04s0834080618
518581BV00002B/42/P

9 780956 452917